"TRUST TO GOOD VERSES"

Roger B. Rollin
J. Max Patrick
Editors

"*Trust to Good Verses*"

HERRICK TERCENTENARY ESSAYS

UNIVERSITY OF PITTSBURGH PRESS

Published by the University of Pittsburgh Press, Pittsburgh, Pa. 15260
Copyright © 1978, University of Pittsburgh Press
All rights reserved
Feffer and Simons, Inc., London
Manufactured in the United States of America

Library of Congress Cataloging in Publication Data

Robert Herrick Memorial Conference, University of
  Michigan, Dearborn, 1974.
  "Trust to good verses".

  Bibliography: p. 237
  Includes index.
  1. Herrick, Robert, 1591–1674—Congresses.
I. Patrick, John Max, 1911–   II. Rollin,
Roger B.   III.   Title.
PR3514.A24   1974   821'.4   77-74547
ISBN 0-8229-3353-5

Contents

Hesperides: Parallelism and Integration

Herrick and His Public

Selected and Annotated Bibliography

Herrick and His Critics

ROGER B. ROLLIN

Sweet Numbers and Sour Readers: Trends and Perspectives in Herrick Criticism

> Thou shalt not All die; for while Love's fire shines
> Upon his Altar, men shall read thy lines;
> And learn'd Musicians shall to honour *Herricks*
> Fame and his Name, both set, and sing his Lyrics.
> (Upon himself," H-366)

It was to honor Herrick's "Fame and his Name" that, on October 11–13, 1974, the original versions of the essays collected in this volume were presented at the Robert Herrick Memorial Conference at the University of Michigan—Dearborn. Held to commemorate the three-hundredth anniversary of the poet's death and attended by scholars from Japan, England, and Canada as well as the United States, this conference was but one indication of recent interest in the author of *Hesperides*. For, as the bibliography appended to this book records, the tercentenary year was also marked by the publication of two critical studies of Herrick's poetry, a scholarly monograph, and a popular biography. This surge of activity was the culmination of a process that had extended over two decades—a reexamination of Herrick's art and of his place in literary history.

Taken together, the essays which follow consolidate a "revisionist" view of Robert Herrick. In essence this view maintains that Herrick is a serious and significant artist rather than a minor if skillful craftsman; that his *Hesperides* is an encyclopedic and ultimately coherent work rather than a miscellany of charming but trivial poems; and that many of those poems exhibit patterns of intellectual significance and emotional depth beneath their polished and seemingly simple surfaces. Some essays support this view by correcting erroneous impressions arising out of the prior consensus about Herrick, which held him to be a decidedly "minor" poet in every respect except, perhaps, his craftsmanship. Other essays serve to broaden and deepen the foundations upon which the "new consensus" rests.

For example, the old commonplace that Herrick's art is steeped in the poetry of classical Greece and Rome is confirmed in new ways by John T. Shawcross and James Tillman, and expanded beyond questions of "sources and influences" into the area of creativity itself by Gordon Braden. Likewise, Herrick's recognized indebtedness to (but ultimate independence of) Ben Jonson receives fresh confirmation in Helen Marlborough's study of a neglected genre of *Hesperides,* its epigrams of praise. Still another truism of earlier Herrick criticism—that the poet's lyrical impulse is central to his art and the chief source of his popularity—is rescued from mere impressionism and given the support of verifiable evidence in the essay by A. E. Elmore.

Other essays directly or indirectly buttress some of the main tenets of the revisionist view of Herrick: that he can be a poet of high seriousness, as capable of searching meditations upon the human condition as of lyrical celebrations of life (T. G. S. Cain, Shonosuke Ishii); that he is a socially conscious and ideologically committed poet as well as a felicitous writer of songs (Claude J. Summers); that his sensibility is not split by a "Christian-pagan" dichotomy but is, rather, "holistic," embodying and transcending both religious impulses (Virginia R. Mollenkott). Another aspect of the new consensus is its recognition of Herrick's self-consciousness as an artist, a self-consciousness which manifests itself in his subordination to aesthetic ends of even the sacred (William Oram) and the erotically profane (Achsah Guibbory). In *Hesperides* as a whole this self-consciousness emerges in Herrick's unobtrusive but deliberate arrangement of his poems: one of these modes of arrangement establishes his persona as a poet who matures as an artist and ages as a man throughout the course of the volume (Avon Jack Murphy); still another mode is based upon the principle of *ut pictura poesis,* setting *Hesperides* forth as a poetic "landscape" whose varied scenes and prospects are "viewed" through the eyes of a visually as well as verbally sensitive persona (Norman K. Farmer, Jr.).

The growth of Herrick's reputation in recent years is amply validated by such studies of the formal properties of his art as are to be found in this volume. J. Max Patrick's scholarly analysis, on the other hand, invalidates the widespread notion that *Hesperides* was, as a publishing venture, a failure, and that as a consequence, Herrick's reputation as a poet must have been negligible during the last two decades of his life.

Even three hundred years later, however, the consensus about Herrick is by no means complete—witness, for example, the diametrically opposed arguments of the essays by William Oram and Virginia Mollenkott. Indeed, the latter's thesis—that Herrick is *essentially* a "religious" poet—will probably generate as much controversy among readers as it did among those attending the Herrick Conference and the scholars who evaluated the manuscript of this volume. The fact that this essay could provoke radically different judgments from students of seventeenth-century literature and the prospect that it could give rise to fruitful critical debate in the future were taken by the editors as positive reasons for its inclusion, even though both had reservations about the essay's methodology and conclusions.

The new consensus represented here, moreover, need not be seen as limiting the possibilities for future investigations into *Hesperides*. The critical approach adopted in the majority of the essays which follow (and in much recent Herrick criticism) is that of Formalism, albeit a formalism flexible enough to accommodate relevant historical and generic considerations. However, such typically formalistic concerns as the poet's prosody, rhetoric, wit, and humor have thus far not received comprehensive treatment. Furthermore, the possible applications to Herrick studies of current developments in such fields as semiotics and structuralism and in contemporary sociocultural, archetypal, and psychological approaches to literature have yet to be fully tested.

One such testing (necessarily preliminary rather than full-scale) will occupy the remainder of this essay. It can be regarded as a kind of prolegomenon to a study of Herrick's poetry which for its theoretical framework would draw upon ego psychology and which would have as its focus the psychodynamics of reader response. Such studies have been infrequent in seventeenth-century scholarship, but they hold out the possibility at least of opening up a new range of insights into the work of Herrick and his contemporaries.

A current trend of literary criticism refocuses attention upon the reader and, specifically, upon that "transaction" between the text and the reader's mind which Norman N. Holland has termed "the dynamics of literary response." As Holland explains his psychoanalytically based theory in *Five Readers Reading*, *"A reader responds to a literary work by assimilating it to his own psychological processes, that is, to his search for successful solutions within his identity theme to the multiple demands, both inner and outer, on his ego"* (p. 128). That Robert Herrick was sensitive to the role readers play in "creating" poetry is evidenced by his poems of advice, exhortation, and warning to those readers, to critics, and to fellow poets and scholars. More than most poets of his age—or of any other—Herrick displays not only a heightened awareness of his readers, but a desire to have them respond positively to his book. And if that response can be enhanced by such devices as direct address, authorial marginalia, or the calculated placement of individual poems, Herrick will oblige. (Over a dozen poems of *Hesperides* contain direct addresses to readers and over two dozen allude to his works being read by others or by the poet himself, and to his own reading in other authors.)

Similarly directive of reader response is Herrick's created persona, whose unifying personality gives *Hesperides* its distinctive "voice." This personality, like any reader's, attains unity and coherence through what ego psychologists would call an "identity theme." Herrick's persona thus offers readers a centered consciousness which they can assimilate into their own, *introjecting* characteristics of that fictive consciousness into their ego systems and *projecting* theirs out into it. In the process readers will find themselves playing a variety of roles—not only such "social" roles as lover, friend, citizen, gentleman, and philosopher, but also such "professional" roles as those of editor, critic, literary theorist, literary historian, and, of course, working poet. Whether one speaks of the capacity of the ego thus to "split" itself deliberately or whether one simply speaks of the creative imagination, Herrick must be singled out as remarkable among poets for the amount of role-playing (and perhaps game-playing) that characterizes his art. Those occasions on which Herrick's artistic self-consciousness expresses itself in poems on poetry, on poets, and on himself as poet constitute—to extrapolate from Avon Jack Murphy's essay—a kind of monodrama within *Hesperides.* In terms of archetypal criticism the plot of that monodrama takes the form of a quest of the poet-hero for his completed opus.

Another type of quest-motif in *Hesperides,* though its pattern is less clear, could be represented as "the search for the father." It is implicit in such poems as those in which Herrick venerates authority figures like King Charles and "Father Johnson"; his poem on his natural father (H-82), one of the most moving in *Hesperides;* his numerous poems to God the Father; and even those poems whose social and political conservatism seem to be unconscious expressions of a "negative Oedipus complex" and of an authoritarian personality as well. The hypothesis that a preoccupation with the paternal is a significant dimension of the identity theme of Herrick's persona then merits fuller consideration. Such facts as Nicholas Herrick's dying (mysteriously) when his son Robert was only a little over a year old and Robert's later uneasy relationship with his uncle, Sir William Herrick, would only lend interest and impetus to an investigation whose ultimate aim would be to shed new light on pervasive psychological motifs in *Hesperides.*

The very distinctiveness of the Hesperidean personality is a quality which in the past has not been celebrated by all of Herrick's readers and critics, nor is it likely to be wherever and whenever the preference is for "anonymous" poets, for "invisible" personae. And it is probable that Herrick's strategy of the dominant and distinctive persona does have the effect of distancing his readers from his poems to some extent. Such distancing can complicate what Norman N. Holland regards as the basic psychological functions of the literary text: (1) to provide materials out of which readers will (mainly unconsciously) produce fantasies that accord with their characteristic psychological processes; (2) simultaneously to provide other materials out of which readers can synthesize psychological strategies of "defense" and "adaptation," whereby they become able to "manage"—cope with, both emotionally and intellectually—whatever fantasies have been generated in their reading.

Some fantasies are essentially wish-fulfillment dreams: Herrick's amatory and pastoral poems, for example, are rich in such materials. But wish-fulfillment fantasies can also have anxiety components. Thus Herrick, the Love Poet, has been charged by critics with being everything from a naive dreamer, spinning mistresses and romances wholly out of his own feverish imagination, to a sexually psychopathic personality, a sensualist, voyeur, or even fetishist. Yet daydreaming about sex is, of course, a thoroughly common human activity, and embodying such dreams in poetry is scarcely less common; it is only rare to do it as well as Herrick does. Whether his re-creation of such dreamwork is conscious, as in *"The Vine"* (H-41), or possibly unconscious, as in the nightmarish parade of grotesques in the grosser epigrams, latent anxieties and wishes generate tension throughout *Hesperides*.

Herrick's reputation as a love poet has suffered because some critics fail to recognize that there are different love-styles as well as different life-styles, or because they are unable to accommodate alternative styles within their own characteristic systems of defense and adaptation. Readers and critics whose conditioning has been to understand love primarily in terms of the total fusion of the ego with the love object—the durable Romantic Ideal—will be inclined to perceive Herrick's amatory poems as lacking in real passion or as insincere—as if passion and sincerity exist solely in the text and not in the interaction between the text and what the reader brings to it.

Another factor in the mixed reader response to Herrick's love lyrics is that, unlike that more praised amatory poet, John Donne, he usually gives names to his mistresses (and sometimes they are the real names of real women) and he often endows them, however slightly, with distinguishing physical and/or psychological characteristics. Thus Herrick's women often seem more than mere narcissistic projections of the poet's ego, more than the typical "she's" belied by false compare routinely encountered in Renaissance verse. It is a question whether, in the love poetry of that period, any fictional mistresses save Shakespeare's Dark Lady have significantly more "reality" than Herrick's Julias, Corinnas, and Elizabeth Wheelers.

Historically, it has been easier for Herrick's readers to respond positively to his "Arcadian strain," his predilection for creating pastoral worlds compounded of Devonshire realities and bucolic fantasies derived from English folklore and from classical pastoral traditions. Such fictive worlds can fulfill the deep-seated needs and desires of not a few readers. Even a fallen Eden such as Herrick's offers materials for "dreaming a dream" in which immediate sensuous gratification, peace, security, and even immortality are afforded. Herrick's Hesperidean garden is many things to many readers, but its appeal for most of them, like the appeal of any of the numerous variations of garden myth, probably derives from the contact such a vision makes with long-repressed memories of the very earliest infantile stages of human life.

On the other hand, no study of the psychological patterns of *Hesperides* should fail to take into account the tensions *within* his bucolic vision—for even temporary regression in service of the ego can entail anxiety as well as gratification—and also the tensions *between* that vision and its alternative, what might loosely be termed Herrick's "urban vision." Psychic aggression and even hostility rather than psychic retreat characterize this aspect of Herrick's art, exemplified in such poems as those attacking Devonshire and its natives, other sorry specimens of humanity, political and literary adversaries, and selected forms of immorality. Works of this type afford quite different kinds of fantasy material and thus some readers will prefer them, perceiving them as more "realistic" than the pastorals or even, somehow, as more "masculine." Whatever the case, such poems offer ready opportunities for venting aggression in ways which the poet's art renders acceptable. Paradoxically, Herrick's epigrammatic exercises in the gross and the grotesque may well be rejected by the very same readers, because one of their characteristic patterns of defense and adaptation may involve setting fixed limits on real-life experience and construing aesthetic experience within somewhat narrow limits of decorum. Conversely, readers capable of responding positively to *Hesperides'* idyllic strain will tend to be more receptive to the "coarse" Herrick as well, for their more adaptive ego systems will be able to accommodate almost as wide a range of fantasizing as the poet's own.

Whatever the fantasy a Herrick poem evokes in a reader, that fantasy is, in psychoanalytic literary theory, also managed by the ego's transformation of the poem's psychological content into intellectual content, into themes and interpretations. Readers will bring such "higher" ego functions as critical expertise and knowledge of literary history to bear to render the fantasy they have synthesized from a poem such as "Corinna's *going a Maying*" (H-178) into an intellectual content that is both characteristic of and pleasurable to them as persons. Thus the *carpe diem* motif of that poem, and the strain of serious Epicureanism which informs the whole of *Hesperides,* will offer readers predisposed to this type of "secondary-process thinking" opportunities to reinforce and re-create their own identities as they read. Much of the scholarly ink spilled concerning Herrick's "Christian-pagan tension" and in particular those critical discussions which have concluded that Herrick is philosophically shallow or spiritually superficial are expressions of some critics' own inabilities to come to terms with his persona's strategies of "secondary-process" defense and adaptation. For those strategies tend to be quite overt in his verse, and consequently readers' egos may well find it less easy to accommodate them than the ambiguities of a Shakespeare, the witty sophistries of a Donne, or the orthodoxies of a Herbert.

Since critics are first of all readers, it is not surprising that, in the past, many of them have proved hardly more adaptive to the considerable. demands *Hesperides* has made upon them than readers with less expertise. For, as was noted at the beginning of this discussion, Herrick's collection is an encyclopedic work whose intimidating size and scope, elusive patternings, and great variety make its reading an extensive and complex psychological transaction. The kind of psychoanalytic approach to *Hesperides* that is outlined here would of necessity be a complicated undertaking in and of itself, and it would not, of course, guarantee to offer up "the definitive Robert Herrick." But if, as has been claimed here, a revised critical consensus about the poet has indeed been reached, that consensus affords an appropriate point of departure for those who would further illuminate Herrick's art; for not without merit is his claim that "all here is good, / If but well read; or ill read, understood."

Hesperides: Visual, Poetic, Musical

NORMAN K. FARMER, JR.

Herrick's Hesperidean Garden: *ut pictura poesis* Applied

"The most pleasant of all outward pastimes," Robert Burton declares, is "to walk amongst orchards, gardens, bowers, mounts, and arbours, artificiall wildernesses, green thickets, arches, groves, lawns, rivulets, fountains, and such like pleasant places."[1] Though he has little to say in this connection about "inward" pastimes, one need look no further than such miscellanies as *Briton's Bowre of Delights* (1591, 1597), *The Arbor of Amorous Devises* (1597), *England's Helicon* (1600, 1614), and *Bel-vedere: or the Garden of the Muses* (1600) to realize that for the seventeenth-century reader a book of poems was often the verbal equivalent of a garden. Indeed, one's experience within such a verbal universe was often regarded in horticultural terms, and for this there was ample mythological precedent in the Hesperidean garden of the Muses.

Henry Hawkins, who sees the physical garden in which Burton would have us walk as an emblem of universal harmony, begs his Genius in *Partheneia Sacra* (1633) to lead the reader into a similar poetic garden: a "goodlie Amphitheatre of flowers, upon whose leaves delicious beauties stand, as on a stage, to be gazed on and to play their parts."[2] Moreover, in its blend of emblematic image with poetry, *Partheneia Sacra* offers both a series of visible "stages" as well as lines to be delivered upon them. Its visual as well as verbal multiformity is thus compatible with Burton's further advice, when he recommends "inspection alone of those curious iconographies of temples and palaces." And when he adds the recreations of both country and city, the "May-games, feasts, wakes, and merry meetings" where men "solace themselves," Burton seems to have prescribed in 1628 much that was to appear in the collected poems of Robert Herrick.

By 1648 there was good reason for Herrick to call his large and multiplex collection *Hesperides*. As G. C. Moore Smith remarked many years ago,[3] the name is conventionally enough used to mean not the nymphs of the gardens, but the gardens themselves. And as Roger Rollin has remarked more recently, "Herrick's book itself [is] the new Hesperides, a garden whose golden fruits take the shape of poems."[4]

In this essay I will explore some of the implications that emerge from this assumption when we apply to it the famous maxim from Horace's *Ars poetica* (lines 361 ff.): "ut pictura poesis," or, roughly translated, "as a painting, so also a poem." While I do not propose to compete with the poet to "Sing of *Brooks*, of *Blossomes*, *Birds*, and *Bowers*" or "Of *April*, *May*, of *June*, and *July*-Flowers," I do intend to offer reasons why Herrick's declared topics require of the reader a view of the poetic performance which embraces the visual as well as the verbal and which allows for reciprocal relations between the two.

In 1675 Edward Phillips wrote that what is "chiefly pleasant in these poems [*Hesperides*] is now and then a pretty Floury and Pastoral gale of Fancy, a vernal prospect of some Hill, Cave, Rock, or Fountain; which but for the interruption of other trivial passages might have made up none of the worst Poetic Landskips."[5] Regrettably, the unimaginative Phillips did not perceive the true nature of Herrick's lyric achievements. But he did, nonetheless, perceive a generic element in the poems that deserves exploration, namely, that of landscape.

"Landskip," writes Henry Peacham in *The Art of Drawing with the Pen and Limning in Water Colours* (London, 1606), "is a Dutch word & it is as much as we shoulde say in English landship, or expressing of the land by hills, woodes, Castles, seas, valleys, ruines, hanging rocks, Citties, Townes, &c, as farre as may bee shewed within our Horizon." Notably, though, landscape is only seldom drawn "by it self, but in respect & for the sake of some thing els." For this reason, "it falleth out among those thing[s] which we call *Parerga*, the accessory elements in a properly subordinated landscape." In a section called "Of the Fairest and Most Beautiful Landskips in the World," which appeared first in the 1612 edition, Peacham explains that landscape is properly associated with traveling because it takes a variety of subjects. Indeed, his list of subject matter appropriate for the landscape artist is quite wide:

If you draw your Landskip according to your invention, you shall please very well, if you shew in the same, the faire side of some goodly Cittie, haven, forrest, stately house with gardens. I ever took delight in those peeces that shewed to the life a countrey village, faire or market, *Berga-mascas* cookerie, *Morrice* dancing, peasants together by the eares, and the like.[6]

Certainly, it is a short step from this formula to Herrick's declared intention to sing "of *May-poles, Hock-carts, Wassails, Wakes,* / Of *Bride-grooms, Brides,* and of their *Bridall-cakes,*" to say nothing of his writing "of *Youth,* [and] of *Love.*" And it is a particularly short step when we make it with Burton's phrases in mind, "to walk amongst orchards, gardens, bowers . . . and such like pleasant places" and to enjoy such recreations as "May-games, feasts, wakes, and merry meetings." The notion of variety and diversity, the mixture of pure "scene" with the activities of those who dwell naturally and properly in a scene, the juxtaposition of fertile and barren, of smooth and rough, of near and far, of mountains and lowlands—all are present in Herrick's lyrics just as they are in the landscapes of the late sixteenth and seventeenth centuries. In short, there is an evident parallel to the theories and effects of the visual arts in the verbal creations of this English poet.

But how is one to discuss this parallel in an appropriate way, without making grand-sounding but facile declarations based solely on a rough parallel of themes treated by the poet and the painters? And how convert one's sense of the rightness of this parallel to a productive reading of the poetic experience that Herrick offers? The larger significances of these questions have been and must continue to be debated along with the manifold subtleties of the visual/verbal reciprocity in late Renaissance culture. But to reach some tentative answers I propose to discuss (1) the pertinence to a reading of *Hesperides* of William Marshall's engraved frontispiece to the 1648 edition, (2) the inferences that may be drawn from the several poems that relate directly to painters and painting, and (3) Herrick's apparent fascination with the visual experience and with the problems posed by iconic and ecphrastic poetry.

William Marshall's engraved frontispiece to *Hesperides* (figure 1) has been described as follows by J. Max Patrick:

[It] shows the bust of a somewhat hooknosed, curly-headed man, in profile, with a moustache. It is usually assumed that the engraver . . . intended this to portray Herrick, but the picture may well be merely a generalized representation of a poet. The landscape surrounding the bust includes the Hill of Parnassus, the Spring of Helicon, Pegasus about to soar from the hill, several trees, and nine naked figures—presumably the Muses. Two of these winged figures are flying with wreaths of flowers—flowers from the Garden of the Hesperides—preparing to crown him. Five others circle in a dance below the largest tree in the garden itself. And two, holding branches of bay or olive leaves, sit in the foreground pointing to a Latin poem on the base of the bust.[7]

On the basis of these observations, I pose three questions.

First, is Marshall's engraving to be regarded simply as an addendum, a piece of random decoration, or are there grounds for assuming that it has a genuine organic relation to the contents of the book? Second, is the portrait of Herrick a true likeness, or has Marshall simply provided a generalized representation of a poet? Third, is there an emblematic cue in this engraving to what we may expect in Herrick's book, to the nature (and genre) of his poetry, and to the vicarious experience one may expect to have with it?

As to grounds for assuming that this frontispiece has an organic relation to the contents of the book, it is important to recognize, first, that *"The pillar of Fame,"* the penultimate poem in *Hesperides,* clearly echoes the visual monument of the frontispiece in both its statement and in its topiary appearance. Second, engraved title pages and frontispieces, which began to appear at a surprisingly late date in book decoration and which reached their peak during the seventeenth century, are commonly of a deliberately symbolic and hieroglyphic nature. Commenting on

Figure 1. *Hesperides* (1648). Courtesy, Humanities Research Center, The University of Texas at Austin.

this phenomenon, Alfred Johnson declares in his introduction to *A Catalogue of Engraved and Etched Title-Pages* that

> the title-page had ceased to be purely decorative and had become a thing of emblems and allegories. The scheme was frequently based on the Roman arch flanked by symbolic figures; in the case of the Greek and Roman classics, the heroes of antiquity; in Bibles, we have Old and New Testament characters; in books of travel, Turks, Persians, and the like. In that age of metaphysical poets a number of symbolic scenes were often imposed on an architectural framework.[8]

This organic importance of the frontispiece or title page may be seen in the striking engraving by Theodore de Bry on the title page of Robert Fludd's *Metaphysica, Physica atque Technica Historia* (Oppenheim, 1617), where we find a vivid emblem of "Times trans-shifting" (figure 2). But what Johnson fails to point out is that, even on title pages purportedly containing portraits alone, there are quite often inset scenes of a distinctly allegorical or emblematic nature (figure 3). This feature is, of course, common in Tudor and Stuart portraiture where, as Roy Strong has observed, "the portrait, being a record of an individual being, is inexorably bound up with that other emanation of renaissance individuality, the *impresa* or emblematic device."[9]

My examination of the numerous frontispieces and title pages engraved by William Marshall—well over a hundred of them—leads me to conclude that the artist truly intended something more than a simple decoration.[10] The frontispiece (figure 4) engraved for the English translation of M. Silesio's *The Arcadian Princesses* (1635) is a good example. On a throne there sits a crowned female representing the figure of Justice. In her left hand she holds a lance with the accompanying inscription *cum Lancea Pugnamus,* and in her right hand she holds a balance with the inscription *cum forma Pauperis.* A man in a hat and ruff with a scroll inscribed *Ira Potentis* weighs down the scales. From behind the throne hands point to scrolls reading (left) *Illinc Praemium* and (right) *Hinc Praelium.* The significance of the engraving is appropriately obscure. But more to the point is the accompanying epigram, "Upon the Frontispiece":

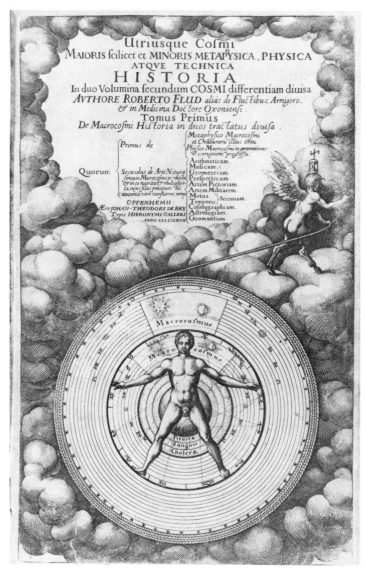

Figure 2.   *Ultriusque Cosmi . . . Metaphysica, Physica atque Tech-nica Historia* (1617). Courtesy, Humanities Research Center, The University of Texas at Austin.

Figure 3. *Eikon Basilike* (1649). Courtesy, Humanities Research Center, The University of Texas at Austin.

> Hee that in words explaines a Frontispiece,
> Betrayes the secret trust of his Device:
> Who cannot guesse, where Mott's and Emblemes be,
> The drift, may still bee ignorant for me.

Another example of the deliberately allegorical frontispiece is Marshall's spectacular engraving for George Wither's *Emblemes* (figure 5). Even more recondite than the engraving for *The Arcadian Princesse*, this one presents two mountain peaks.

Figure 4. *The Arcadian Princesse* (1635). Courtesy, Humanities Research Center, The University of Texas at Austin.

Figure 5. *Emblemes* (1635). Courtesy of The Newberry
          Library, Chicago.

At the foot, a grotto where children are playing. From it on the right young men and women make their way up smooth paths past the temple of Venus and thence to stony regions where men are fighting and others are strung up on gallows, to the summit where the figure of Death stands. From dark clouds appear snakes and animal heads. On the left a man sets off alone up a steep and treeless path; he encounters figures representing Faith, Hope, and Charity, and goes past a church covered in crosses; outside it stands a priest in a rochet. The scenery becomes pleasanter, and near the top is a city—Jerusalem. Above perches an eagle carrying a boy.[11]

Once again though, the picture is accompanied by a poem which is designed to engage the reader in speculation about deep mysteries. It reads in part:

> If any thinke this Page will, now, declare
> The meaning of those Figures, which are there,
> They are deceiv'd. For Destinie deneys
> The utt'ring of such hidden Mysteries,
> In these respects: First This contayneth nought
> Which (in a proper sense) concerneth ought,
> The present-Age: Moreover, tis ordain'd,
> That none must know the Secrecies contain'd
> Within this piece; but they who are so wise
> To find them out, by their own prudencies.

The examples given thus far belong to that category of graphic representation that is sometimes called the *allegorical tableau*. The term is particularly useful in the present connection because a *landskip* is also a tableau, and I must stress the fact that *picture* may include outright visual representation of natural objects, iconic verbalizations about the appearance of natural objects, or even a category that lies somewhere between the two—between the domains, as it were, of the purely visual and the purely verbal. In the allegorical tableau, "the governing principles may be considered to be more or less naturalistic pictorial representation on the one hand, and on the other some kind of organization in space which is not naturalistic but artificial, schematic, or diagrammatic." An interesting and well-known example is the title page of Hobbes's *Leviathan* (figure 6). Here, however, in-

Figure 6. *Leviathan* (1651). Courtesy, Humanities Research Center, The University of Texas at Austin.

stead of an outright natural representation alone or a hieroglyphic and visually enigmatic representation alone, we encounter a combination of these, with a verbal message as well. To
an extent, the entire title page is held together as a conceptual
device by the presence of the printed words. Indeed, the words
"form a real part of the total ensemble and interact with the
picture by the fact that they lie in the areas adjacent to it, advertising that 'Leviathan' and the Commonwealth' are to be applied
to the pictorial design to give it a special dimension. This spatial
interaction of picture and visual display of words, sometimes
outside the picture and sometimes set more or less within it, is
common." But the verbal element, with all its capacity for
weighted intensification, is nonetheless an equal to the visual
element in a spatial frame that is entirely nonrealistic. This is to
say that the space inside the pictorial element is denaturalized
and is "made subordinate to the overall schema of picture-and-
word representation." While "all real or dramatic actions take
place in time, real or imagined, respectively" in the allegorical
tableau there is no human time element at work. It may well
involve figures pictured in some sort of action, but it remains
"basically a diagram felt as committed to space in such a way as
to be free of time, like a geometrical triangle or square."[12]

As we return to the frontispiece of *Hesperides* with these points
in mind, we may no longer be willing to regard it as mere decoration. Rather, we shall understand its function as a cuing device
to the uniquely iconic quality of the poems that follow,[13] and we
shall anticipate the pictorialism in those poems to be organic
rather than merely ornamental. Before proceeding to that point,
however, I must address one question that I believe to be of
substance, namely, Is the portrait on this title page *in fact* a
representation of Robert Herrick, or is it the generalized representation of *a* poet? The question is substantive, for if the portrait is an imitation of nature—i.e., a reasonably accurate visual
likeness of Herrick—then its presence in the emblematic field of
this tableau informs the reader to be alert to a continuing relation
between the poet's own Hesperidean fiction and its informing
realities, a relation displayed in another mode by the poet's use

of the visual and the verbal. The blend of realism and allegory in the frontispiece warns against any simplistic reading of the poems and suggests that they in fact seek a balance between the modalities of naturalism and allegory.

Since there are, to my knowledge, no other portraits of Herrick, the test of verisimilitude in this case lies in the purely circumstantial evidence that purported portraits by William Marshall do indeed attempt to offer accurate representations. I will select one example, that of Marshall's frontispiece to Sir John Suckling's *Fragmenta Aurea* (1646) (figure 7). Fortunately, the visual accuracy of this engraving can be compared with the fine portrait of Suckling by Van Dyke (figure 8). Marshall has demonstrably captured the essential features of Suckling's face: the direct and frank look about the eyes, the set of the mouth, and the structure of cheekbones and nose. Though there is admittedly a certain degree of idealization in each picture, it is clear that for Marshall, while portraiture may be *symbol* and *allegory*, it is an attempt at a natural likeness. And further examination of Marshall's other engravings, such as those of Robert Baron, Charles I, George Villiers, John Hall, and William Lilly, reveals his close attention to the idiosyncratic features of individual faces.[14] It is my conclusion, then, that the engraving contains a genuine portrait and, therefore, that Marshall has sought expression through the visual medium of complexities we may expect to discover as we turn to the verbal *Hesperides*.

As we scan the frontispiece (figure 1), we perceive that a large bust of the poet rests upon an ornate pedestal occupying the entire foreground of the picture. The bust and pedestal rest, in turn, upon a stone slab that bears a commendatory Latin inscription by John Harmar. The practice here is quite in keeping with the Renaissance habit of including inscriptions in works of visual art in order to intensify the significance of the visual.[15] To ensure our attention to the verses, two *putti* (each bearing a laurel branch symbolic of eternity and triumph) point to the inscription, and the apt juxtaposition of picture and word immediately characterizes the piece as an allegorical tableau. We are not, therefore, to expect *natural* representation in the picture as a

Figure 7. *Fragmenta Aurea* (1646). Courtesy, Humanities Research Center, The University of Texas at Austin.

Figure 8.   Sir John Suckling by Anthony Van Dyck. Copyright The Frick Collection, New York.

whole. But at the same time, we may assume that the bust in the spatial frame of our picture *does* depict Robert Herrick.

Our perception of the frontispiece may now be said to "occur" within a perceived setting that is located between the strictly visual and the strictly verbal, a condition that is especially propitious for creativity.[16] The garden in which the memorial statue is placed is appropriately denaturalized; and yet it retains the visual components of a *locus amoenus:* the trees, groves, rolling hills, pleasant valley, and a spring welling from beneath the hill closest to the foreground. Here the iconology of the picture takes precedence over any traditional notion of landscape. We know, for example, that the hill must be Helicon and that the spring flowing from its base is Hippocrene, the waters of which are released by the hard hoof of Pegasus and are sacred to the nine Muses. As the mythological residue of the image sinks into consciousness, we notice that it is toward Helicon that the bust of the poet faces. And perhaps with equal appropriateness it is toward Herrick that Pegasus himself faces as he rears majestically upon Helicon. The reciprocal interrelatedness of the poet, the mountain, and the winged horse (which George Sandys "mythologizes" as Fame in his commentary upon book 5 of Ovid's *Metamorphosis*) crosses simultaneously the boundaries of space and time. Instead of framing his portrait of the poet in a conventional cartouche (as he had done with the portrait of Suckling), instead of leaving the bust in a starkly unadorned and unframed setting (as he had done with the bust of Henry Carey, Earl of Monmouth) (figure 9), and instead of using the far more conventional architectural setting, Marshall has "framed" the image of Herrick with symbols that define the *condition* the poet has achieved through his poetry—inspired composition (the association with Pegasus), responsiveness to classical traditions and conventions (the association with Helicon and the Muses), and eternal fame (the association with the *putti* and again with Pegasus). In so doing, Marshall has in effect linked the frontispiece of *Hesperides* with "The pillar of Fame" at its conclusion. There, in a topiary poem that combines the visual and the verbal, thus contrasting with the engraving's combination of the verbal and the visual, Herrick writes:

HENRICUS
Dom: CARY; Baro
de Lephingtō; Com: de
MONMOVTH

W.Marshall fecit.

Præ nob: Ord: Baln: EQVES.

Figure 9.   Henry Carey, Earl of Monmouth. By permission of The
Huntington Library, San Marino, California.

Fames pillar here, at last, we set,
Out-during *Marble, Brasse,* or *Jet,*
  Charm'd and enchanted so,
  As to withstand the blow
    Of   overthrow:
    Nor shall the seas,
    Or OUTRAGES
    Of storms orebear
    What we up-rear,
    Tho Kingdoms fal,
  This   pillar   never   shall
  Decline or waste at all;
But stand for ever by his owne
Firme and well fixt foundation.

We do not, I think, see the memorial statue of Robert Herrick in an actual representation of the Garden of Hesperides. For one thing, there is none of the traditional Hesperidean iconography in the picture—nothing about the famous apples, the eleventh labor of Hercules, the dragon, and so on. But as we ponder the relation of this pictured garden, this *locus amoenus,* to the title that faces it on the opposite page, we come gradually to the recognition that Herrick's "Hesperides" is the following collection of poems, the poems toward which, incidentally, the poet's gaze directs us as we turn over the facing leaf and commence to read.

As we walk about (i.e., "read") the garden, we can understand that our experience is quite often to be the verbal equivalent to *seeing,* an understanding which rests squarely on the Horatian doctrine, *ut pictura poesis.* A preponderance of the poems are to be read as speaking pictures, as *landskips* (in the general meaning of that term) where scenes of village life and rustic pleasures mingle with tales of the fairy kingdom and descriptions of trees and flowers, or they are to be read simply as iconic poems in which the poet contemplates an already-formed graphic representation. In still another sense, the large number of epigrams that pervade *Hesperides* also argues for the principle of poetry as speaking picture, especially if we call to mind the inscriptive nature of that poetic genre, which was to make some object "speak" to the beholder. In this respect, nearly all the "Julia" poems function as individual inscriptions elaborating the *image* of Julia.

Herrick's conscious and deliberate application of the *ut pictura poesis* principle is arguable, initially, on the basis of the poem addressed to his nephew—himself an artist—in which the poet compiles an impressive list of major painters; the list is comparable to nothing in the works of contemporary poets. Second, it is arguable on the basis of *"To his Honoured Kinsman, Sir Richard Stone"* (H-496), which poses the tantalizing possibility that Herrick took as his primary *schema* the famous statue gallery of the Earl of Arundel. And finally, it is arguable from the advice-to-a-painter poems in which he demonstrates uncommon skill in manipulating the reciprocal demands of the verbal and the visual.

"To his Nephew, to be prosperous in his art of Painting" (H-384) is addressed, in all probability, to Henry Stone, a son of Nicholas Stone of Devon, who was himself the outstanding English mason-sculptor of the period. Henry, known as a copyist of Van Dyke and other painters, appears to have spent the greater part of his thirty-seven years in Holland, France, and Italy. Moreover, he also composed a modest treatise called *The Third Part of the Art of Painting,* which we may reasonably speculate was a book known to his uncle. Whatever his ultimate merits as an artist or a theorist, he is linked by Herrick with the very greatest of the Renaissance painters:

> On, as thou hast begunne, brave youth, and get
> The Palme from *Urbin, Titian, Tintarret,*
> *Brugel* and *Coxie,* and the workes out-doe,
> Of *Holben,* and That mighty *Ruben* too.
> So draw, and paint, as none may do the like,
> No, not the glory of the World, *Vandike.*

Herrick's avuncular enthusiasm appears to have overcome any genuine critical awareness of his nephew's promise as a painter, for Henry Stone is virtually unknown for any artistic accomplishments. Nonetheless, this poem is grounded in a familiarity with important artists that must betoken interest in the visual arts. Certainly, works by Holbein, Rubens, and Van Dyke were widely known in the London of Herrick's youth and early maturity, and we may safely surmise that he, like so many others, was familiar with portraits by Holbein and Van Dyke, to say nothing of Rubens' famous ceiling at Whitehall. Indeed, Peter Paul Rubens was a close friend and avid collector of works by Jan (sometimes known as "Flower") Bruegel. Through copy-work done by his nephew and through social contact with artists, Herrick could have had direct experience with works by these painters. Coxie, however, is more of a problem than the others. Herrick probably refers to Michiel Coxie (1499–1592), who worked at Malines and Brussels and was a member of the Accademia di S. Luca at Rome. Coxie is mentioned by Vasari, whose *Lives of the Painters* may well have given Herrick some of his familiarity with the names of artists. Moreover, Coxie's drawings were an early source of inspiration to Rubens. If the reference is not to Michiel Coxie, it is probably to one of his sons, Michiel II, or grandsons, Michiel III or Mattys.[17] With the exception of Coxie, each of the artists mentioned was handsomely represented in the collection of the Earl of Arundel. And this fact, based on the famous Arundel inventories, raises the question whether Herrick had some first-hand familiarity with that collection, the most extensive and most famous of its kind in seventeenth-century England, and rivaled only by the collections of King Charles himself.[18]

That Herrick may have seen some of the Earl's collection is suggested in *"To his Honoured Kinsman, Sir* Richard Stone":

> To this *white Temple* of my *Heroes,* here
> Beset with stately Figures (every where)
> Of such rare *Saint-ships,* who did here consume
> Their lives in sweets, and left in death perfume.
> Come thou *Brave man!* And bring with Thee a Stone
> Unto thine own *Edification.*
> High are These Statues here, besides no lesse
> Strong then the Heavens for everlastingnesse:
> Where build aloft; and being fixt by These,
> Set up Thine own *eternall Images.*

The fundamental image in this poem, that of a *"white Temple of . . . Heroes,"* figuring significant achievement and the honors attendant upon that achievement, may well come from the pictorial formula used in the portrait (by Daniel Mytens) of the Earl of Arundel in his statue gallery (figure 10). Saxl and Wittkower speculate that this is not a representation of the Earl's collection at Arundel House but is, rather, the repetition of a visual *schema* developed in Italy and used by artists elsewhere.[19] Nonetheless, whether this picture is the representation or simply the idealization of a place, Herrick's poem relies for its own effect on something far more impressive than verbal panegyric alone. It invites the reader to *see* a pantheon—a white temple of heroes where statuary towers over the head of the beholder. And the fact that he refers to "this" temple of heroes that is "here beset with stately figures" suggests a degree of specificity that can be accounted for only in terms of an actual place (Arundel house?) or an actual picture (the portrait of the Earl in his statue gallery?), or a piece of iconic writing.

Neither of these two poems conveys an inner sense of the *ut pictura poesis* dictum. They are only circumstantial bits of evidence revealing Herrick's awareness of the pantheon of painters and, perhaps, of the statue gallery—itself an important visual metaphor—dedicated to the fame of heroic men. But in his two poems written according to the "instruction-to-a-painter" *topos*, we may perceive first-hand Herrick's ability to bridge the two arts on the basis of the *ut pictura poesis* assumption. The first of these in *Hesperides* is *"To the Painter, to draw him a Picture"* (H-108), one of the earliest English poems of its kind:[20]

> Come, skilfull *Lupo*, now, and take
> Thy *Bice*, thy *Umber*, *Pink*, and *Lake*;
> And let it be thy Pensils strife,
> To paint a Bridgeman to the life:
> Draw him as like too, as you can,
> An old, poore, lying, flatt'ring man:
> His cheeks be-pimpled, red and blue;
> His nose and lips of mulbrie hiew.
> Then for an easie fansie; place

Figure 10. The Earl of Arundel by Daniel Mytens. Courtesy,
Lord Arundel and The Tate Gallery, London.

A Burling iron for his face:
Next, make his cheeks with breath to swell,
And for to speak, if possible:
But do not so; for feare, lest he
Sho'd by his breathing, poyson thee.

The speaker's direct address to Lupo immediately locates the event in human or dramatic time. A patron has approached the artist with instructions for the composition of a picture. In these lines our attention goes rather automatically to the verbal event (perhaps even the "narrative" event) of which we are only vicarious participants. "Come," "take," and "let" are spoken within the precincts of this narrative framework. But a curious thing happens after "let." It is to be "thy Pensils strife, / To paint a Bridgeman to the life." By putting the emphasis on the pencil, the instrument, Herrick removes attention from the person, the artist; to a degree, the artist fades from view while the medium of pictorial creation achieves an autonomy of its own. In line 5, "Draw" momentarily returns us to an awareness of the dramatic moment. But the ensuing description of the proposed portrait exerts an unavoidable pull toward the iconic. Lines 5–9, then, are virtually ecphrastic. They constitute a description of an object that resides in the stilled ("still," to use the pun so effectively employed by both Keats—in "Ode on a Grecian Urn"—and Eliot—in "Burnt Norton") world of plastic forms. Indeed, the language of the poem is the device whereby the effect of "stillness" is created and maintained. Spatial concerns have overcome for the moment all temporal concerns: before us we see the face of an old, poor, lying, flattering man with pimpled cheeks discolored as much by the outer elements as by the inner disease of a mean and crafty disposition. In line 9, the imperative, "place," temporarily reasserts the dominance of the original dramatic moment, and in line 11, "make" reinforces our sense of resumed temporal progression of events. But the suspense generated in lines 11–12 is based almost wholly on visual perception vicariously entertained. We are expected to "see" in our minds' eyes the painter's ultimate, anticipated triumph—that of creating an illusion which seems on the verge of actually speaking. This, after all, was the achievement of Zeuxis, who, according to tradition, painted a thoroughly lifelike image of Helen, and of Apelles and Praxiteles, who both rendered perfect and all-but-breathing images of the celebrated courtesan, Phryne. But it is at just this point that the speaker in the dramatic, temporal framework of the poem hesitates and, in doing so, he calls us back from *pictura* to *poema*. Reversing direction, which has been toward the iconic creation of a living picture much in the tradition of Philostratus' *Imagines*—the supreme achievement of verbal verisimilitude—he warns the painter that an image so true to life "Sho'd by his breathing, poyson thee."

The deeper resonances of the joke would be lost if we did not participate fully in the assumption on which it is based. For example, all the theoretical ingredients of the *ut pictura poesis* formula are there: the doctrine of *imitation*, the doctrine of *invention*, and the doctrine of *expression*. Verbally, we have followed the imitation of a dramatized event. But closely associated with that event we have been invited to participate vicariously in a visual *compositione*. The *dispositio*, or blocking out of the poem's rhetorical course, has paralleled the *circonscriptione*, or the outline drawing of the caricature as it is created "by the Pensils strife." And the *elocutio* of the poem—its actual spoken performance—is the appropriate medium for the punch line, in which we learn that such an accurate visual likeness as has emerged through the medium of words comes dangerously close to being as disgusting as the model in person.[21] Moreover, the description of the painting, the iconic element in the poem, has also brought the reader vicariously into the midst of the most popular of the Renaissance *paragoni*, the strife between nature and art.[22] The visual and the verbal have, in effect, fought it out. And though in this instance the verbal would appear to have won, it is only because the visual threatens to reproduce actuality so vividly that the capacity of art to sustain illusion will be destroyed. As Jean Hagstrum has remarked in *The Sister Arts:*

The competition between painter and poet achieved philosophic and artistic status during the Renaissance largely because it represented a profound and far-reaching conflict of interest and idea, a conflict that itself may be said to have had a part in the making of the modern world. For poetry, the newly won position of painting carried a challenge; it, like painting, must seek to render the wholesome and vivacious realities of life and nature. But the prestige of painting also implied something subtler and more profound. The greatest power of painting, as it was understood by the Renaissance mind, was the power of making physical detail—and physical detail only—express order, character, meaning, morality, and purpose.[23]

And it is this enormously vital power of the visual that competes with poetry in Herrick's lyric.

"*The Eye*" (H-133) is Herrick's only other poem using the "instruction-to-a-painter" *topos*. But here, instead of framing the presentation of instructions within a clearly dramatized situation, Herrick launches immediately into them:

> Make me a heaven; and make me there
> Many a lesse and greater spheare.
> Make me the straight, and oblique lines;
> The Motions, Lations, and the Signes.
> Make me a Chariot, and a Sun;
> And let them through a Zodiac run:
> Next, place me Zones, and Tropicks there;
> With all the Seasons of the Yeare.
> Make me a Sun-set; and a Night:
> And then present the Mornings-light
> Cloath'd in her Chamlets of Delight.
> To these, make Clouds to poure downe raine;
> With weather foule, then faire againe.
> And when, wise Artist, that thou hast,
> With all that can be, this heaven grac't;
> Ah! what is then this curious skie,
> But onely my *Corinna's* eye?

As we read this poem, the precise *descriptio* calls instantly to mind a well-known set of visual *topoi* from the category of popular imagery commonly termed "le monde et les créatures." The subject of hundreds of broadside engravings and woodcuts, to say nothing of emblems, the composite subject of Herrick's proposed "picture" includes (either directly or indirectly) the four elements, the seven planets, the seasons, the months, and the signs of the zodiac. In addition, it includes day and night as well as popular meteorology.[24] As the conventional diagram of the universe begins to unfold, the cyclical progression of the seasons is compounded by the cycles of day and night until at last we reach that circle beneath the moon where clouds "poure downe raine." Not until the fourteenth line of the poem is the dramatic frame of reference established by the speaker's recognition of the "wise Artist" who presumably stands before him. And even then, in an interrogative that unfolds in a leisurely, rhetorically periodic manner before us, we learn that this carefully structured and infinitely manifold universe is "onely my *Corinna's* eye."

The method here is comparable to that of an emblem, a genre which required of poems that they be "speaking pictures" and which required of pictures that they be visual poems. The first thirteen lines are deliberately and systematically iconic, recalling such standard depictions of the universe as Fludd's title page (figure 2). But instead of describing a picture that imitates reality in its *natural* form, it describes a hieroglyphic image. When we read the final line of the poem, the unmistakable symbol of the universe is metamorphosed into Corinna's eye, which becomes (in both senses of the term) the universe. Notably, after achieving the proper symbolic image, Herrick turns to the resources of language—in this instance the calculated effect of the interrogative mode—to reveal the significance of the emblem. Once again, we should be lost without some knowledge of the *ut pictura poesis* maxim as our guide. For Corinna's eye, *"The Eye,"* is itself a multiplex picture that "speaks" several messages simultaneously. Each element in the emblem *is* an aspect of the universe. And the manifold universe cannot help but manifest itself in the singleness of *this* beautiful eye.

Thus far we have prepared ourselves to "walk" about in Herrick's Hesperidean garden to the extent that we know to "see" as well as to "read." From the emblematic frontispiece to the two "painter" poems we have learned that in order to relate to Herrick's verbal world we should perform the poems vicariously in a manner that allows verbalization to blend subtly with verisimilitude.[25] Indeed, it would seem to be just such a blend that Herrick himself found so pleasing in Sir John Denham's "Cooper's Hill," a poem that he praised in *"To* Master Denham, *on his Prospective Poem"* (H-673). And once we have learned the trick, we are prepared to see that this has probably been a significant part of the poet's intention from the beginning. In the much discussed *"Arguments of his Book"* (H-1), for example, he systematically proceeds through the links in the conventional great "chain of being" from the world of inanimate to animate nature, then to the world of man, to the world of God's mysterious cause-and-effect, and (at last) to the realms of Hell and Heaven.[26] He has signaled, in short, that his garden of poetry—the virtual realm—figures the realm of actuality even to the extent of expressing the way one *perceives* actuality. That is to say, his poems are not so much *about* anything; rather, they are experiences in and of themselves which relate us to the actual experience we have with the surrounding universe and even with *pictures* of the universe. This is why one's perambulations in the Hesperidean garden depend so much upon a reciprocal interplay of the visual and the verbal, the one being perceptual and the other being conceptual. The difference between Herrick and, say, Donne or Cleveland in this regard is not so much that between one who is a "Cavalier" and others who are "Metaphysicals." Rather, it is to be seen in Herrick's deliberate foreshortening of visual conceits which Donne and Cleveland tend to leave deliberately unresolved. For such poets as those, *catachresis* commonly prevents images from coming altogether on a common ground; the compass image from "A Valediction: forbidding mourning" is illustrative. In a subtle way, Robert Herrick also brings many disparate things into the precincts of the poem. But instead of *catachresis,* Herrick employs the more radical principle of *ut pictura poesis,* whereby it is the visual and the verbal that are yoked together and not, as Samuel Johnson complained of the metaphysicals, "heterogeneous ideas . . . yoked by violence together." And so smoothly does he miter the joints in this fusion of the visual and the verbal that the reader interested only in "nature" poetry misses the art altogether.

By way of conclusion, I shall illustrate what I believe to be some of the more exquisite subtleties of Herrick's blend of the visual and verbal in the "Oberon" poems, in the "Julia" poems, and in a selective sampling of others where his poetry embraces *topoi* common to the painting of the period. It is Andrew Marvell who is commonly believed to have most fully developed the ec-phrastic potential of poetry during the seventeenth century in England. Rosalie Colie has made a strong case for Marvell's use of the Horatian maxim in such poems as "The Gallery," "The Unfortunate Lover," "The Garden," and "Upon Appleton House." And it is she who has most convincingly called attention to Marvell's spectacular use of *topoi* common to contemporary landscape painting and emblems and to his employment of visual devices related to scalar shifts and optical illusions. She sees "scalar disruption," for example, when "grasshoppers are seen to contemn the men 'beneath' them," an image based on the fact that "the grasshoppers are sitting, in their usual small shapes, on top of the grass grown taller than men. Inverted, but not inverted; and the poet involves himself in this scene as a figure wandering in this world."[27] In addition, she demonstrates that Marvell's imagery includes deviations in perspective, metamorphoses, and anamorphoses. But neither Colie nor anyone else, to my knowledge, has pointed out that Robert Herrick often works in a similar way, particularly in the "Oberon" poems. What is remarkable is that he did so many years before Robert Hooke's *Micrographia* (London, 1665), which made more fashionable the theme of "small things seen as great."

In his dedication of "Oberons *Feast*" (H-293A) to Thomas Shapcott, Herrick identifies his interest in *"things that are / Curi-ous, and un-familiar."* In the very first line of the poem proper he is able to begin the ecphrasis with "A Little mushroome table spred." It is too easy, perhaps, from our own modern perspective to view the scene as something like a doll's house, a plaything. But such a view would be misleading, for Herrick is engaged in a determined effort to create a particular illusion through words. As he proceeds through the miniature delicacies of the feast—the "Moon-parcht grain of purest wheat," the "pure seed-Pearle of

Infant dew," the "hornes of paperie Butterflies," and the "little Fuz-ball-pudding," the "Late fatned" moth, and "The unctuous dewlaps of a Snaile"—we respond fully to the verbal pictures precisely because they link something in the actual world of scalar relationships and objects of normal size to the item in the fairy world. Cows in our world do have dewlaps; they are also sizable creatures, and their dewlaps have considerable bulk and weight. To speak, then, of the dewlaps on snails is to require significant proportional adjustment on the part of the reader. At once he must visualize himself to be of so small a size that the snail—normally an insignificantly small thing itself—becomes the equivalent of a cow. To me, this is as spectacular a verbal feat as Marvell's conceptualization of grasshoppers standing upon grass that waves above one's head. In Herrick's poem, though, a tiny object in the actual world of scalar relationships has been superimposed upon the virtual in a deliberately dislocative and disruptive way. As *pictura,* "Oberons *Feast*" requires a significant optical adjustment, one that we now probably take too much for granted as a consequence of our experience with telescopes, binoculars, microscopes, and cameras.

In "King Oberon his Cloathing," which I believe to have been written by Herrick and not Sir Simeon Steward,[28] we find exactly the same ecphrastic impulse and the same scalar disruption. But there is, in addition to the visual, a tactile element that intensifies the verisimilitude of the verbal picture. Oberon's "Roabes for Reuelling" are "a cob-webb shirt more thinne / Then ever spider yet could spinne." One waistcoat is made "Of the Trowt-flies guilded wing," but it is discarded because those dressing the king fear that "even with its weight" it will "make him sweat." As in the previous poem, where the reader was invited to project a scalar image of himself into the poem by means of the unusual imagery, the reader is here invited to imagine how delicate he would have to be in order for the wings of trout-flies to make him sweat. And when we read that the lace on Oberon's doublet is "Drawne by the unctuous Snailes slowe trace," we are likewise compelled to adjust ourselves mentally to a world of relativity where something seemingly so insubstantial in our actual experience takes on the permanence of substance in the world of pure verisimilitude.

The effects created here by words seem curiously parallel to those created by Jan Bruegel in his spectacularly vivid flower paintings as well as in his landscapes. In Herrick's *"The Fairie Temple"* (H-223), for example, the following lines manifest a clarity of the visualized object, a vividness of texture and color, and a tightly woven sense of spatial interdependencies that beg acceptance of the speculation offered above of Herrick's first-hand knowledge of painting. Of the tiny altar we read that its

> Linnen-Drapery is a thin
> Subtile and ductile Codlin's skin;
> Which o're the board is smoothly spred,
> With little Seale-work Damasked.
> The Fringe that circumbinds it too,
> Is Spangle-work of trembling dew,
> Which, gently gleaming, makes a show,
> Like Frost-work glitt'ring on the Snow.   (ll. 60–67)

Further, "the *Fairie-Psalter* [is] Grac't with the Trout-flies curious wings, / Which serve for watched Ribbanings." Herrick's technical grasp of surfaces, textures, and proportional relationships is analogous to that of Bruegel (figure 11). Indeed, the all-encompassing nature of the theme in these incredibly detailed paintings in *The Five Senses* series prompts the question whether Robert Herrick's *Hesperides* is not also a tour of the senses that combines pastoral scenes, imaginary landscapes, pictures-within-pictures, perspectives, mythological creatures, and still life. Certainly, Herrick's vivid flower poems, *"To Cherry-blossomes"* (H-189), *"How Lillies came white"* (H-190), *"To Pansies"* (H-191), *"On Gelli-flowers begotten"* (H-192), and the remarkably colorful *"The Lilly in a Cristall"* (H-193), reflect an awareness of an interest in still life of the sort done by Jan Bruegel and collected so avidly by Peter Paul Rubens.

And there is a great deal more of an ecphrastic nature in the poems to Julia, where Herrick's striking sensuality depends wholly upon the perception of textures, surfaces, and intimate

Figure 11. "Sight" from *The Five Senses* by Jan Bruegel. Courtesy, The Prado, Madrid.

physical detail. *"On* Julia's *Picture"* (H-374) gives us a clue, for it is a purely iconic poem that is about a picture and not the object of the picture:

> How am I ravisht! When I do but see,
> The Painters art in thy *Sciography?*
> If so, how much more shall I dote thereon,
> When once he gives it incarnation?

On the basis of the strong visual element in the "Julia" poems, I am led to speculate that when Herrick declares his intention "to sing of cleanly-*Wantonnesse*" he is doing so on the grounds that in iconic poetry the visual illusion is sustained only by the fragile temporality of language (the very epitome in art of *"Times trans-shifting"*). Notably, this epigram ("How am I ravisht") relies upon the same principle that we observed in *"To the Painter, to draw him a Picture."* Through the art of the painter, it is assumed that the image will suddenly spring into life; it will assume a natural life through the medium of art. And when (in H-349) he writes: "Fain would I kiss my *Julia's* dainty Leg, / Which is as white and hair-less as an egge," or (in H-230):

> Display thy breasts, my *Julia,* there let me
> Behold that circummortall purity:
> Between whose glories; there my lips Ile lay,
> Ravisht, in that faire *Via Lactea,*

we become acutely aware that the declaration and the image are indeed so far apart that they are forever prevented from losing the delicacy of illusion—of artful representation—that is the universal hedge against pornography.

On the basis of the foregoing, it is proper to declare that Robert Herrick not only understood the workings of the visual imagination but that he consciously developed a poetic technique compatible with the operation of such imaginative faculties. Thematically, *Hesperides* is a large and complex landskip which the poet is at pains to define in *"The Argument of his Book"* and to redefine throughout by means of the poetic experiences he holds up to his readers. Like the painted landscapes that were so popular during the seventeenth century,[29] Herrick's poems encompass natural scenes,[30] objects seen in nature,[31] celebrations and village environs,[32] and pastorals.[33] And interspersed generously about this poetic landscape are several hundred epigrams, poems in a genre derived from the lineated inscription which, during the Renaissance, appeared everywhere: upon tablets, shields, and plaques, upon temporary structures made for pageants and processions, and—in the art of painting—as bearers of cryptic, *impresa*-like messages such as the famous "Et in arcadia ego" of Nicholas Poussin's paintings by that title.

In the midst of this variety and poetic ripeness, Herrick's Hesperidean garden is most certainly one whose golden fruits take the shape of poems. Moreover, it is a garden created according to the ancient formula *ut pictura poesis*, and one in which we may (in the most vivid sense) "walk amongst" the verbal equivalent of "bowers, mounts, and arbours, artificiall wildernesses, green thickets, . . . rivulets, fountains and such like pleasant places."

NOTES

1. Robert Burton, *The Anatomy of Melancholy*, ed. Holbrook Jackson, 3 vols. (London, 1961), II, 74–75.

2. (London, 1963), p. 2.

3. "Herrick's 'Hesperides,' " *Modern Language Review*, 9 (1914), 373–74.

4. *Robert Herrick* (New York, 1966), p. 29.

5. *Theatrum Poetarum, or A Compleat Collection of the Poets* (London, 1675), p. 162.

6. Quoted in H. V. S. Ogden and M. S. Ogden, *English Taste in Landscape in the Seventeenth Century* (Ann Arbor, 1955), pp. 5–7. See also Luigi Salerno, "Seventeenth-Century English Literature on Painting," *Journal of the Warburg-Courtauld Institute*, 14 (1951), 234–58.

7. *The Complete Poetry of Robert Herrick*, ed. J. Max Patrick (New York, 1968), pp. 7–8. The poems are quoted from this edition.

8. (Oxford, at the University Press for the Bibliographical Society, 1934), pp. vii–viii.

9. *The English Icon: Elizabethan and Jacobean Portraiture* (New Haven, 1969), p. 30.

10. Margery Corbett and Michael Norton, *Engraving in England in the Sixteenth and Seventeenth Centuries* (Cambridge, 1964), pp. 102–92.

11. Ibid., p. 186.

12. Walter J. Ong, "From Allegory to Diagram in the Renaissance Mind: A

Study in the Significance of the Allegorical Tableau," *Journal of Aesthetics and Art Criticism,* 17 (1959), 423–41.

13. Ronald Berman, "Herrick's Secular Poetry," *English Studies,* 52 (1971), 20–30, argues persuasively but in a much more restricted theoretical context for the hieroglyphic character of Herrick's poetic imagery.

14. See, for example, Corbett and Norton, plates 54, 57, 58, 60, and 68. It may be objected that Marshall's engraving of John Milton for the 1645 edition of the *Poems* bears the following verses (translated from the Greek by W. R. Parker, *Milton: A Biography* (Oxford: Clarendon Press, 1968), p. 289.

> You, who really know my face,
> Fail to find me in this place.
> Portraiture the fool pretends,
> Laugh at the result my friends.

But while Milton objected to the artist's interpretation of his features, he did not deny that he was the object of the artist's endeavors.

15. John Sparrow, *Visible Words: A Study of Inscriptions in and as Books and Works of Art* (Cambridge, 1969).

16. The concept of such "occurrence" and a definition of its enabling conditions are uncommon in the vocabulary of philological criticism and New Criticism. They are best approached through the concept of "liminality" in Arnold van Gennep, *The Rites of Passage,* trans. Monika B. Vizedom and Gabrielle L. Caffe (Chicago, 1960), and the extended discussion of that term by Victor Turner, *The Ritual Process: Structure and Antistructure* (Chicago, 1969) and *Dramas, Fields, and Metaphors: Symbolic Action in Human Society* (Ithaca, 1974), as well as in his essay, "Myth and Symbol," *The International Encyclopedia of the Social Sciences.* In this essay, Turner says, "Myths are liminal phenomena: they are frequently told at a time or in a site that is 'betwixt and between.' " "Liminality is a period of structural [social] impoverishment and symbolic enrichment." "Liminality is pure potency." In an unpublished paper, "Liminality, Play, Flow, and Ritual: An Essay in Comparative Symbology," he extends his discussion of liminality to include the concept of "liminoid" ("-oid" deriving from the Greek "-eidos," which means "like" or "resembling"): "In the so-called 'high' culture of complex societies, the liminoid is not only removed from a rite of passage context, it is also 'individualized.' The solitary artist creates the liminoid phenomena, the collectivity experiences collective liminal symbols. This does not mean that the maker of liminoid symbols, ideas, images, etc. does so *ex nihilo*; it only means that he is privileged to make free with his social heritage in a way impossible to members of cultures in which the *liminal* is to a large extent the sacrosanct." Herrick, I propose, is inviting his reader into a comparable situation which lies in the particularly fruitful region for re-creativity "betwixt and between" the visual and the verbal.

17. Ulrich Thieme and Felix Becker, *Allgemines Lexikon der Bildenden Künstler* (Leipzig, 1913).

18. Mary Hervey, *The Life of Thomas Howard, Earl of Arundel* (Cambridge, 1921).

See also, Fritz Grossmann, "Notes on the Arundel and Imsteuraedt Collections," *Burlington Magazine,* 84 (1944), 151–54; 85 (1944), 173–76.

19. Fritz Saxl and Rudolph Wittkower, *British Art and the Mediterranean* (London, 1948).

20. There is a relatively complete checklist of poems using this *topos* by Mary Tom Osborne, *Advice-to-a-Painter Poems, 1633–1856* (Austin, 1949). Among discussions of poems, mainly those of Marvell, see Michael Gearin-Tosch, "The Structure of Marvell's 'Last Instructions to a Painter,' " *Essays in Criticism,* 22 (1972), 48–57; and Earl Miner, "The 'Poetic Picture, Painted Poetry' of 'The Last Instructions to a Painter,' " *Modern Philology,* 62 (1966), 288–94.

21. The fullest discussion of the Horatian maxim is Rensselaer W. Lee, *Ut Pictura Poesis: The Humanist Theory of Painting* (New York, 1967). However, specific parallels between the theoretical *dicta* of poets and painters are discussed by Creighton E. Gilbert, "Antique Frameworks for Renaissance Art Theory: Alberti and Pino," *Marsyas,* 3 (1943–45), 87–106.

22. Jean H. Hagstrum, *The Sister Arts: The Tradition of Literary Pictorialism and English Poetry from Dryden to Gray* (Chicago, 1958), p. 66.

23. Ibid., p. 70.

24. Achille Bertarelli, *L'imagerie populaire italienne* (Paris, 1929); Samuel Chew, *The Pilgrimage of Life* (New Haven, 1962).

25. Such vicarious performance requires alertness to the cues the poet includes in his poem, cues that give not only the literary expectations which are appropriate but the implicit social context as well. See, in this connection, Roger D. Abrahams, "Folklore and Literature as Performance," *Journal of the Folklore Institute,* 9 (1972), 75–94. In an extended discussion of "Corinna's *going a Maying*" Abrahams explains how Herrick "uses the traditional seasonal ceremony as the setting for a poem" and how, through that reference, he "has been able to call upon more of the resonances of the base-metaphor comparing life with the passage of the seasons." He approaches Herrick's poem with the assumption that "if there can be art in life, then it seems no problem to also see the utility of calling the life-artist a performer and to regard his manipulation of the latencies of life-style as performance. Such usage recognizes that just as there is a difference between an art of life and the art of art because the latter is considerably more self-conscious and stylized, so there will be distinctions made in the realm of performance. But this perspective allows us to see that rather than there being a hard-and-fast line between such interactions, there are crucial continuities." Cf. discussions by Turner, above n. 16.

26. I am indebted to my colleague, R. V. LeClercq, for this observation.

27. Rosalie L. Colie, *"My Ecchoing Song": Andrew Marvell's Poetry of Criticism* (Princeton, 1970), p. 205.

28. Norman K. Farmer, Jr., "Robert Herrick and 'King Oberon's Clothing': New Evidence for Attribution," *The Yearbook of English Studies,* 1 (1971), 68–77.

29. See Ogden, n. 6 above, and Wolfgang Stechow, *Dutch Landscape Painting of the Seventeenth Century* (London, 1968).

30. *"A Country Life: To his Brother"* (H-106), *"To Springs and Fountains"* (H-413), *"To* Dean-bourn*"* (H-86), *"To Meddowes"* (H-274), and *"Faire dayes: or, Dawnes deceitful"* (H-202).

31. *"The Lilly in a Cristal"* (H-193), *"Divination by a Daffadill"* (H-107), *"To Groves"* (H-449), *"To Daffadills"* (H-316), *"To the Willow-tree"* (H-262).

32. *"The Hock-cart, or Harvest home"* (H-250), "Corinna's *going a Maying"* (H-178), *"Twelfe night, or* King *and* Queene*"* (H-1035), *"Ceremonies for Candlemasse Eve"* (H-892), *"Ceremonies for Christmass"* (H-784), *"The Wake"* (H-761), *"The Wassaile"* (H-476), *"A New-years gift sent to Sir* Simeon Steward*"* (H-319), *"An Epithalamie to Sir* Thomas Southwell*"* (H-149A).

33. *"A Beucolick, or discourse of Neatherds"* (H-716), "Charon *and* Phylomel, *A Dialogue sung"* (H-730), *"An Eclogue, or Pastorall between* Endimion Porter *and* Lycidas Herrick*"* (H-492), *"A Pastorall sung to the King"* (H-421).

AVON JACK MURPHY

Robert Herrick: The Self-Conscious Critic in *Hesperides*

Robert Herrick has been largely neglected as a literary critic because he is a different type of critic from an Addison or a Wellek. In essence, his criticism is "I"-centered: the more than one hundred poems in *Hesperides*[1] which make direct statements about the definition, technique, function, composition, and reception of art all reflect the poet's analysis and judgment of himself.[2] In a slightly different context, Joan Webber has written, "By seventeenth-century literary self-consciousness, I mean the writer's crucial and unremitting awareness that he is the subject of his own prose. . . . As a writer, he is explicitly interested in his own prose and often comments exclusively upon it, becoming his own first critic."[3] This approach may be applied generally to the way Herrick uses the device of a persona-critic throughout *Hesperides*.[4] He seems to have arranged his poems so that one who reads through the volume gradually acquires a sense of the persona's developing literary self-consciousness. This persona is groping toward confidence in his own artistry and control, an assurance in the immortalizing power of poetry, and a mature realization of what *Hesperides* can and does become. The development operates through a three-part sequence: (1) the opening (H-1 through H-8), (2) the large middle section (H-9 through H-1122), and (3) the conclusion (H-1123 through H-1130).

The frontispiece to the 1648 edition placed the focus on the poet himself: his bust is centered on a pedestal of fame; at the bottom of the pedestal the inscription to the poet is framed by two pointing Muses in mirror postures; the poet's chest is flanked by various balancing details; and in the air two flanking Muses prepare to crown him with wreaths. It is thus no surprise that the persona opens the volume itself with eight poems tentatively implying principles which he will observe while evaluating his own art. The persona here mixes tones and topics with a premonition of the ultimate complexity of his art and with some insecurity about how his art is to be managed.

In *"The Argument of his Book"* (H-1) Herrick *seems* to have his upcoming performance well in hand, as implied in the choice of stylistic devices which not only befit formal announcement of one's literary program but also suggest deliberate control by the speaker: the strong yoking of disparate topics through alliteration; the series of "I sing of" and "I write of" phrases; and even a semi-sonnet structure.[5] However, the suggestions of mysterious changeability in *"Times trans-shifting,"* changing flower colors, and the coming of nightfall and fairy activities following human social activities indicate that the persona cannot have everything in his poetic universe under absolute control.

The second poem, *"To his Muse,"* shows a more conscious uncertainty. He argues that his verse will be safe from severe criticism only if he restricts it to pastoral themes. But several clues tell us that such a restriction will be invalid. Two such clues are the overly artificial alliteration in "piping please / The poore and private *Cottages*" and the self-doubt implied in the word "perhaps," which is slipped into "There, there, (perhaps) such Lines as These / May take the simple *Villages.*" Even stronger evidence is the impossibility of "sitting still," already suggested in the opening poem by his reference to *"Times trans-shifting"* and his saying, "I write of *Hell*; I sing (and ever shall) / Of *Heaven"*—this is how far his *"Mad maiden"* will roam.

The third poem, the first *"To his Booke,"* similarly pictures a roaming child to suggest further relaxation of bounds in letting others read his work: "On with thy fortunes then, what e're they be; / If good I'le smile, if bad I'le sigh for Thee." Having thus exposed himself to the world, the persona in the last five poems of this opening section adopts various tones—quiet pride, abusiveness, celebration—as he considers his readers. The eruptive vehemence of "May every Ill, that bites, or smarts, / Perplexe him in his hinder-parts" and "The Extreame Scabbe take thee" reflects an attempt to suppress the fear expressed in *"To his Muse"* that somewhere lurks a critic eager to misinterpret these verses. *"When he would have his verses read"* (H-8) suddenly switches us from epigrammatic bite to intense ceremony. The persona now picks up the more positive note of celebration found in *"The Argument"* as he describes the timing, setting, and structure of a poetic reading.[6] Instead of a man peering nervously from within his rural cell, we now find a persona confidently using words like "holy incantation," "Enchantments," and "sacred," along with classical references, to indicate the substantiality, mystery, and broad power of his poetry.

Herrick's grouping of eight critical poems at the beginning does more than announce that this section is a prologue. It also highlights the abrupt rhythm with which the persona finds his first thoughts about his own poetry erupting and clashing; he announces, he withdraws, he opens up, he attacks, he calls for celebration. This is the rhythm through which one evolves the principles by which he will judge art. The rhythm is an intensely personal matter, because the artistic self-consciousness of the persona is just beginning to develop. He thus confines himself to *his* developing book and *his* readers. At this stage he has not yet fully spelled out his aesthetic (there is, for example, no specific reference here to one of Herrick's dominant themes, the immortalizing power of verse), but he has established some general principles which will underlie the critical writing in the rest of *Hesperides:* the importance of readers' impressions, the ceremony and ritual of poetry, the mystery and sacredness of poetry, the development of significant content under a cloak of superficiality, the paradoxical *"cleanly-Wantonnesse,"* clarity, multiplicity, etc. Realizing that one must assume risks if he is to create and discuss art, the persona is ready to "make" his book.

In the second section of *Hesperides,* the critical poetry is found at intervals, but we should never forget that the persona is analyzing himself as he brings into his garden social occasions, mistresses, friends, relatives, and much else. Approximately twenty poems focus squarely on various literary figures. The praise in these poems is highly generalized: Mildmay Fane should publish his verses because otherwise they are concealed gems (H-459); John Denham possesses a Virgilian wit and will influence other poets (H-673); Leonard Willan can pen comedy or tragedy in prose or verse (H-955); John Hall seems incredibly young to write so well (H-956). Herrick does not make other points or provide substantial supportive detail, because, again, he is not that kind of critic.[7] Rather, the few qualities praised are always related to critical positions which are significant to him. Reinforced by classical precedent (Herrick even brings Horace directly into the argument with Fane), the persona perceives his subjects' works in terms of his concern about immortality and inspiration. Thus, he urges Fane to publish because only then will come that "publick praise" so vital to the artist's survival; Willan's versatile productivity assures that "Posterity will pay thee what I owe," namely survival, again, through praise. The mere presence of John Selden's literary spirit assures immortality for Hesperidean topics, book, and author (H-365). He attempts to trace the root of literary inspiration as he marvels at the mysterious *"mighty influence"* driving the Apollonian John Hall. William Alabaster seems inspired by "the spirit of the Gods" (H-763).

These poems on other writers are strategically spaced throughout the volume. The curt dismissal of unidentified poetasters referred to as Pievish, Prat, and Nis in three two-line epigrams spaced at regular intervals (H-410, H-692, and H-896) subtly suggests that throughout *Hesperides* the persona judges unworthy of consideration "the Worst" poets, whose verses are fit only "to make Paper-kites." Much more emphatic is the positive focus shown in *"The Apparition of his Mistresse calling him to* Elizium" (H-575).[8] Here in the middle of a book immortalizing numerous subjects, one of the many revelations is that the power to achieve poetic immortality (suggested in this very poem by such poeticized images as "eternall May," "perpetuall Day," "th'Enamel of the light," and "endlesse Roses") ultimately derives from one's inspiration. Homer, Anacreon, and Jonson are described through such terms as "incantation," "Raptures," "rage," and "Radiant fire." Herrick and Anacreon "drink and dance together"; Jonson is "thy Father." Connotations of mystery, sacredness, paternity, camaraderie, and ceremony establish the focus on these other writers as wellsprings of inspiration.

The dominant position of Jonson emphasized in *"The Apparition"* is made even clearer by the number and spacing of poems devoted exclusively to him as a source of inspiration. Six poems (H-382, H-383, H-604, H-653, H-910, and H-911) are grouped roughly in pairs at the beginning, middle, and end of *Hesperides,* thus suggesting that throughout the volume Jonson is for the persona a major source of power, his "Saint *Ben.*"[9] The two stanzas of the last of these poems, *"An Ode for him,"* appropriately assume the shape of pillars on the printed page; their end position and shape look forward to *"The pillar of Fame."* Thus, Herrick has arranged these and other poems on various authors to good critical advantage.

Only about a fifth of Herrick's directly critical poems involve assessments of other writers. The great majority reflect the persona's assessment of his own book. He will on rare occasions evaluate himself by writing an aesthetic definition. For instance, when in *"Art above Nature, to* Julia" (H-560) and *"Delight in Disorder"* (H-83) he commends "wild civility," he is isolating a principle underlying the artistic tensions found in much of his book. This principle recurs in such contexts as the tribute to Jonson's inspiration, which "made us nobly wild, not mad" (H-911), or even the structure of *Hesperides,* which is controlled yet seems so uncontrolled.

The persona often analyzes himself as in numerous poems he tells subjects how his art will immortalize them. The poems are so arranged that he seems to become more explicit about the poetic structure within which these people will achieve immortality as he becomes surer of what his volume is becoming. (This is not to imply that Herrick originally wrote the poems in the present order, but he does seem to have arranged them purposefully.) The elegy on his father, placed early in *Hesperides,* ends without any reference to the book itself: "Rise from out thy Herse, / And take a life immortall from my Verse" (H-82). The notion of a book in progress gradually becomes clearer in later poems: Edward Fish will live eternally "in this my rich Plantation" (H-392); Thomas Shapcott's name will be "Writ in the Poets Endlesse-Kalendar" (H-444); Penelope Wheeler comes "Next . . . / Here, in my Book's Canonization" (H-510); a friend can "Looke in my Book, and herein see, / Life endlesse" (H-906); and near the end Thomas Herrick is welcomed "though late" into "my great and good foundation" (H-983). Finally, we have one of the last poems, to Michael Oldisworth:

> Nor thinke that Thou in this my Booke art worst,
> Because not plac't here with the midst, or first.
> Since Fame that sides with these, or goes before
> Those, that must live with Thee for evermore.
> That Fame, and Fames rear'd Pillar, thou shalt see
> In the next sheet *Brave Man* to follow Thee.
> Fix on That Columne then, and never fall;
> Held up by Fames *eternall Pedestall*.   (H-1092)

Here the persona becomes explicit; he explains precisely where the man is placed in the book, as he himself looks ahead thirty-seven poems to *"The pillar of Fame."* The explicitness, positive boldness, and wittiness befit a persona who has gradually acquired the confidence that through his own powers he has ensured "Fame" for himself and his subjects. This is a poet convinced of his success.

The strongest evidence of the persona's developing critical self-awareness is the dozens of poems in which he plays the role of author addressing his muse, his book, his readers, or himself about his work as it evolves. These poems are a rhythmically unfolding total reflection of a self-conscious artist's creative self. Viewed in their entirety, they reveal a progression from unsure first steps, to fatigue, and finally to the edge of quiet triumph.

In the early poems of this type, the persona, unsure of how his *"Bride, the Bashfull Muse"* (H-84) will be received, nervously asks readers to "See, and not see . . . / Wink at small faults" (H-95). His insecurity sometimes expresses itself in virulent hostility toward critics; for instance:

> Thy long-black-Thumb-nail . . .
> A fellon take it, or some Whit-flaw come
> For to unslate, or to untile that thumb!   (H-173)

Or it may erupt into incredulous anger that worthless ballads "(Bred from the dung-hils, and adulterous rhimes,) / Shall live, and thou [his book] not superlast all times?" (H-405). We also sense it in odd juxtapositions, as when a broken-lined poem discussing his inability to compose immediately precedes the flawlessly ordered *"His Poetrie his Pillar"* (H-211). The persona does not yet feel assured that a contemporary reading public can accept the poem which focuses on mistresses, epigrammatically plays upon a topic and drops it, or falls flat in comparison with other verses in the same book. At this point, although he can assert the mystery of art in poems like those on sack (H-128 and H-197), he seems to fear that his accomplishment might be interpreted as a number of discrete productions, each open to individual attack, rather than as a unified whole (the precise structure of which he himself is not yet fully aware).

A cluster of poems focusing on creative fatigue and implications of death[10] signals transition into a broader, more controlled, more mature outlook on *Hesperides*. The persona no longer alarmedly views the hostility his poems might incur. There are no more diatribes against critics; his strongest relevant thought is simply to avoid "Those faces (sower as Vineger)" (H-868). Gaining confidence in his artistic worth, he instead develops a consistent touch of humor. He now relishes the comic effect of odd juxtapositions, as when a poem asserting "nor will I tell or sing / Of *Cupid,* and his wittie coozning" is followed by *"Upon* Jone *and* Jane" (H-659), which opens, *"Jone* is a wench that's painted; / *Jone* is a Girle that's tainted." Such outrageous comedy never arises in the first half of the volume. The sheer variety in his lines can now occasion jests rather than panic; he playfully boasts of his verse:

> Adopted some; none got by theft.
> But all are toucht (like lawfull plate)
> And no Verse illegitimate.   (H-681)

The persona's growth is evident also in his controlled vision of the structure which he has been creating. He describes in *"Not every day fit for Verse"* (H-714) his three stages of composition:

lack of inspiration → sudden "holy fier" of creativity → return to noncreativity. The persona who can write this no longer feels the panicky defeatism of earlier complaints like *"The Poet hath lost his pipe"* (H-573). Once he has written, his responsibility is to await further inspiration, which will come. Confidence in his inspiration implies acceptance of several major principles. (1) The verse is all to be taken seriously. (2) The poet cannot be held totally accountable for what goes into his book. (This principle can partially deflect blame for unchaste poetry and can lead to a rationale for God as the author of poems, which Herrick develops more explicitly in *His Noble Numbers*.) (3) Different inspirations create a great variety in poetic length, theme, and tone. The security with which the persona accepts these principles in the second half of the book fully prepares us for the confidence and clear-sightedness of such late lines as "The bound (almost) now of my book I see, / But yet no end of those therein or me" (H-1019). We are ready for the concluding poems.

The final eight-poem movement, like the opening poems, focuses exclusively on personal reactions to the book. The persona will "write no more" (H-1124) of love and life, two topics embracing most of his themes. Instead, he asserts his triumph by setting up physical death as foil to artistic immortality. There has been even stronger evidence of physical decay throughout the last half of *Hesperides*,[11] but Herrick has kept it out of the critical verse, so that for some time a decline in the persona's physical health has corresponded to his rising confidence in his ability to achieve poetic immortality. The two trends at last come together when the first of these eight poems, *"The mount of the Muses"* (H-1123), contrasts "the Laurell Crowne" physically presented by men and the "one / Not subject to corruption" bestowed by the Muses. In the next five poems "my dust," "The Muses will weare blackes, when I am dead," and other phrases tell us that the body has almost given up.

The context for *"The pillar of Fame"* (H-1129) is established by the persona's becoming the addressee rather than the addresser in *"The mount of the Muses,"* his resolve to write no more, and the announcements of his death. Through a virtuoso stroke Herrick has removed his "dead" persona from the scene to focus entirely on *his own* art. The name "Herrick" has sporadically occurred in connection with various roles, but the distinctive presence of the persona has tended to keep the focus away from the poet himself. Now the lines in their control assure triumph for Herrick:

> This pillar never shall
> Decline or waste at all;
> But stand for ever by his owne
> Firme and well fixt foundation.

The definitions of "his" and "its" in the *Oxford English Dictionary* warrant interpreting "his owne / . . . foundation" as referring to *Hesperides* itself, which now, as the poem claims, effectively guarantees him immortality as an artist.

The focus on Herrick is reinforced by the relationship between this emblematic poem and the emblematic 1648 frontispiece. "Fames pillar" is shaped like the engraved monument, wide at the top and bottom and narrow in the middle. Although the two final lines of *Hesperides* (H-1130) are numbered as a separate poem by Patrick, it seems clear that in the 1648 edition, where they are printed without a title,[12] those lines are not supposed to be totally separate. Rather, they are an epigram appended to the base of the pillar exactly as the Latin verse to Herrick is inscribed on the foundation of the bust in the frontispiece. Referring to the engraved wreaths being presented to the bust of the poet, John Harmar's Latin proclaims: "A denser shade of leaves thy brows should bind; / A laurel grove is due to such a mind."[13] Herrick has arranged for his leafy "*Coronet*" earlier (H-1128); the two concluding lines cap his clever self-congratulation with more seeming humility than would a repetition of Harmar's bombast. Herrick has anchored his estimate of himself by making the end of his book mirror its opening, thus reinforcing the notion of the circular coronet he has fashioned for himself through his art.

The literary criticism in *Hesperides* is extremely valuable for what it tells us of Herrick's art. He is no Spenserian numerologist, but we should not be surprised to find critically effective structures in the work of a poet who carefully revises, remarks on his care in several poems, and knows where a given poem fits into the structure of his book as a whole. Close reading of *Hesperides* reveals the subtle use of a persona who reflects in detail the growth of a critical self-consciousness through a carefully structured sequence of reactions. Herrick has proved himself to be a sound literary critic as well as a successful poet.

NOTES

1. "*Hesperides*" refers in this paper to the first book of the 1648 edition; I am not discussing *His Noble Numbers*. Quotations from Herrick are followed by "H" (*Hesperides*) and appropriate poem numbers from *The Complete Poetry of Robert Herrick*, ed. J. Max Patrick (New York, 1963).

2. For views on the aesthetics underlying Herrick's critical stance, see, for instance, Leah Jonas, *The Divine Science: The Aesthetic of Some Representative Seventeenth-Century English Poets* (New York, 1940), pp. 228–42; Roger B. Rollin, *Robert Herrick* (New York, 1966), particularly ch. 7, "*The Pillar of Fame* and *This Sacred Grove*: The Theme of Immortality"; and Richard John Ross, " 'A Wild Civility': Robert Herrick's Poetic Solution of the Paradox of Art and Nature" (Ph.D. dissertation, University of Michigan, 1958). Rollin's chapter thoroughly investigates the background and poetic use of Herrick's major aesthetic theme; he offers several full explications in discussing such topics as the pastoral mediation between art and life, "wild civility," Jonson's influence upon Herrick's craftsmanship, and art as religion and salvation.

3. *The Eloquent "I": Style and Self in Seventeenth-Century Prose* (Madison, 1968), p. 4.

4. Herrick's persona is discussed by John L. Kimmey, "Order and Form in Herrick's *Hesperides*," *JEGP*, 70 (1971), 255–68; and "Robert Herrick's Persona," *SP*, 67 (1970), 221–36. Kimmey shows a much deeper understanding of Herrick's overall structure and the psychology of a developing persona than do most of Herrick's critics. In this study I differ from him mainly in focusing on one aspect of the persona's place within the design of *Hesperides*, an aspect which should be investigated to provide a still clearer insight into Herrick's achievement; Kimmey and I also differ in assessing the implications of some individual poems (for instance, "The pillar of Fame," H-1129). See also Rollin, *Herrick*, passim.

5. Robert B. Hinman analyzes sonnet implications in "The Apotheosis of Faust: Poetry and New Philosophy in the Seventeenth Century," in *Metaphysical Poetry*, ed. Malcolm Bradbury and David Palmer (Bloomington, 1971), pp. 160–63. Herrick is, of course, responsible for the themes, imagery, verse forms, sound patterns, etc., through which his persona may speak. However, in poetry of formal announcement (like H-1) or argumentativeness (like H-2), the author can

make the persona characterize himself through rhetorical decisions which seem to issue not so much from the author as from the speaker placed in a dramatic role. The same principle applies in Marvell's "To his Coy Mistress," wherein the decision to employ a deductive structure, improbable comparisons, and shocking imagery of physical decay belongs properly to and thereby characterizes the persona given the role of seducer.

6. On Herrick's ceremony, see Robert H. Deming, "Robert Herrick's Classical Ceremony," *ELH*, 34 (1967), 327–48.

7. It is true that most versified criticism written during the middle years of the seventeenth century is no more detailed. For instance, the commendatory verses bound with John Hall's essays say no more about the youthful Hall than does Herrick; A. Holden expresses the general view that "Thy Nineteen / Makes five and forty blush" (*Horae Vacivae, or, Essays. Some Occasionall Considerations* [London, 1646], sig. A10ʳ). However, such massive evidence as many critical poems prefixing the 1633 edition of Donne's *Poems* and many contributions to the 1638 *Jonsonus Virbius* strongly demonstrates that by the 1640s there was ample precedent for poets to write fully detailed commendations if they so desired. Herrick quite simply—and, I believe, consciously—chooses not to.

8. For a rather full treatment of many suggestions in "The Apparition," see Rollin, *Herrick*, pp. 192–98. Because I am interested mainly in the place of this poem in the overall structure of *Hesperides* and for the sake of concision, just one of its major themes is touched upon here.

9. The import of this six-poem series is reinforced by the spacing and theme of four poems (H-117, H-185, H-492, and H-1071) on Endymion Porter as patron and, therefore, source of poetic inspiration, the persona's "chiefe Preserver."

10. These poems are *"The bad season makes the Poet sad"* (H-612), *"To Vulcan"* (H-613), *"Glorie"* (H-623), and *"To his Verses"* (H-626); in the midst of these falls the noncritical *"His own Epitaph"* (H-617). On the persona and death, see especially Kimmey, "Robert Herrick's Persona," pp. 226–29; and Rollin, *Herrick*, pp. 32–47.

11. As Kimmey notes (ibid.), in the second half of the book the persona complains frequently of weakening vision and other bodily ills, discovers that his physical condition will no longer let him enjoy youth and love, and prepares for his own funeral.

12. Most other editors print the lines as part of the same poem.

13. Translated by Alexander B. Grosart, ed., *The Complete Poems of Robert Herrick*, 3 vols. (London, 1876), I, cclxxi.

A. E. ELMORE

Herrick and the Poetry of Song

About twelve hundred of the more than fourteen hundred poems which Herrick published in a single volume in 1648 are
written exclusively in rhyming couplets of a single and unvary-
ing meter—iambic pentameter, iambic tetrameter, or truncated
iambic tetrameter (that is, with the initial syllable of each line
omitted).[1] For convenience these twelve hundred will here be
called "uniform" poems. The approximately two hundred poems
containing any variation at all from the uniform patterns (apart
from an occasional unsystematic foot substitution or feminine
ending) will be called "varied" poems. The latter thus constitute
only about one of every seven poems in *Hesperides* and *Noble
Numbers*.

Yet an examination of representative modern anthologies reveals a surprising and suggestive fact. Varied poems account for
virtually *half* of all Herrick's poems in the anthologies—47 percent,
to be exact, as opposed to only about 15 percent (one out of seven)
in Herrick's original volume. Assuming that anthologists try to
select the best poems (their only other standard being representa-
tiveness, from which they clearly depart in Herrick's case), one
must conclude that the work now generally considered Herrick's
best contains a significant disproportion of varied poems.

Furthermore, such poems figure even more disproportionately
among the works considered to be Herrick's *very* best: "Corinna's *going a Maying*" (H-178), "*To the Virgins*" (H-208), "*Upon
Julia's Clothes*" (H-779), and "*His Letanie, to the Holy Spirit*" (N-
41). It is chiefly on these poems that Herrick's reputation among
the literate public rests[3]—and all four of them are varied. If scholars and critics were to expand their lists of Herrick's very best
work, they would probably add "*To live merrily, and to trust to*

Good Verses" (H-201), *"To Daffadills"* (H-316), *"His Lachrimae or Mirth, turn'd to mourning"* (H-371), *"The Night-piece, to* Julia" (H-619), *"The Transfiguration"* (H-819), *"An Ode for him* [Ben Jonson]" (H-911), and *"The White Island"* (N-128). Many lists would probably also include *"To Musique, to becalme his Fever"* (H-227), *"To* Anthea, *who may command him any thing"* (H-267), *"To Meddowes"* (H-274), *"The mad Maids song"* (H-412), *"To Blossoms"* (H-467), or *"The* Hag" (H-643). All these poems, too, are varied.

Which of the uniform poems would appear on such lists? Probably the leading candidates (judging from anthologies, critical studies, and the like) would be *"The Argument of his Book"* (H-1), *"Cherrie-ripe"* (H-53), *"Delight in Disorder"* (H-83), the poem *"To* Julia" which begins "How rich and pleasing thou my *Julia* art" (H-88), *"His fare-well to Sack"* (H-128), *"The Hock-cart"* (H-250), *"Oberons Feast"* (H-293A), *"The Apparition of his Mistresse calling him to* Elizium" (H-575), *"The bad season makes the Poet sad"* (H-612), and *"His Tears to* Thamasis" (H-1028)—undeniably an admirable collection, but not so extensive as that of the varied poems and, with a notable exception here and there, not what most would regard as Herrick at his very best. (The most notable exception for many recent critics would be *"The Hock-Cart,"* whose reputation has grown steadily in recent years.)

The varied poems are disproportionately represented not only in anthologies and critical studies but also in songbooks. L. C. Martin identifies twenty-one poems from Herrick's 1648 volume that appear in seventeenth-century manuscripts of song collections.[4] All but two of these are found in autograph manuscripts of Henry or William Lawes, each of whom is the subject of a laudatory poem by Herrick. Herrick himself identifies two additional poems not found on Martin's list as having been set by Henry Lawes. Likewise he identifies Robert Ramsey and Nicholas Laniere as composers for yet two other poems—the same Laniere, almost certainly, whom Herrick praises elsewhere.[5] Thus, putting aside the two poems on Martin's list which were not set by men whom we can now identify as known to Herrick, we are left with twenty-three poems set by composers whom Herrick names in *Hesperides* and *Noble Numbers* and in every case (except Ramsey's) also explicitly praises. This very small sample, composing well under 2 percent of all the poems in Herrick's original volume, includes three which figured in the earlier discussion of Herrick's most highly regarded work—"*To the Virgins*," "*To Anthea, who may command him any thing*," and "*The Night-piece, to Julia*." Several others among the twenty-three, it could be argued, are of only slightly less quality and they also are frequently anthologized—e.g., "*The Cheat of Cupid*" (H-81), "*The Bag of the Bee*" (H-92), "*To a Gentlewoman, objecting to him his gray haires*" (H-164A), and "*The Willow Garland*" (H-425). These seven poems, and indeed seventeen of the twenty-three, are varied—74 percent of the total.

Considering Herrick's numerous references to music and specifically to the setting and singing of his own poems, and considering that virtually all of the poems for which tunes have survived were set by men he seems to have known, we may reasonably assume that all, or very nearly all, of these twenty-three poems were written as songs—that is, with the conscious expectation that they would be set to music and sung. Considering further that seventeenth-century composers like Laniere and Ramsey and the Lawes brothers have left behind ample evidence of their ability to set poems written exclusively in rhyming couplets of a single meter, we may also reasonably assume that Herrick *chose* to write prosodically varied and (for him) untypical poems when he anticipated a musical setting.

Indeed various kinds of evidence strongly associate the varied poems in general with the genre of song. The association by no means represents an exact overlap, since a quarter of the song poems are uniform and since there is no reason to believe that every one of the two hundred varied poems was written for a musical setting. But the mark of prosodic variety is revealing. It tends to shift the burden of proof, especially when it is combined with the other kinds of evidence we are about to observe.

Probably the single best piece of evidence that a given poem was written for, or as for, musical setting is the presence of ballad measure. Of the seventeen varied songs we have been considering, four are written entirely in ballad measure, a fifth ("*The admonition*," H-330) is written largely in it, and a sixth ("*The Cheat of* Cupid") is written in an unusual but only slight variation of it. Ballad measure refers to the 4,3,4,3 rhythmical pattern which characterizes the four-line stanzas of many of the traditional ballads collected by Professor Child. Although this pattern was originally accentual rather than metrical, later imitators translated it into iambic tetrameter alternated with iambic trimeter. In like manner the original rhyme scheme of *a b c d* was often modified in the seventeenth century to *a b a b*. Herrick's ballad measure scans metrically and employs the *a b a b* rhyme scheme, but these adaptations do not alter the fundamental virtue of this stanza type for a poem written to be sung—the virtue that the poet can vocalize his lyrics as they develop to any one of dozens of familiar, traditional ballad tunes, thus eliminating any worries about whether he has produced a poem which will yield gracefully to setting and singing. Anyone can test that virtue by singing "*To the Virgins*" or "*To* Anthea," two of the four poems in this group which are written entirely in Herrick's version of ballad measure, to the tune of, say, "Barbara Allen." For that matter one can sing "*To the Virgins*" or "*To* Anthea" to the tune of Jonson's "Drinke to me, onely," since that most popular of all seventeenth-century songs is also written in ballad measure. When one surveys the entire two hundred varied poems rather than just the seventeen we have been considering, one finds that at least forty of them, or 20 percent, are written exclusively in this measure.

Most of these forty poems contain a second piece of evidence—numbered stanzas. In all, nearly sixty poems in *Hesperides* and *Noble Numbers* contain numbered stanzas, and every one is a varied poem. Those which are not in ballad measure very often display an even more complex structure, with highly varied line lengths and a strikingly unusual rhyme scheme—as, for example, "*To Blossoms*" and "*To Daffadills*." When one considers that the numbered stanzas are functional in a song and therefore clearly more appropriate than for a poem written merely to be read, one's awareness of a likely link between the varied category and the category of song can only be reinforced.

A third piece or kind of evidence grows out of this one. Those poems with highly varied line lengths and very unusual rhyme schemes (often, though not always, marked by numbered stanzas) have proven extremely attractive to composers from Herrick's day to our own. Four of the seventeen songs set by Herrick's acquaintances contain more than two line lengths and at the same time more than two rhymes. Inasmuch as Herrick wrote very few poems that meet this description, four of seventeen is a revealingly large proportion. After the rediscovery of Herrick in the nineteenth century, following more than a century of neglect, composers again turned to his poems, and again they favored out of all proportion to their actual numbers those with extreme variety in rhyme and meter. One of these, *"To Daffadills,"* has been set by more composers than any other poem by Herrick.[6] *"To Blossoms"* and *"To Primroses fill'd with morning-dew"* (H-257) have also been popular choices. In short, extreme prosodic variety seems to mark a poem as a song just as ballad measure does.

These richly varied poems are often further marked by intensely melodic effects such as internal rhyme, double rhyme, ritualistic repetition, and the skillful alternation of masculine and feminine endings.

> 2. Thou sweetly canst convert the same
>   From a consuming fire,
>   Into a gentle-licking flame,
>   And make it thus expire.
>   Then make me weep
>   My paines asleep;
>   And give me such reposes,
>   That I, poore I,
>   May think, thereby,
>   I live and die
>   'Mongst Roses.   (H-227)

The stanza just quoted is from *"To Musique, to becalme his Fever,"* a poem not known to have been set in Herrick's own day. Yet it has been set by a number of more recent composers. It displays a highly varied prosodic structure, further marked by rich melodic effects, and, of course, its very subject is music. When Herrick writes specifically about or to music or specifically entitles a poem a song, in most cases the connection appears to be more than merely verbal.

A final piece of evidence is that the songs tend toward a singleness and simplicity of tone and meaning, no matter how complex the form and the melodic effects. Images and symbols are typically limpid and conventional.

> 2.   The glorious Lamp of Heaven, the Sun,
>   The higher he's a getting;
>   The sooner will his Race be run,
>   And neerer he's to Setting.   (H-208)

Like "Old Time" in the same poem, the sun here is neither mythologized nor metaphorized in a way that requires the reader to pause and reflect. If there is a subtle suggestion of Apollo, it is unnecessary to an immediate apprehension of the lines. By contrast, uniform poems often employ images that call attention to themselves and require the reader to analyze—or at least to think twice. For example, *"Comfort to a Lady upon the Death of her Husband"* (H-259) presents the sun as a goldsmith: "Dry your sweet cheek, long drown'd with sorrows raine; / Since Clouds disperst, Suns guild the Aire again." Another such poem, *"To the most vertuous Mistresse* Pot, *who many times entertained him"* (H-226), uses the same image as but one part of an elaborate conceit.

> When I through all my many Poems look,
> And see your selfe to beautifie my Book;
> Me thinks that onely lustre doth appeare
> A Light ful-filling all the Region here.
> Guild still with flames this Firmament, and be
> A Lamp Eternall to my Poetrie.
> Which if it now, or shall hereafter shine,
> 'Twas by your splendour (Lady) not by mine.
> The Oile was yours; and that I owe for yet:
> *He payes the halfe, who do's confesse the Debt.*   (H-226)

In both these poems Herrick invites us to watch the metaphor maker at work, seeking and exploiting illustrations for the moral which will conclude his little sermon. But in those poems which we know were set to music and those which are most like them in form and language, he presents images so simple, clear, and decorous that they draw almost no attention to themselves, require no tracing out of verbal and logical implications. Even when the theme is Herrick's familiar one of short life and eternal oblivion, the reader or listener is invited, not to contemplate or brood, but only to acquiesce. The hypnotic power of Herrick's songs may owe as much to the seemingly inevitable clarity and simplicity of his images as to his exquisite manipulation of sounds.

The method of compiling evidence given above is necessarily suggestive rather than exhaustive and scientifically precise. In our attempt to steer between the Scylla of deadly mathematical precision and the Charybdis of unsupported impressionism, our argument has taken us to the following point: one category of Herrick's poems, representing only 15 percent of *Hesperides* and *Noble Numbers,* supplies about half of the selections in modern anthologies, over half of Herrick's most highly regarded poems, and three-fourths of the poems which were set to music by contemporaries specifically identified in his own verses. Other evidence suggests that many more, perhaps most, of the remaining poems in this varied category were also intended as lyrics for eventual if not immediate setting and singing.

What conclusions can be drawn from these data? First, one must conclude that Herrick anthologized is a very different poet from Herrick collected. Only then can one make the necessary discounting of generalizations about Herrick's poetry derived from a partial or anthology-based reading. Take for example this generalization by Sue Maxwell, writing in *Poet Lore:*

When Swinburne, in his preface to Herrick's poems, says of the author, "The apparent or external variety of his versification is, I should suppose, incomparable," he is stating a very phenomenal fact in a very quiet way. The expounders of prosody have found his poetry a wholesale house from which they can select whatsoever styles they will to display as models for their customers. His monometers, dimeters, trimeters, etc., are retailed in discussions of poetic form.[7]

The implication is that Herrick is a poet who regularly displays enormous prosodic variety. Actually, however, if one may continue Maxwell's not altogether happy metaphor, only one specialty shop in Herrick's general store displays any such variety. Even in that shop the variety has certain clearly defined limits. For example, Herrick almost never departs from the dominant iambic foot; only one poem in *Hesperides* and *Noble Numbers* is written essentially and predominantly in a non-iambic foot. My purpose in this study, however, is not to lament the picture that anthologizers give us of Herrick. I am only recommending that we not confuse the Herrick who wrote the most varied poetry (that is, Herrick at his most visible and generally admired) with the Herrick who wrote the collected or typical poetry.

The second conclusion one can draw is that Herrick is generally at his best as a song writer. This will not, of course, come as a revelation to students of seventeenth-century poetry, but it is a conclusion arrived at more systematically than Swinburne's hyperbolic announcement in his preface to Pollard's 1891 edition of Herrick's poetry:

Herrick, of course, lives simply by virtue of his songs; his more ambitious or pretentious lyrics are merely magnified and prolonged and elaborated songs. Elegy or litany, epicede or epithalamium, his work is always a song-writer's; nothing more, but nothing less, than the work of the greatest song-writer—as surely as Shakespeare is the greatest dramatist—ever born of English race.[8]

Contemporary scholars would put the case more cautiously, in all probability agreeing with the high assessment of Herrick as song writer, but disagreeing with the contention that only his songs have merit. Still, if Swinburne errs, he remains generally on the side of the angels. For Herrick is quintessentially a songwriter and most of his very best work, as we have observed, falls into the category or genre of song.

The final conclusion of this study is that Herrick's songs, meaning those poems written for setting and singing, may well be so generically marked in strictly internal and poetic ways (as opposed to external and musical ways such as appearance in a seventeenth-century songbook) that one can speak of the genre of the song as one speaks of the genre of the tragedy or the masque or the ballad or the carol—that is, speak of it literally and critically, without necessarily referring to its performance. Herrick's anthologists, like other admirers of the poet, seem drawn to that small category of varied poems—not merely or even primarily because prosodic variety is intrinsically appealing and certainly not because they associate these poems with remembered tunes—but because so many of the varied poems embody and express an artistic wholeness, a fully realized form. Although anthologists or other readers may not be as conscious of the form as when they read a sonnet by Shakespeare or a dramatic monologue by Browning, this does not negate the power of the form to affect a reader's total response. Herrick, or so this study concludes, found his "natural" and best form in the song, and we pay him a high and subtle flattery when our anthologies and critical studies focus, however unwittingly, on that genre. Herrick knew his own strength, knew that his chief enduring appeal would be to the lover and to the musician.

> *Upon himself.*
> Thou shalt not All die; for while Love's fire shines
> Upon his Altar, men shall read thy lines;
> And learn'd Musicians shall to honour *Herricks*
> Fame, and his Name, both set, and sing his Lyricks.   (H-366)

What Herrick may not have foreseen is that the unlearned musician in his readers also responds to the same lyrics and, in doing so, helps to fulfill the poet's joyful prophecy of undying fame.

NOTES

1. The precise figures are 205 varied poems out of the 1,404 poems in *Hesperides*. Several objections might be made to my figures and to my conclusions.

The first would be that anthologists favor short poems over long ones for practical rather than esthetic reasons. But by most standards of "long"—from poems of over 20 lines to those of over 150 lines—the anthologies in my survey statistically *over*represent Herrick's longer poems. Furthermore, the latter are more often varied than uniform: for example, of the 87 poems longer than 20 lines, 48 are varied and 39 are uniform; of the 16 poems longer than 60 lines, 9 are varied, 6 uniform; of the 7 longer than 100 lines, 5 are varied, 2 uniform; of the 3 longer than 150 lines, all are varied.

Another objection might be that many of Herrick's poems are epigrams, which are always uniform (iambic-pentameter couplets for the most part) and almost always shunned by anthologists. Here my response is that anthologists have simply made negative judgments about the quality of these poems. Even if one concedes (as I do not) that the 450 epigrammatic distichs should be set aside as a special case not involving a judgment of quality, the ratio of varied poems to the "total" poems would only be lowered from one out of about seven to one out of about five—still a significant degree of disproportion.

To object that the epigrams are omitted because they are "occasional" or "out of fashion" ignores the fact that Jonson's epigrams are regularly anthologized and widely admired.

2. The representative anthologies are: M. H. Abrams et al., eds., *The Norton Anthology of English Literature*, 2nd ed., rev. (New York, 1974); Howard Foster Lowry and Willard Thorpe, eds., *An Oxford Anthology of English Poetry*, 2nd ed., rev. (New York, 1956); J. William Hebel and Hoyt H. Hudson, eds., *Poetry of the English Renaissance* (New York, 1929); Roy Lamson and Hallett Smith, eds., *Renaissance England: Poetry and Prose from the Reformation to the Restoration* (New York, 1942); Miriam K. Starkman, ed., *Seventeenth-Century English Poetry*, 2 vols. (New York, 1967), II; Alexander M. Witherspoon and Frank J. Warnke, eds., *Seventeenth-Century Prose and Poetry*, 2nd ed. (New York, 1963); and Helen C. White et al., eds., *Seventeenth-Century Verse and Prose*, 2nd ed. (New York, 1971).

3. Norman Ault in *Seventeenth Century Lyrics* (New York, 1950) described *"To the Virgins"* as "easily the most popular poem of the century" (p. xii); it is still among the best known of all poems. Cleanth Brooks's very influential study, *The Well Wrought Urn* (New York, 1947), has helped to make the often subtle charms of *"Corinna's going a Maying"* accessible to generations of undergraduates. *"Upon Julia's Clothes"* is often cited as an example of the skillful use of diction in creating a perfectly controlled poem. *"His Letanie . . . "* is the only one of Herrick's *Noble Numbers* which is almost universally anthologized.

4. "Introduction" to *The Poetical Works of Robert Herrick*, ed. L. C. Martin (Oxford, 1956), pp. xxvii–xxx. One learns from *Grove's Dictionary of Music and Musicians* (see note 5, below) that *"The Curse. A Song"* (H-138B), one of the two poems on Martin's list not set by the Lawes brothers, was set by John Blow. Although the song achieved considerable popularity which it retained until the middle of the eighteenth century, it could not have been set earlier than the 1660s, some fifteen years after the publication of *Hesperides*; furthermore, Herrick makes no references of any kind to Blow. The remaining poem not set by the Lawes brothers, *"To Musick. A song"* (H-254), was set by a composer whose name, if it is known at all, I have been unable to locate. These two poems, the first of which is uniform and the second of which is varied, would make very little difference in the proportions of one kind of poem to the other. Instead of seventeen varied poems in a total of twenty-three, or 74 percent, one would have eighteen in twenty-five, or 72 percent.

5. All titles and quotations are from *The Complete Poetry of Robert Herrick*, ed.

J. Max Patrick (New York, 1963). The poem in praise of Henry Lawes is H-851 and that in praise of William is H-907. The two poems set by Henry Lawes are N-96 and N-97; the poem set by Ramsey is H-181; the poem set by Laniere is H-213A. "Rare *Laniere*" is favorably alluded to in the poem to Henry Lawes (H-851).

6. Eric Blom, ed., *Grove's Dictionary of Music and Musicians*, 10 vols. (London, 1954). See especially IV, 255.

7. Sue Maxwell, "Robert Herrick, the Metrician," *Poet Lore*, 52 (1946), 353.

8. A. C. Swinburne, "Preface" to *Robert Herrick: the Hesperides & Noble Numbers*, ed. Alfred Pollard (London, 1891), p. xi.

Hesperides: Eros, Flux, and Stasis

ACHSAH GUIBBORY

"*No lust theres like to Poetry*": Herrick's Passion for Poetry

The speaker in Herrick's poetry often seems something of a voyeur. He gains his pleasure from watching Julia bathe, or is aroused by glimpses of her breasts or visions of her swelling petticoats. He is typically an observer rather than an active participant in these poems—acted upon by her beauty, her fragrant smells, her singing—and his delight is at once aesthetic and sexual. In *Hesperides*, there is a close relationship between art, particularly poetry, and what Herrick calls "lust." Both the creation and the effects of poetry are associated with "lust"—in the sense of "sexual appetite or desire" as well as the more general meanings of "pleasure" and "vigor" or "fertility." For Herrick, poetry is the product of a heat which is almost sexual, and his poems themselves become objects of his love, capable of arousing a delightful excitement that is similar to sexual passion and possibly superior to it.

Herrick frequently describes the creation of poetry in sexual terms. In *"His fare-well to Sack"* (H-128), he praises this wine for its ability to arouse the "Lust" which is essential for creating poetry. Sack has the power to "awake / The frost-bound-blood, and spirits; and to make / Them frantick with . . . raptures."[1] Horace and Anacreon would never have been famous had not sack filled them with this "fire and flame." Since a poet must be passionately aroused in order to write well, Herrick demands those things which will induce such a state of excitement. In a poem *"To Sir* Clipseby Crew" (H-620), he begs of him:

> Give me wine, and give me meate,
> To create in me a heate,
> That my Pulses high may beate.

> 2.   Cold and hunger never yet
>   Co'd a noble Verse beget.

Wine and food are primarily valued because they raise the "heate" which is as necessary for begetting a good poem as it is for fathering a child.

As Herrick's language suggests, the impulse which leads to poetic creation is similar to that which drives men to procreation. It is partly mere physical passion, but it is also a desire to compensate for the brevity of life. Like the procreative urge, the "creative impulse of the artist" springs from the powerful "tendency to immortalize himself," as Otto Rank has suggested in his essay on "Life and Creation."[2] The children Herrick begets are his poems. In *"Upon his Verses"* (H-681), he vouches for the legitimacy of his "off-spring":

> These are the Children I have left;
> Adopted some; none got by theft.
> But all are toucht (like lawfull plate)
> And no Verse illegitimate.

By publicly recognizing these poems as his own, he ensures that, like other mens' sons, they will carry on his name. His poems are thus the progeny who provide him with an immortality.

Herrick's poems not only provide him with children; they are also his mistresses, the actual objects of his love. His book is a "Bride" adorned with "richest jewels" (H-194). In *"Master Herrick's Farewell unto Poetry"* (S-4), he addresses poetry as his lover and compares their abrupt parting to that of two lovers who, meeting secretly at night, are suddenly forced to separate.

Herrick's love for poetry is manifested in numerous poems about his mistresses. He often thinks of his poems as if they were the beautiful maids he admires and adores. In *"The bad season makes the Poet sad"* (H-612), he complains that the unfortunate political situation has made him

> Dull to my selfe, and almost dead to these
> My many fresh and fragrant Mistresses:
> Lost to all Musick now.

Sharing in the general sadness and "faintings" of "the Land," he has lost his delight in "Musick" and his "Mistresses." Here as elsewhere in *Hesperides* (see, for example, H-1, H-332, and H-778), music seems to be symbolic of lyric poetry, and the implicit connection between music and his mistresses in these opening lines suggests that these mistresses are themselves associated with his lyric poems. His present state of being "almost dead to" these maids reflects his poetic lethargy during this "bad" political "season." These suggestions are reinforced by the conclusion of the poem in which Herrick claims that, if Charles were to "Rule" again and the "golden Age" were restored, he would again "delight": "And once more yet (ere I am laid out dead) / *Knock at a Starre with my exalted Head.*" Echoing Horace, but perhaps also alluding to the poems in *Hesperides* as stars, Herrick in this last line may imply that he would again write exalted lyric poetry, no longer "Lost" to music or "dead" to his mistresses.

Herrick's association of his poems with his "many fresh and fragrant Mistresses" may help to explain some of the special qualities of his poems to various mistresses—in particular, the Julia poems. The women in these poems seem physically flawless. As Herrick presents them, they are like ripe, unblemished fruit, or even perfect works of art, and his interest in them seems largely aesthetic. Indeed, the special beauty these mistresses offer is the kind he defines in *"The Lilly in a Christal"* (H-193)—the beauty of nature which has been transformed by art.

In this poem, Herrick insists that nature alone is not so pleasing as when it is adorned and even veiled by art. As Richard J. Ross and, more recently, Roger B. Rollin have demonstrated,[3] Herrick typically insists on the importance of refining nature through art. The lily or the rose, though attractive in itself, becomes even more beautiful and alluring when "Tomb'd" in a *"Christal* stone" or partially covered by a "Cobweb-Lawne." Similarly, cream is aesthetically uninteresting until a strawberry is set in it:

> Put Purple Grapes, or Cherries in-
> To Glasse, and they will send
> More beauty to commend

> Them, from that cleane and subtile skin,
>   Then if they naked stood.

All this is used as an argument to convince a woman that she will be more enticing if she is draped in soft, transparent clothes than if she is merely naked. This poem, however, is more than an argument against nakedness. It also defines the kind of beauty with which Herrick is concerned in the poems about his mistresses. This beauty is a delicate mixture of art and nature, but it is primarily the art which stirs the sensual and erotic feelings. Herrick is fascinated with the ways in which beauty enhanced by artifice or even by "aesthetic accident" can arouse in the viewer a delight which is almost sexual.

> You see how *Amber* through the streams
>   More gently stroaks the sight,
>   With some conceal'd delight;
> Then when he darts his radiant beams
>   Into the boundlesse aire.

As Paul R. Jenkins has acutely observed, Herrick "is interested in strange optical effects (cherries under glass, pebbles in streams), in the dynamics of voyeurism, in visceral sensations and how to prolong them."[4] The strawberry placed in cream draws the sight by actually "wantoning with it." Art applied to nature "stir[s] / More love" in men than nature's "proper excellence" does by itself.

In his poems about Julia, Herrick tends to see her as an art object as well as a sexual object. In "*Art above Nature, to* Julia" (H-560), her clothes and the artful arrangement of her hair appear to attract him as much or more than Julia herself. When he sees the "Dresse / Of flowers set in comlinesse," "the ascent of curious Lace," and the flowing of her "airie silks," he "must confesse" that his "eye and heart / Dotes less on Nature, then on Art." Herrick is clearly interested in the sexuality of aesthetics. Even when he is moved by a vision of Julia naked, he views her nudity in artistic terms. When he watches her bathing ("*Upon* Julia's *washing her self in the river*," H-939), she looks like "*Lillies*" surrounded by "Christall." This comparison—of Julia half-hidden in the river with the lilies encased in crystal—recalls Herrick's description, in *"The Lilly in a Christal,"* of the way in which nature's beauty is enhanced by the veil of art. The "Lawne of water" (H-939) has an aesthetic effect, transforming Julia's already attractive nakedness into even more irresistible beauty, making Herrick so "fierce" with desire that he throws himself into the "streames." In *"The Lawne"* (H-416), her skin itself becomes a kind of clothing "Which so betrayes her blood, as we discover / The blush of cherries, when a Lawn's cast over." *"Upon the Nipples of* Julia's *Breast"* (H-440) again presents the kind of beauty Herrick praises in H-193, the beauty of nature improved by art: her nipples are like "a red-Rose peeping through a white," or "a Cherrie (double grac't) / Within a Lillie," or a "Strawberry . . . halfe drown'd in Creame." The fact that Julia represents the perfect work of art, a synthesis of art and nature which is capable of arousing the greatest delight and passion in the viewer, suggests that Herrick's aesthetics is complex and subtle. The art ravishes him, but the actual woman is the "medium" in which this art works. He woos her, but through her, art.

Herrick's mistress is symbolic, not just of art in general, but also specifically of poetry. Julia's lips are sweet and clean, "As if or'e washt in Hippocrene," a fountain sacred to the Muses (H-857). Indeed, there is a close connection between Herrick's idealized mistress and his ideals for his own poetic art. A good poem shares the qualities of a woman who has achieved refinement. In *"A request to the Graces"* (H-914), he asks the Graces to see if any of his words are "guilty here of incivility." If they are, they should be refined, just as a coarse and ill-bred girl should be taught graceful arts:

> Let what is graceless, discompos'd, and rude,
> With sweetness, smoothness, softness, be endu'd.
> Teach it to blush, to curtsie, lisp, and shew
> Demure, but yet, full of temptation, too.

Not only does Herrick use the metaphor of language as a woman, but also the actual qualities he describes as prerequisites for

good verses are similar to those he lists in his poem defining
"What kind of Mistresse he would have" (H-665):

> Be the Mistresse of my choice,
> Cleane in manners, cleere in voice:
> Be she witty, more then wise;
> Pure enough, though not Precise:
> Be she shewing in her dresse,
> Like a civill Wilderness;
> That the curious may detect
> Order in a sweet neglect:
> Be she rowling in her eye,
> Tempting all the passers by:
> And each Ringlet of her haire,
> An Enchantment, or a Snare,
> For to catch the Lookers on.

The "sweetness" and "smoothness" of his ideal poems in part
correspond to the "cleane" manners and "cleere" voice of the
ideal mistress; and, indeed, Herrick claims in *"To his Muse"* (H-
84) that his *"Virgin-Verses"* are "cleane." Moreover, like his
"Tempting" mistresses (H-665), his poems must be enticing,
"full of temptation" (H-914). Both should possess the "cleanly-
Wantonnesse" he mentions in *"The Argument of his Book"* (H-1),
for a good poem should be able to stir a kind of pleasurable lust
in the reader. In *"A request to the Graces,"* Herrick, paraphrasing
Martial, remarks that *"Numbers ne'r tickle, or but lightly please, /
Unlesse they have some wanton carriages."* If they are "Precise,"
they will never elicit the desired response. Poetry at its best has
an almost erotic effect: it tickles and arouses like a demure but
temptingly coquettish mistress. Herrick apparently recognized
that his own poetry had some such qualities, for, in *"To his
Book"* (H-899), he humorously addresses *Hesperides* as a promis-
cuous woman who, now that she is in print, wants to "shew
[her] nakedness to all."

Not only do his mistress-like poems "tickle" the reader, but
they may also be capable of arousing in Herrick new poetic fires.
Again Herrick's metaphor is sexual. On the literal level, his

lightly self-mocking poem, *"To his Mistresses"* (H-19), is about his sexual impotence: "Old I am, and cannot do / That, I was accustom'd to." But Herrick's descriptions in H-128 and H-620 of his ability to create poetry in terms of sexual potency suggest that this poem may also in part be read as referring by analogy to his lack of inspiration for composing poetry. He calls to his mistresses, his "pretty *Witchcrafts*," to bring *"Magicks, Spels, and Charmes,* / To enflesh my thighs, and armes." Herrick calls his poems "enchantments" in *"When he would have his verses read"* (H-8), and his conception of the magical quality of poetry, noted by Rollin,[5] as well as his association of his mistresses with his lyrics in *"The bad season makes the Poet sad,"* leads one to suspect that these enchanting mistresses may in fact correspond to his own poems. His plea for help from his mistresses would thus reveal his hope that his poems might be capable of miraculously renewing his ability to create. Perhaps they can "beget / In . . . [his] limbs their former heat" (H-19).

The ability to write a good poem and the ability to court a mistress successfully both require the ability "to do." In a delightful poem, *"The Vision"* (H-1017), Herrick dreams he sees Anacreon—his face flushed, a vine around his head, his hair shining with oil, and his mouth running over with wine. He is so drunk that when the beautiful "young *Enchantresse*" standing by his side teases him, "Tapping his plump thighes with a *mirtle* wand," he is unable to respond fully to her advances. Though he kisses and hugs her, he is too tipsy to make love: "being cup-shot, more he co'd not doe." Anacreon's failure to keep his mistress happy symbolizes the loss of his poetic powers, as his subsequent loss of his "Crown" makes clear. Angered at his inability to perform the part of a proper lover, his mistress snatches away his "Crown," apparently the crown of laurel worn by poets, and gives it instead to Herrick. In this wish-fulfillment fantasy, Herrick presumably takes over Anacreon's place in art as well as in love, for her handing over the "wreath" implies not only that she is transferring her amorous favors to Herrick but also that she wants him to assume the laureateship. As a "young *Enchantresse*," this mistress is probably symbolic of poetry itself, and her giving him the laurel crown suggests poetry's power to offer immortal fame to the poet. This dream-poem thus reflects Herrick's hope that he will gain poetic immortality just as Anacreon did.

Finally, poetry not only can confer immortality on the poet-lover, but like a good mistress she can continue to provide pleasures for her lover even in his old age. Her magical charms can renew his youthful vigor. In one of his best poems, *"His age, dedicated to his peculiar friend, Master* John Wickes, *under the name of* Posthumus" (H-336), Herrick most fully reveals his belief in this special power of poetry. In a beautiful and touching fantasy, he imagines himself as an old man, "bruised on the Shelfe / Of Time" (ll. 74–75), sitting by the fire with his "old leane wife" (l. 84), "foretelling snow and slit, / And weather by our aches" (ll. 86–87). In order to assuage his pains, he asks his young son, Iülus, to recite some of the poems he wrote in his younger days— a poem on Julia's breast, *"The Lilly in a Christal,"* and a poem "of a higher text" (l. 100). Although he is old, these poems are able to "beget" (l. 101) in him "a more transcendant heate" (l. 102) than Helen of Troy was ever able to arouse in old men with "her loving Sorceries" (l. 106). Poetry's seductive power is greater than that of the most beautiful woman. His poetry revives in him the heat of his youth, and for a few moments he becomes like a young, lusty rooster, ready to engage the whole barnyard:

> I'le reare
> Mine aged limbs above my chaire:
> And hearing it,
> Flutter and crow, as in a fit
> Of fresh concupiscence, and cry,
> No lust theres like to Poetry.   (ll. 107–12)

Art, more than natural woman, is what arouses Herrick's concupiscence, and thus the delights poetry offers can seem superior to those afforded by sex itself; for, as Freud observed in "The Relation of the Poet to Day-Dreaming" and as Bacon recognized long before,[6] the poet can create in his poems an ideal world which at least partly fulfills those wishes the actual world leaves unsatisfied. Good poetry is like an eternally youthful woman: she never loses her vital powers, and she offers to her lovers a very special opportunity to transcend the ruins of time.

NOTES

1. Quotations from Herrick's poems follow *The Complete Poetry of Robert Herrick*, ed. J. Max Patrick (New York, 1963 and 1968).

2. "Life and Creation," in *Art and Artist* (1932; rpt. New York, 1968), p. 38.

3. Richard J. Ross, " 'A Wilde Civility': Robert Herrick's Poetic Solution of the Paradox of Art and Nature" (Ph.D. diss., University of Michigan, 1958), and Roger B. Rollin, *Robert Herrick* (New York, 1966), pp. 172–77.

4. "Rethinking What Moderation Means to Robert Herrick," *ELH*, 39 (1972), 64.

5. Rollin, *Herrick*, pp. 24, 195.

6. See Sigmund Freud, "The Relation of the Poet to Day-Dreaming," in *On Creativity and the Unconscious* (New York, 1958), pp. 44–54; and Francis Bacon, *Advancement of Learning*, in *The Works of Francis Bacon*, ed. James Spedding, R. L. Ellis, and D. D. Heath, 14 vols. (London, 1857–74), III, 343.

JOHN T. SHAWCROSS

The Names of Herrick's
Mistresses in *Hesperides*

Fourteen names are employed for Herrick's mistresses in the various poems that comprise *Hesperides*. There are, of course, other names in the poems, but they are not used in the same way. Compare, for example, *Lucie* in H-649 or *Joan* in H-864.[1] Some of the names, like Silvia, had previously appeared in pastoral poetry; some, like Sappho, have allusive qualities; and still others, like Julia, are most memorable because of Herrick himself. In the past the main concern of critics has been the question of the mistresses' reality or unreality. Edmund Gosse, in *Seventeenth Century Studies*,[2] rejected the reality of all but Julia, but F. W. Moorman, in *Robert Herrick: A Biographical and Critical Study*,[3] found Julia also a poetic fiction, largely because there is no biographical development of an affair in the many poems in which she figures. Besides, for Moorman the "fanciful classical names . . . suggest the fictitious character of those who bear them."[4] But there are other avenues to arrive at the same conclusion which say more about Herrick's art and the "meaning" of his poems.

No one has examined the etymologies of the names, for example, and then related the meanings to what Herrick does in the poems in which they appear. This is what I propose to do here. (See the Appendix to this essay for a list of these names and their appearances in Herrick's poems.) My examination argues that the names were sometimes employed for their onomastic value and that we therefore cannot conclude that each necessarily depicts a different mistress, whether real or fictitious. Herrick may not have conceived of fourteen different mistresses—Perenna may represent the same idea as, say, Corinna; and he may not have intended any single name as always applying to the same character—perhaps not all Antheas, for example, are the same Anthea.

Irene appears only in the title and first line of H-566. The name is French from the Latin and in turn from the Greek, meaning *peace*. Herrick quite clearly chose the name for irony:

> Angry if *Irene* be
> But a Minutes life with me:
> Such a fire I espie
> Walking in and out her eye,
> As at once I freeze, and frie.

We catch the Petrarchan oxymoronic clichés, but we miss much of the ironic humor between "anger," "fire," and "peace" if we do not pay attention to the name. Further, substituting "peace" for "Irene" in the poem leads to additional meaning for the love / war paradox so frequently employed as a theme in seventeenth-century poetry: if peace is with me but for a minute, I become angry, for peace demands so much passionate action to be maintained that I am immobilized and destroyed at the same time. The connotations of sexual climax for a minute's duration cause an equation of sexual exhaustion with peace. While "Walking in and out her eye" modifies "fire," it is a squinting modifier attached to "I." The foot, implied by "walking," is not only more applicable to "I" than to "fire"; it is a commonplace symbol for the male sexual organ. As lover, then, the poet is torn between immobility in order to extend the "Minutes life" and extreme passion which too readily would consume him.

Myrrha is used twice; it comes from the Latin, meaning a *myrrh tree*, from the Greek for the Arabian myrtle. In H-132 she is "hard-hearted"; in H-39, which cites seven of the mistresses, she is praised for her voice. Remembering the myrrh tree and the way in which it drips gum, we understand the picture the poet is admonishing Myrrha to present in H-132:

> Fold now thine armes; and hang the head,
> Like to a Lillie withered:
> Next, look thou like a sickly Moone;
> Or like *Jocasta* in a swoone.

> Then weep, and sigh, and softly goe,
> Like to a widdow drown'd in woe:

She is "insensible" and "hard-hearted" like a tree; but like the myrrh tree she can become soft by melting into sweet, spicy gums. The last lines of the poem allude to Ecclesiastes 12:1. Herrick writes:

> thou art
> Insensible . . . of those evill dayes that be
> Now posting on to punish thee.

The Preacher has said, "Remember now thy Creator in the days of thy youth, while the evil days come not, nor the years draw nigh." Myrrha is apparently growing older, and the poem takes on a much more obvious *carpe diem* cast. She is a "Faire Maid," but she is told to appear "like a Virgin full of ruth, / For the lost sweet-heart of her youth"—again a comment on her aging, and we should note that she would only be *like* a virgin. And this aging makes clear why she might be "like to a widdow" or "like *Jocasta*." The lily, symbol of both life and death, has become withered as her aging is envisioned, and the moon, symbol of the female, has become sickly. The context of the poem thus narrates a familiar story: the woman who has resisted the poet's advances is admonished to envision her older age in order to ensure her succumbing to his sexual desires. One way to become soft like the Gods—the adjective "easie" applied to the Gods implying also "morally lax"—is to exude, like the myrrh tree, aromatic, slightly pungent gums, the sexual application being patent.

The etymology of *Biancha*, Italian *white* from Old High German meaning *shiny, bright*, is significant in H-98, "*Being once blind, his request to* Biancha":

> When Age or Chance has made me blind,
> So that the path I cannot find:
> And when my falls and stumblings are
> More then the stones i'th'street by farre:
> Goe thou afore; and I shall well
> Follow thy Perfumes by the smell:

> Or be my guide; and I shall be
> Led by some light that flows from thee.
> Thus held, or led by thee, I shall
> In wayes confus'd, nor slip or fall.

One can classify Biancha in this poem as a woman beloved who functions as inspiration, but the name more clearly has metaphoric significance in H-897, "*To* Biancha, *to blesse him*":

> Thwart all Wizzards, and with these
> Dead all black contingencies:
> . . . All will prosper, if so be
> I be kist, or blest by thee.

And consider its importance in H-991, "*To* Biancha":

> Ah *Biancha!* now I see,
> It is Noone and past with me:
> In a while it will strike one;
> Then *Biancha,* I am gone.
> Some *effusions* let me have,
> Offer'd on my holy Grave;
> Then, *Biancha,* let me rest
> With my face towards the East.

Biancha, as whiteness and brightness and shiningness, is coupled with seeing, with noon, with striking the poet, with effusions, contrastively with the darkness of the grave, with the rising sun and thus with resurrection. Biancha could be again a beloved mistress, who inspires; or, as symbolic brightness and ascendant sun, she stands for a principle by which man lives and is able to conquer physical decline and death.[5]

Herrick's well-known *Corinna* is found in five poems; the name is a diminutive of Cora, which means *maiden*. The etymology of the name is pertinent enough therefore in all five poems. Kore, the Greek form of the name, was the daughter of Demeter, the goddess of agriculture, and thus represents all the female offspring of the Earth Mother, all maidens. But in myth Kore was taken by Hades to the underworld, where she was renamed Persephone (Latin Proserpina). Demeter refused to enflower the earth until the return of her daughter; Zeus decreed that she should return to earth for two-thirds of the year and live with her husband Hades one-third of the year. The story mythologized the seasons and the endless cycle of time: winter (in Hades), spring, summer, and autumn (on earth). Thus Persephone became the goddess of seasons, and Kore (or Cora) signified the maiden from whom the endless cycle of life would spring. All this is of clear significance to H-178, "Corinna's *going a Maying*," a poem frequently read in terms of mythic cycle. But this relationship between the unchanging alternations of spring-summer, autumn-winter inherent in the name has not been noted, for example, in H-232, entitled *"The Changes to* Corinna":

> Be not proud, but now encline
> Your soft eare to Discipline.
> You have changes in your life,
> Sometimes peace, and sometimes strife:
> You have ebbes of face and flowes,
> As your health or comes, or goes;
> You have hopes, and doubts, and feares
> Numberless, as are your haires.
> You have Pulses that doe beat
> High, and passions lesse of heat.
> You are young, but must be old,
> And, to these, ye must be told,
> Time, ere long, will come and plow
> Loathed Furrowes in your brow:
> And the dimnesse of your eye
> Will no other thing imply,
> > But you must die
> > As well as I.

Note the agricultural image of "plow" and "Furrowes," and thus the implication that the dimness of her eye is a metaphor for the decline of the sun in winter. As J. Max Patrick notes, we have the similar equation of the heavens with Corinna's eye in H-108, *"The Eye,"* an advice-to-a-painter poem.

Lucia, meaning *light*, from the Latin, appears in seven poems and seems to have some pertinency in four of them. In H-207 carnations, which are usually white, pink, and red, are said to play hide or seek in Lucia's cheek; that is, in the whiteness of her complexion, in the flush which may come over her, or in the blush which she might experience. But *light* also shows such gradations of color as the sun rises or the sun descends. The word *carnation* derives from the Latin for *flesh* and thus indicates further word play in the poem. We probably, however, think of carnation as a red only, and the reference to Lucia as woman and as light therefore suggests the advance of time as Lucia reacts coyly to the poet's amorous play and as the light of day descends all red with hope of a fair tomorrow.

A similar reference is found in H-729 where Lucia is dabbled in dew, as at morning. As Lucia lifts her skirts to avoid wetting their hems and reveals "her decent legs," so light of day creeps over the land and allows one to discern some of the scene. But Lucia does not reveal all as the poet would have wished, just as the rising sun also casts shadows.

In H-814 the soul of Lucia is in Purgatory, for she has been too fiery, like the sun. We are requested to shed tears to cool her and thus effect the purgation. Perhaps it is significant that the next poem is *"The Cloud,"* which "is no other then the Bed / Where *Venus* sleeps (halfe smothered.)" And in H-973, *"Crutches,"* to read Lucia as metaphoric light gives fuller meaning to the poem:

> Thou seest me *Lucia* this year droope,
> Three *Zodiaks* fill'd more I shall stoope;
> Let Crutches then provided be
> To shore up my debilitie. . . .
> Yet with the bench of aged sires,
> When I and they keep tearmly fires;
> With my weake voice Ile sing, or say
> Some Odes I made of *Lucia*.

Perenna implies *lasting for years, perpetualness*, and Anna Perenna was the protector or bestower of the returning year. The six occurrences in Herrick's poems play with these meanings. There is irony in the use of the name in H-220, H-471, and H-976.

> H-220: Dear *Perenna*, prethee come,
> And with *Smallage* dresse my Tomb:

Adde a *Cypresse*-sprig thereto,
With a teare; and so *Adieu*.

Smallage is celery or parsley, and note the pun on "a dew.")

H-471: How long, *Perenna*, wilt thou see
Me languish for the love of Thee?
Consent and play a friendly part
To save; when thou may'st kill a heart.

H-976: I a *Dirge* will pen for thee;
Thou a *Trentall* make for me:
That the Monks and Fryers together,
Here may sing the rest of either:
Next, I'm sure, the Nuns will have
Candelmas to grace the Grave.

We should note that "Candlemas" is the Feast of Purification for Mary after the birth of her son Jesus. "Nuns," of course, connotes whores. Perenna has apparently resisted the poet's seductions, and so supposed celibates people the poem. Rather than giving life, Perenna denies it—perpetually. The anti-Roman Catholic bias of the poem indicates its further satiric meaning.

There is direct importance of the name to H-255, "*To the Western wind*":

1. Sweet Western Wind, whose luck it is,
(Made rivall with the aire)
To give *Perenn'as* lip a kisse,
And fan her wanton haire.

2. Bring me but one, Ile promise thee,
Instead of common showers,
Thy wings shall be embalm'd by me,
And all beset with flowers.

The western wind, of course, will bring gentle rains in spring and is thus precursor of the returning year and the rebirth of vegetation. As earth mother, Perenna, her lip kissed and her hair stroked, will bring forth life. There is also a play on "embalmed," meaning that the western wind will be made fragrant and will be immortalized by the poet's words, as in the poem being read.

Electra, from the Greek for *shining* or *brilliant* as in reference to the beaming sun, occurs in twelve poems. The whiteness and shiningness of H-105 are clearly pertinent; and H-404 is a vers on the meaning of the name:

> When out of bed my Love doth spring,
> *'Tis but as day a kindling:*
> But when She's up and fully drest,
> 'Tis then *broad Day throughout the East.*

Herrick may have used the name for its contrast with night in H-56, H-152, H-534, and H-767.

The six uses of *Dianeme,* from the Greek, meaning *of divine origin,* may all have onomastic significance. But H-828 is the only interesting one, for Dianeme allows the poet to bleed with the darts of love without moving to stanch the flow. Like man, beset with troubles but unheeded by the gods, the poet says:

> If thou compos'd of gentle mould
>   Art so unkind to me;
> What dismall Stories will be told
>   Of those that cruell be?

Oenone, from the Latin, derived from the Greek, meaning *wine,* and *Perilla,* meaning *little pear,* from Vulgate through Spanish, offer no meaningful word play. *Sappho,* a frequent name for a mistress in pastoral poetry, is simply the name of the Greek lyric poet. Only H-362, "*Upon* Sapho, *sweetly playing, and sweetly singing,*" seems to make a connection. A common name is *Silvia,* Latin for *wood* or *inhabiting woods.* Although we might think that the etymology could be integrated into the poetry, none of the seven poems in which it occurs hint at the meaning.

Remaining are the two very important mistresses *Anthea* and *Julia.* The first comes from the Greek, meaning *flowering,* a *flower* or *blossom,* and thence *to be brilliant* or *to shine.* It was an epithet of both Juno and Venus. The second is the feminine form of *Julius,* the name of a Roman gens, probably resulting from a contraction of *Jovilios,* meaning *pertaining to* or *descending from Jupiter* (as father-god). The *bright* and *shining* meaning of *Anthea* can be seen in H-104, "*To* Anthea *lying in bed*":

So looks *Anthea,* when in bed she lyes,
Orecome, or halfe betray'd by Tiffanies:
Like to a Twi-light, or that simpring Dawn,
That Roses shew, when misted o're with Lawn.
Twilight is yet, till that her Lawnes give way;
Which done, that Dawne, turnes then to perfect day.

Its *flower* meaning and use as epithet for Juno lie behind H-155,
"Love perfumes all parts":

If I kisse *Anthea's* brest,
There I smell the Phenix nest:
If her lip, the most sincere
Altar of Incense, I smell there.
Hands, and thighs, and legs, are all
Richly Aromaticall.
Goddesse *Isis* cann't transfer
Musks and Ambers more from her:
Nor can *Juno* sweeter be,
When she lyes with *Jove,* then she.

Perhaps there is a reference to the story of Venus and Mars in
H-678, and Herrick puns on "push-pin," a child's game and also
a steel point having a projecting head for sticking into a wall:

Come *Anthea,* know thou this,
Love at no time idle is:
Let's be doing, though we play
But at push-pin (half the day:)
Chains of sweet bents let us make,
Captive one, or both, to take:
In which bondage we will lie,
Soules transfusing thus, and die.

Venus and Mars, it will be remembered, were found in coition
by her husband, Hephaestos, who cast a chain cover over them
so that they would not escape the gods' derision. The phallicism
of push-pin is clear in association with "play," "sweet bents,"
"soules transfusing," and "die."

In H-781 Juno and "the *Naked Graces,*" who were in attendance
on Venus, are cited as well as roses. The Graces were Aglaia

(Brilliance), Thalia (Bloom), and Euphrosyne (Mirth). H-1054
deals with flowers specifically:

> Sick is *Anthea,* sickly is the spring,
> The Primrose sick, and sickly every thing:
> The while my deer *Anthea* do's but droop,
> The *Tulips, Lillies, Daffadills* do *stoop;*
> But when again sh'as got her healthfull houre,
> Each bending then, will rise a proper flower.

Julia appears in seventy-three poems and is implied as subject
of four others. She is associated with a ruler (queen) or goddess
in six (H-11, H-88, H-414, H-539, H-819, H-974). The title of
H-539, for example, is *"To* Julia, *The* Flaminica Dialis, *or* Queen-
Priest"; and in H-974 she is "the Queen of *Peace and Quorum."*
One is struck, though, how often she is associated with flowers,
particularly roses (H-9, H-11, H-45, H-78, H-182, H-295, H-441,
H-719, H-734, H-824, H-876, H-939, H-1070, H-1090) and with
perfumes or spices (H-32, H-179, H-251, H-327, H-414, H-445,
H-485, H-719, H-805, H-856, H-870, H-957). H-957 (and with this
we should compare H-974) refers to the altar of incense built by
Aaron (Exodus 30). Anthea, too, as has been noted, is associated
with flowers and often they are roses; and H-155 (cited above)
refers to the "Altar of Incense." Are Anthea and Julia really distinct? In any case, in reference to Julia in H-957, the altar and its
vessels must needs be sanctified so "that they may be most holy:
whatsoever toucheth them shall be holy" (Exodus 30:29). The
perfume "shall be unto you most holy" (vs. 36) and "it shall be
unto thee holy for the Lord" (vs. 37). First, however, because "he
that toucheth the dead body of any man shall be unclean seven
days" (Numbers 19:11), Julia, like Aaron in Leviticus 16:4, must
sanctify her hands, after which, again like Aaron in Leviticus
16:13, she may "put the incense upon the fire before the Lord,
that the cloud of the incense may cover the mercy seat that is
upon the testimony, that he die not." Julia is apparently offering
atonement for the poet's death and thus becomes his redeemer;
in various poems the poet feigns death and charges Julia with
rites for his salvation (as in H-627). What is particularly interest-

ing in H-957, though, is that according to Exodus 35:27–28 it is "the rulers" who bring "spice, and oil for the light, and for the anointing oil, and for the sweet incense."

This salvational view of Julia, as one descended from Jupiter who discharges oblations for Herrick's pardon for his sin—with the key being her perfumes and spicery—should cause us to re-read a poem like H-327:

> For my embalming, *Julia,* do but this,
> Give thou my lips but their supreamest kiss:
> Or else trans-fuse thy breath into the chest,
> Where my small reliques must for ever rest:
> That breath the *Balm,* the *myrrh,* the *Nard* shal be,
> To give an *incorruption* unto me.

And note the possibility of sexual intercourse as death and the play on the temple of the soul and the temple of death in H-445:

> Besides us two, i'th'Temple here's not one
> To make up now a Congregation.
> Let's to the *Altar of perfumes* then go,
> And say short Prayers; and when we have done so,
> Then we shall see, how in a little space,
> *Saints* will come in to fill each Pew and Place.

The emphasis on "now" and "short Prayers," "then" and "in a little space" (with double meaning of time and anatomy) points to Julia's womb as symbol of the temple of the soul and of death, and thus of immortality, a reading which adds meaning to H-327 above as well.

Related to all this is the last poem addressed to Julia, H-1095, *"His last request to* Julia." Here Herrick refers to Psalm 38:18, "For I will declare mine iniquity; I will be sorry for my sin." The book which Julia is asked to clasp is both his book of poetry and the book of life: they are coterminous for him.

Turning now to two random poems concerned with mistresses who are unnamed, we see how etymology and the poems themselves lead to possible identifications. H-54, *"To his Mistresses,"* reads:

> Put on your silks; and piece by piece
> Give them the scent of Amber-Greece:
> And for your breaths too, let them smell
> Ambrosia-like, or *Nectarell:*
> While other Gums their sweets perspire,
> By your owne jewels set on fire.

The first couplet recalls poems to Julia and to Anthea; the second couplet, with its immortal allusions, suggests Perenna; and the final couplet certainly indicates Myrrha. H-665, "*What kind of Mistresse he would have,*" gives hints of Myrrha, Corinna, Julia, and perhaps Electra.

"*Upon the losse of his Mistresses*" (H-39) lists seven of the names we have been looking at. Julia is called stately and is said to be "prime of all," which certainly the great frequency of her appearance bears out. Sappho is "next" and called "a principall"; in number of times cited she is fourth after Julia, Anthea, and Electra. Anthea and Electra follow in order in the poem, the former described as "smooth," with skin that is "white, and Heavenlike Chrystalline"; the latter simply noted as "sweet." Next is Myrrha, called "choice . . . for the Lute, and Voice," followed by Corinna, whose wit and "graceful use of it" are recalled, and Perilla accompanies her. The omission of Biancha, Dianeme, Irene, Lucia, Oenone, Perenna, and Silvia is not significant. Half of all the mistresses are included in the poem as having been lately lost, and half are not. If there were truly biographical importance within these poems and if a biographical story were being told, clearly this poem would not appear in the collection where it does. And we cannot infer that the seven omitted are simply less important or other versions of the seven who are listed.

Herrick seems to have used the names at times with etymological significance, at times not. Occasionally he assigns a poem to one when etymology would suggest another would have been more appropriate, and perhaps this is some evidence that we cannot be sure that each of the fourteen mistresses is distinct. For example, H-362 to Sappho, playing and singing, would have been appropriate to Myrrha, according to what is said of her in

H-39, although the historical Sappho may have directed the choice of name. And H-740 to Sappho sounds etymologically more like Corinna, with its specific reference to Proserpina. Yet this approach to the poems does lead to more textural readings and to a conclusion that few would argue with today: concern over the reality or unreality of any of the mistresses is simply misplaced effort. A more important conclusion that the evidence of this paper reinforces is that Herrick is a self-conscious artist, who is not given to rigidities of technique, intent, or meaning.

APPENDIX

Numbers in italics refer to the numbered poems in *The Complete Poetry of Robert Herrick*, ed. J. Max Patrick (New York, 1963). Numbers in roman refer to lines. Poems in brackets refer to Julia but do not cite her in title or text.

Anthea, *22*: title, 1, 10; *33*: 1; *39*: 4; *55*: title, 2; *74*: title, 1; *104*: title, 1; *155*: 1; *267*: 1; *678*: title, 1; *761*: 1; *781*: title, 13; *854*: title; *1006*: title, 1; *1054*: title, 1, 3.
Biancha, *87*: 1; *98*: title; *897*: title; *991*: title, 1, 4, 7.
Corinna, *39*: 9; *133*: 17; *178*: title, 29, 42, 70; *232*: title; *575*: 40.
Dianeme, *103*: title, 2, 9; *160*: title; *403*: title; *538*: title; *684*: title; *828*: title.
Electra, *39*: 7; *56*: title; *105*: title; *152*: title; *404*: title; *534*: title; *567*: title; *663*: title; *746*: title; *767*: title, 19; *836*: title; *875*: title.
Irene, *566*: title, 1.
Julia, *9*: title, 9; *11*: title; *23*: 3; *27*: title, 1; *32*: 1; *35*: title, 14; *39*: 3; *45*: 3; *49*: 1; *53*: 5; *59*: title, 1; *67*: title; *75*: 4; *78*: 8; *88*: title, 1; *114*: title, 2; *115*: title, 13; *150*: 1, 3; *156*: title, 1; *172*: title, 1; *175*: title; *179*: title, 1; *182*: 1, 6, 10; *204*: title; *230*: title, 1; *251*: 1; *284*: 1; *295*: 1; *322*: title, 2; *327*: title, 1; *342*: title, 2; *347*: title; *348*: 3; *349*: 1; [*350*]; *399*: 10; *414*: title, 5; *416*: 2; *440*: title; *441*: 9; *445*: title; *484*: title, 1; [*485*]; *491*: 2; *499*: title, 1; *539*: title, 1; *560*: title; *584*: title, 1, 3, 5; *619*: title, 16; *627*: title; *687*: 3; *700*: 1; *719*: title, 2; *734*: title; *741*: title; [*742*; *743*]; *779*: title, 1; *805*: 1; *811*: 9; *819*: 2; *824*: title, 2; *841*: 3; *856*: title, 2; *857*: title, 1; *870*: title (+); *876*: 2; *881*: title; *898*: title; *939*: title, 2, 3; *957*: 2, 3; *968*: 2; *974*: title; *1069*: title, 1; *1070*: title; *1090*: title; *1095*: title, 3, 5 (twice).
Lucia, *41*: 4, 12; *207*: 5; *599*: title, 1; *690*: 1; *729*: title, 1; *814*: 2; *973*: 1, 14.
Myrrha, *39*: 8; *132*: title.
Oenone, *446*: title; *790*: title, 1; *833*: title.
Perenna, *16*: title; *220*: title, 1; *255*: 3; *471*: title, 1; *976*: title; *1081*: title.
Perilla, *14*: title, 1, 5, 9; *39*: 11; *154*: title, 9; *1020*: title, 2.
Sappho, *39*: 4; *118*: title, 7; *258*: 3; *362*: title; *591*: 2; *691*: title; *740*: 1; *803*: title, 1; *866*: title, 1, 3; *985*: title, 1.

Silvia, *10:* title, 1, 5; *62:* title, 1; *570:* title, 13; *651:* title; *705:* title, 7; *908:* title, 1
936: title, 1.

NOTES

1. My references throughout the essay and in the Appendix are to the numbered poems in *The Complete Poetry of Robert Herrick,* ed. J. Max Patrick (New
York, 1963).

2. (London: Kegan Paul, Trench, 1883), p. 136.

3. (London: John Lane, 1910), pp. 70–71.

4. Ibid., p. 72.

5. Cf. p. 96, remarks on *Electra.*

T. G. S. CAIN

"*Times trans-shifting*":
Herrick in Meditation

Of all the subjects to which he draws attention in the introductory poem to *Hesperides*, "*The Argument of his Book*,"[1] none so dominates Herrick's work as the one which he calls there "*Times trans-shifting*." It is a subject to which he returns again and again in his attempt to come to terms with the inevitability of human transience and death; and a significantly large proportion of his finest poems are motivated in whole or in part by a desire to slow down or defeat the process of time, whether through marriage and regeneration, through the stasis of ceremony, or through the immortality of poetry. Even his title is, in all probability, a part of this attempt to soften the impact of time by placing his poems in an enclosed garden, set outside the transient world in the light of an "eternal May." The tercentenary of that inevitable death, which none of these stratagems could avoid, was a peculiarly fitting occasion on which to draw attention to a number of fine poems which make no such attempt to soften the blows of "*Times trans-shifting*," but which, on the contrary, meditate on the facts of transience and death without compromise and without offer of consolation, not even the slender solace of *carpe diem* to which Herrick is ready at other times to resort.

Though I have used the word *meditate*, and though some of these poems do indeed seem to draw on Christian meditative disciplines, they are not Christian meditations on death in the manner of Herbert or Donne, or of Herrick's own "*Meditation upon Death*" (N-230) from *His Noble Numbers*.[2] Their ostensible concern is with the fate of the body, not the soul. They make no promise of resurrection, only of the inevitability and universality of death. It is, though, just this spirit of uncompromising contemplation and acceptance to which I wish to draw attention, and which, more than any specific use of the spiritual exercises of the Christian tradition, justifies us in describing them as serious meditative poems. They are Herrick's own powerful and original contribution to the tradition of the *ars moriendi*, and as such worthy to be placed beside the work of the great devotional poets of the seventeenth century. Indeed, in their refusal to deal with the themes of immortality and resurrection, they can convey at their best a keener sense of all that is lost in life than we find in the more overtly Christian meditation where, even in the most tactful hands, that loss may seem to have been all too easily accepted. Their firm contemplation of a death which simply leaves us to lie in cold obscurity and rot gives them a serious dignity which we may not expect to find in *Hesperides,* but which in the context of Herrick's abiding preoccupation with transience makes their achievement all the more impressive.

If Herrick had had to look outside of the Christian tradition for a model for such a poem, he would probably have turned most naturally to Horace—not the Horace of the *carpe diem* odes, but the Horace who so frequently reminds his reader that "omnes una manet nox" (*Odes* 1.28.15), without necessarily mitigating that disturbing fact with any comforting reminder of the pleasures of life. Three of the *Odes* in particular seem likely models for a fine group of poems in *Hesperides* in which Herrick reminds his mistresses of the transience of their beauty and the inevitability of their death. These are 1.25 (*Parcius iunctas*), 4.10 (*O crudelis adhuc*), and 4.13 (*Audivere, Lyce*). Of these it is 4.10, addressed to the youth Ligurinus, which is closest of all to Herrick. Here the details of the process of aging are recorded with the same concision and the same sense of their ruthless inevitability that we frequently find in Herrick's treatments of the subject:

> O crudelis adhuc et Veneris muneribus potens,
> insperata tuae cum veniet pluma superbiae
> et, quae nunc umeris involitant, deciderint comae,
> nunc et qui color est puniceae flore prior rosae
> mutatus, Ligurine, in faciem verterit hispidam:
> dices "heu," quotiens te speculo videris alterum,

"quae mens est hodie, cur eadem non puero fuit,
  vel cur his animis incolumes non redeunt genae?"[3]

If we set this against Herrick's *"To a Gentlewoman, objecting to him his gray haires"* (H-164A), the indebtedness of the one to the other becomes obvious enough:

Am I despis'd, because you say,
And I dare sweare, that I am gray?
Know, Lady, you have but your day:
And time will come when you shall weare
Such frost and snow upon your haire:
And when (though long it comes to passe)
You question with your Looking-glasse;
And in that sincere *Christall* seek,
But find no Rose-bud in your cheek:
Nor any bed to give the shew
Where such a rare Carnation grew.
Ah! then too late, close in your chamber keeping,
        It will be told
        That you are old;
By those true teares y'are weeping.

This is a creative imitation of Horace, resembling his poem not simply in the echoes of the rose-bud and the mirror, but in its relentless vision of the ravaging processes of time, a vision set out in both poems with a concision that makes it all the more telling. In Herrick's poem in particular, the crisp, undeviating rhymes, the simple, largely monosyllabic vocabulary, and the unhesitating, if unobtrusive, rhythms all contribute to the effect of somber inevitability which is crowned by the masterly change of rhythm in the last four lines—lines which, for all their simplicity, constitute a more powerful and more clinching ending than do Horace's slightly anticlimactic questions. Herrick has taken his model and turned it superbly to his own idiom and purposes. As much can be said of the still more concise and devastating statement of *"To* Dianeme" (H-160), where all the pride of beauty is placed uncompromisingly in the perspective of time's trans-shifting by comparison with the small jewel which will outlast it:

> Sweet, be not proud of those two eyes,
> Which Star-like sparkle in their skies:
> Nor be you proud, that you can see
> All hearts your captives; yours, yet free:
> Be you not proud of that rich haire,
> Which wantons with the Love-sick aire:
> When as that *Rubie,* which you weare,
> Sunk from the tip of your soft eare,
> Will last to be a precious Stone,
> When all your world of Beautie's gone.

Within the brief compass of this poem, all of Herrick's skill in the presentation of sensuous beauty has been mustered to make the contrast with the small, hard stone all the more starkly convincing. The lesson that the ruby has to teach is driven home quietly but remorselessly.

"*To* Dianeme" may well have grown out of a much longer and almost certainly earlier poem of Herrick's on the same theme; this is "*Upon a Carved Cherrystone Sent to Wear in the Tip of the Lady Jemmonia Walgrave's Ear, a Death's Head on the One Side and Her Face on the Other*" (S-5).[4] This too deals with a stone to be set in "your ear's soft tip," but a stone which has a more immediately obvious role to play as the starting point of a meditation on death. Carved as a *memento mori,* a "Janus, looking double way," it furnishes a "scripture how you live and die." Jemmonia must read this scripture to learn that, as surely as the cherrystone has lost its fleshy covering,

> So must that fair face of yours
> (As this looking-glass assures)
> Fade and scarce leave to be shown
> There ever lived such a one.

A little later Herrick repeats the lesson still more explicitly, and once more the even, relentless rhythms are used to underline it:

> This lesson you must pierce to th' truth
> And know (fair mistress), of your youth,
> Death with it still walks along
> From mattins to the evensong,

> From the pickax, to the spade,
> To the tomb where't must be laid.

The object of the meditation and its charnel-house imagery both relate this poem more to such traditional didactic meditations on the same theme as Skelton's "Uppon a Deedmans Hed" than to Horace. The same is true of another long meditation on death which starts from an equally appropriate object, *"His Winding-sheet"* (H-515), where Herrick goes with a not altogether ironic resignation to meet the shroud which is "the Wine, and wit / Of all I've writ." It is, in fact, the strong didactic element in Herrick's poems on death and transience that marks off his independence from his Horatian models, so that, while lacking none of the latter's sophistication, a poem such as *"The Changes to Corinna"* (H-232) stands clear from the dramatic, personalized, and bitter context of Horace, and speaks instead with the impartial, resigned voice of the teacher, a voice more gently urbane in its way than Horace's own:

> Be not proud, but now encline
> Your soft eare to Discipline.
> You have changes in your life,
> Sometimes peace, and sometimes strife:
> You have ebbes of face and flowes,
> As your health or comes, or goes;
> You have hopes, and doubts, and feares
> Numberlesse, as are your haires.
> You have Pulses that doe beat
> High, and passions lesse of heat.
> You are young, but must be old,
> And, to these, ye must be told,
> Time, ere long, will come and plow
> Loathed Furrowes in your brow:
> And the dimnesse of your eye
> Will no other thing imply,
> > But you must die
> > As well as I.

There is no question in this admirable poem, as there is in Horace, of the unpalatable truth being used to retaliate against a cruel mistress, though that still remains the distant fictional frame of the poem. Instead, the tone is the even, almost impersonal one of age and wisdom speaking to youth, offering the "discipline," simple but profound, that will be necessary if experience is to be understood, to be seen by the individual in its proper perspective. Thus Corinna is reminded in the first ten lines that her life is a matter of continual change, of shifting states of both mind and body. It is through this recognition of the unstable nature of all human experience that Herrick leads Corinna, and his reader, to the larger lesson, placing these smaller transiencies in the larger perspective of inevitable age and death. Once again the lesson is driven home with quiet but implacable finality, a finality enforced by the insistent rhythms and rhymes of the closing lines.

The gentle, reasoning tone of this poem makes it easier to recognize as a didactic meditation on the transience of life than is the case in "*To* Dianeme" or "*To a Gentlewoman*," where traces of the cruel mistress still linger. It is true of all three poems, though, that they are much more meditations on time than they are love lyrics, that they are more concerned with teaching both poet and reader to accept a single, simple but unpalatable fact than with persuading a coy mistress to reconsider her position. Nor is the term *meditation* a misplaced one: though they may not take their principles of structure directly from the exercises of religious meditation in the way that Louis L. Martz has argued so many other seventeenth-century poems do,[5] the quiet firmness with which they confront the transience of life is reminiscent of both the tone and the achieved spiritual state, a state of mild acceptance, that are sought for at the final stage of most such meditations. That the understanding and acceptance of death do not take place in a Christian context should not blind us to their strong meditative element.

In another closely related group of poems dealing with time and death the meditative cast of Herrick's thought is still more apparent. In both "*To* Dianeme" and "*Upon a Carved Cherrystone*" we have seen him fixing on an inanimate object in order to discover for his reader the truths which these objects can teach.

The ruby and the cherrystone are the starting points for a meditation; they are also parts of that great glass, the *speculum creatu-
rum*, in which the multifold mysteries of the ways of God to man
are laid open for those who are willing and able to read from
them as in a book. Thus the cherrystone is a "scripture" which
Jemmonia Walgrave is exhorted to read. It was not, however,
necessary for the cherrystone to be carved before the meditative
man could read it: instead he could, like the exiled Duke in *As
You Like It*, read the simple Book of Nature, and find "tongues in
trees, books in the running brooks, / Sermons in stones, and
good in every thing." Indeed, he did not have to wait for exile
like the Duke before he began to learn from the *speculum creatu-
rum*. For him, it was present in the more convenient form of the
garden, which, both because of its associations with Eden and
the "garden enclosed" of the Song of Solomon, and because of its
obvious associations of beauty and tranquillity, came to be
closely linked with the practice of meditation during the seventeenth century.[6] It is of course not without significance in this
respect that *Hesperides* itself is named after an enclosed garden.

The garden had much to teach the meditative man, but the
most common lesson of all was, as we might expect, the recognition of the transience and fragility of all earthly things. John
Parkinson is typical in the conclusions he draws from the
flowers: "The frailty also of Mans life is learned by the soone
fading of them before their flowering, or in their pride, or soone
after, being either cropt by the hand of the Spectator, or by a
sudden blast withered and parched, or by the revolution of time
decaying of its own nature: as also that the fairest flowers or
fruits first ripe, are soonest and first gathered."[7]

In an atmosphere conducive to meditation, flowers, blossoms,
and fruits offered the contemplative man the lesson of transience
as in the clearest of books. Frequently in *Hesperides* Herrick
writes in a way that seems to presuppose a familiarity with this
meditative commonplace: it helps to explain, for example, the
studied, if not altogether successful naiveté of *"Divination by a
Daffadill"* (H-107), the very simplicity of which invites us to place
it in a tradition of such "divinations":

> When a Daffadill I see,
> Hanging down his head t'wards me;
> Guesse I may, what I must be:
> First, I shall decline my head;
> Secondly, I shall be dead;
> Lastly, safely buryed.

Herrick's meditations on the lesson are not always as simple as this. Two factors in particular make his reading of the Book of Nature more complex: one is his identification, in a number of poems, of woman with the flowers of the garden. The other is his apparent debt, in some poems, to the Christian meditative exercises of the Counter-Reformation.

The sense of an active interpenetration between woman and the natural world is one that runs through much of Herrick's poetry. It is seen at its clearest and most convincing in the epithalamia and "Corinna's *going a Maying*" (H-178), where the young virgin seems to draw to herself all the regenerative, life-giving forces of the *anima mundi* which are active in the spring. It is not surprising, therefore, that we should find him making the worlds of woman and nature interpenetrate each other in a similar manner when he is writing, not about rebirth, but about death. The relationship we see between flower and woman in these poems is not simply an emblematic one: the ripe and beautiful virgin and the flower are close to each other in being especially close to the sources of all life and beauty in what Thomas Vaughan called the "Universal Spirit of Nature."[8] Even in so apparently simple a poem as "*To a Bed of Tulips*" (H-493), where the relationship between flowers and virgins seems at first an arbitrary emblematic one, the more profound identification is in fact present:

> 1. Bright Tulips, we do know,
>   You had your comming hither;
>   And Fading-time do's show,
>   That Ye must quickly wither.
>
> 2. Your *Sister-hoods* may stay,
>   And smile here for your houre;

> But dye ye must away:
> Even as the meanest Flower.

3.   Come Virgins then, and see
>   Your frailties; and bemone ye;
>   For lost like these, 'twill be,
>   As Time had never known ye.

It is the personification involved in the mode of address, and especially the second stanza's reference to *"Sister-hoods,"* that is crucial here. The tulips have already been deftly but firmly associated with the human world before the relationship they bear to it is made more explicit—and more simple—in the final stanza. Indeed, the poem would retain all its poignant significance for man without that stanza, just as does *"To Violets"* (H-205), where the association is complete without ever having to be overtly stated:

1.   Welcome Maids of Honour,
>   You doe bring
>   In the Spring;
>   And wait upon her.

2.   She has Virgins many,
>   Fresh and faire;
>   Yet you are
>   More sweet then any.

3.   Y'are the Maiden Posies,
>   And so grac't,
>   To be plac't,
>   'Fore Damask Roses.

4.   Yet though thus respected,
>   By and by
>   Ye doe lie,
>   Poore Girles, neglected.

It is, once again, the tact with which Herrick introduces the world of the human into that of the flowers which helps the reader to accept the association made here. It is never labored, and for that reason never seems unlikely or unreasonable. Instead, its brief assured manner and its delicacy of statement and movement demand a respect greater than that which could be given to a piece of attractive whimsy. In being the "Maids of Honour" to spring, the violets are at once linked to both the human world and to the forces of nature's regeneration, forming through that dual association a suggestive link between real maids and the spring that is reminiscent of "Corinna's *going a Maying*." Unlike "Corinna" though, this poem is more concerned with death than with regeneration, and in this context the fact that the violets are "Maids of Honour" "More sweet then any" of the other virgins who wait upon the spring only makes the lesson they offer more devastating. It is made still more so by the simple restraint with which Herrick relates the inevitable decay of the violets in the final stanza, where the "Maids of Honour" have fallen to become "Poore Girles," and where the quiet movement of the verse gives to the last word, "neglected," a weight far beyond the reach of any whimsy.

Another poem, actually called in this case *"A Meditation for his Mistresse"* (H-216), follows a different strategy, in that it depends for its effect on the insistent, explicit repetition of the relationship between the world of woman and of nature. By showing how the lesson of transience can be read in a whole succession of comparisons between the two, Herrick gains for his theme a gathering weight of inevitability, until the last stanza draws together its implications for all mankind:

1. You are a *Tulip* seen to day,
   But (Dearest) of so short a stay;
   That where you grew, scarce man can say.

2. You are a lovely *July-flower*,
   Yet one rude wind, or ruffling shower,
   Will force you hence, (and in an houre.)

3. You are a sparking *Rose* i'th'bud,
   Yet lost, ere that chast flesh and blood
   Can shew where you or grew, or stood.

4. You are a full-spread faire-set Vine,
   And can with Tendrills love intwine,
   Yet dry'd, ere you distill your Wine.

5. You are like Balme inclosed (well)
    In *Amber,* or some *Chrystall* shell,
    Yet lost ere you transfuse your smell.

6. You are a dainty *Violet,*
    Yet wither'd, ere you can be set
    Within the Virgins Coronet.

7. You are the *Queen* all flowers among,
    But die you must (faire Maid) ere long,
    As He, the maker of this Song.

Whether or not we feel that the inclusion of the "Balme" of the fifth stanza is intrusive amongst the list of flowers, we must, I think, recognize that few poems in English convey so complete a sense of the brevity of all life as does this one. It is a profoundly serious poem, not just in intent, but in realization. And yet the very grace and brevity which are the means of this realization make it difficult for the modern reader, unaccustomed to seeing such graceful lyric delicacy subserving, indeed enacting, a serious meaning, to recognize it for what it is. Where we look for a tough reasonableness beneath its slight lyric grace, we find that that grace is more than slight, that it has become in fact the vehicle of a moral awareness which it would be crass to call tough, or even stringent, but which we must certainly call serious in its apprehension of transience and decay.

What justifies Herrick in calling this poem a meditation is not simply its framework, the reading of the Book of Nature, but the quiet, unflinching acceptance of the lesson taught by that book. The method of meditation itself, however, is a relatively simple one when compared to the spiritual disciplines recommended by many writers of the Counter-Reformation, or even those set out by Herrick's own bishop, Joseph Hall.[9] It is the contemplative method of the emblem books, out of which come such poems as Wither's "The Marigold," that Herrick is developing here in his own peculiarly graceful and telling way. But while we may safely conjecture that the stringency of many meditative exercises would have been uncongenial to his religious temperament, there are occasions when he appears to make more use than we might expect of relatively complex meditative techniques.

One such is the cumbrously titled "*Mistresse* Elizabeth Wheeler, *under the name of the lost Shepardesse*" (H-263). Though the self-consciously sophisticated pastoralism of the title scarcely alerts the reader to the poem's more serious dimensions, the suggestion, present from the start, of the tone of George Herbert should help counter the assumption that we are simply reading a fanciful compliment. Indeed, this poem, like one or two others in *Hesperides* (most notably "*The Olive Branch*," H-187), might well be described as a secular parody of Herbert, so closely does it resemble him in both tone and structure.[10] The figure of Love with whom Herrick here walks and talks in the garden is not, of course, the same figure with whom Herbert talks in *The Temple*, but this major difference apart, it is the similarities that are striking. The colloquial tone, the garden setting, and the dramatized narrative leading to the final statement of the lesson to be learned all bring Herbert's meditative technique vividly to mind:

> Among the *Mirtles*, as I walkt,
> Love and my sighs thus intertalkt:
> Tell me, said I, in deep distresse,
> Where I may find my Shepardesse.
> Thou foole, said Love, know'st thou not this?
> In every thing that's sweet, she is.
> In yond' *Carnation* goe and seek,
> There thou shalt find her lip and cheek:
> In that ennamel'd *Pansie* by,
> There thou shalt have her curious eye:
> In bloome of *Peach*, and *Roses* bud,
> There waves the Streamer of her blood.
> 'Tis true, said I, and thereupon
> I went to pluck them one by one,
> To make of parts an union;
> But on a sudden all were gone.
> At which I stopt; Said Love, these be
> The true resemblances of thee;
> For as these flowers, thy joyes must die,
> And in the turning of an eye;
> And all thy hopes of her must wither,
> Like those short sweets ere knit together.

The meditation, as Loyola and others advise, is best begun with what Loyola calls a "composition of place," the bringing into dramatic focus of the situation that is the subject or the starting point of the meditation. In Donne or Herbert this may often take the form of an abrupt and arresting opening, but it could also take the quieter, more explicit form of description with which Herrick's poem opens: "Among the *Mirtles*, as I walkt." In the same way Herbert's poem "Christmas" begins "All after pleasures as I rid one day."

Herrick is precise: his setting is the garden, and his subject the search for earthly beauty in the form of the shepherdess. Love's answer to his question as to where he can find her, "In every thing that's sweet, she is," is accurate enough. But the questioner fails to recognize that her transience, and the transience of his love for her, are both implied by Love's statement. It is only when he goes to pluck the flowers and sees them die in his hand that he begins to understand, and Love can draw out the truth to which this pastoral meditation has led, that "as these flowers, thy joyes must die, / And in the turning of an eye." Any reader familiar with seventeenth-century poetry cannot fail to be reminded by the plot of this poem of Herbert's "Life." There too Herbert's persona makes a posy of flowers without appreciating the transience of their beauty, and there too, as he sees them wither in his hand, he draws out the lesson which they hold for man:

> I took, without more thinking, in good part
> Times gentle admonition:
> Who did so sweetly deaths sad taste convey,
> Making my minde to smell my fatall day;
> Yet sugring the suspicion.

It is significant that it should be this poem which Martz chooses to demonstrate the way in which Herbert's poetry reflects the "formal process of meditation," which he defines earlier in his book thus: "Without expecting any hard and fast divisions . . . we should expect to find a formal meditation falling into three distinguishable portions, corresponding to the acts of memory, understanding, and will—portions which we might call composition, analysis, and colloquy."[11] We cannot, it is true, follow this threefold structure through "*Mistresse* Elizabeth Wheeler": indeed, in Herbert it is rather less clear than Martz suggests. Nevertheless, there are strong suggestions in Herrick's poem of the formal meditative framework Martz describes. Certainly, the opening "composition of place," the long colloquy with Love, the process through which misunderstanding is turned into true knowledge, and the final statement of the lesson learnt are all characteristic of the meditative poem. What is uncharacteristic is the presence of earthly rather than heavenly love, and the pastoral framework which accompanies it. Even this is less surprising, though, if we consider how close the two kinds of love could come, not just in fashionable Neoplatonism, but even in the work of a serious devotional writer such as Francois de Sales.[12] Though de Sales or Herbert might well have had reservations about the amatory, pastoral framework of Herrick's poem, no Christian could have objected to the conclusions it reaches. For the closing lines of the poem do not simply involve the hopelessness of Herrick's love for this particular woman; they recognize too the inevitable brevity of all earthly love and beauty. And although the Christian obverse of the lesson—the affirmation of the eternity of heavenly love—is not given, it is worth noting that even Herbert in "Life" feels it unnecessary to go beyond the recognition of transience, so clear for any Christian are the further implications of the lesson taught by the flowers.

Though they would still, no doubt, have regretted the absence of any explicit Christian reference, Herbert and de Sales would have found still less to object to in the final group of poems to be discussed here, "*To Primroses fill'd with morning-dew*" (H-257), "*To Daffadills*" (H-316), and "*To Blossoms*" (H-467). In these poems the mistress is no longer involved in the meditation; instead, as in "*To Violets*," Herrick addresses the flowers directly in a way that de Sales himself had suggested when he wrote that in meditation it may be useful to address oneself "even, as David in the Psalms, and other saints in their prayers and meditations, to inanimate creatures."[13] Perhaps the best gloss on Herrick's strategy, however, is to be found in Ralph Austen's book *The Spiritu-all use of an Orchard*, where he enlarges on the statement that "Fruit-trees though they are dumb companions, yet (in a sence) we may discourse with them," by saying:

We enquire of, and discourse with Fruit trees when we consider, and meditate of them, when we search out their virtues and perfections which God hath put into them, when we pry into their natures, and properties, *that is speaking to them.*

And when we (after a serious search) do make some use and result of what we see in them, when we collect something from them concerning the *Power, Wisdome, Goodnesse, and Perfections of God,* or our duty to God, *that is the answer of the Fruit-trees;* then Fruit-trees speak to the mind, and tell us many things, and teach us many good lessons.[14]

In *"To Primroses fill'd with morning-dew"* we find Herrick doing precisely what Austen recommends, "enquiring of" the primroses, prying into their natures, and discoursing with them:

1.   Why doe ye weep, sweet Babes? can Tears
                Speak griefe in you,
                Who were but borne
            Just as the modest Morne
            Teem'd her refreshing dew?
        Alas you have not known that shower,
                That marres a flower;
                Nor felt th'unkind
            Breath of a blasting wind;
            Nor are ye worne with yeares;
                Or warpt, as we,
                Who think it strange to see,
        Such pretty flowers, (like to Orphans young)
        To speak by Teares, before ye have a Tongue.

2.   Speak, whimp'ring Younglings, and make known
                The reason, why
                Ye droop, and weep;
            Is it for want of sleep?
            Or childish Lullabie?
        Or that ye have not seen as yet
                The *Violet?*
                Or brought a kisse

> From that Sweet-heart, to this?
> No, no, this sorrow shown
>   By your teares shed,
>   Wo'd have this Lecture read,
> That things of greatest, so of meanest worth,
> Conceiv'd with grief are, and with teares brought forth.

Although this poem concerns itself with transience rather than with death, it provides a clear example of Herrick reading the Book of Nature, and turning the meditative techniques of his contemporaries to his own purposes. We can see the threefold structure Martz describes more clearly here than in *"Mistresse Elizabeth Wheeler,"* as Herrick moves from composition through the analysis of the situation, exploring possible explanations, to the conclusion, the "lecture" which the primroses have to teach him. This conclusion corresponds to the colloquy with which we would expect the typical meditative poem to end; as in Herbert's "Life" or King's "A Contemplation upon flowers," though, the colloquy is not with God but with the flowers themselves.

In its use of the meditative disciplines, *"To Primroses"* is closely related to two more poems in which Herrick uses the garden as a starting point for a meditation on death. These are *"To Daffadills"* and *"To Blossoms." "To Daffadills"* is the simpler of the two in that the middle stage of the meditation, the analysis of the situation, has largely disappeared: the colloquy with the flowers is carried on from a position in which the transience of both daffodils and man has been accepted. There is no spiritual struggle, no mistaking of the lesson to be read, simply the quiet, firm, but graceful statement of the persona's acceptance of the situation. The daffodils are merely being asked to wait a little longer until man, too, dies:

> 1.   Faire Daffadills, we weep to see
>   You haste away so soone:
>   As yet the early-rising Sun
>   Has not attain'd his Noone.
>   Stay, stay,
>   Untill the hasting day
>   Has run

> But to the Even-song;
> And, having pray'd together, we
> Will goe with you along.

2.　 We have short time to stay, as you,
> 　　We have as short a Spring;
> As quick a growth to meet Decay,
> 　　As you, or any thing.
> 　　　We die,
> As your hours doe, and drie
> 　　　Away,
> Like to the Summers raine;
> Or as the pearles of Mornings dew
> Ne'r to be found againe.

If "To Daffadills" is the final stage of a meditation whose previous stages of question and debate we have hardly been allowed to see, "To Blossoms" gives us the whole process in a threefold development which reflects the influence of the meditative disciplines more clearly than any other poem in *Hesperides*. In it, Herrick's persona moves through the stages of misunderstanding and rebellion to an acceptance of time and death that is as complete as it is convincing. In doing so, he follows one of the most commonly advocated patterns of meditation, that of deliberately cultivating unreasonable, mistaken, or even blasphemous thoughts in order to strengthen oneself against temptation. Martz discusses the immensely popular *Spiritual Combat*, attributed to Lorenzo Scupoli, as the most important source of this method, but it is a commonplace of devotional advice. Its employment by Donne in his Holy Sonnet, "If poysonous mineralls, and if that tree," and by Herbert in such poems as "The Collar" or "The Crosse" make it familiar to all readers of seventeenth-century poetry. In each of these poems, angry rebellion, the refusal to accept God's order, is put forward in order that it may be overcome. In the first two stanzas of "To Blossoms," Herrick's persona too fails to accept the natural order of things, first questioning, and then defying it, before returning, like Donne and Herbert, to a quiet acceptance of that order:

1.   Faire pledges of a fruitfull Tree:
      Why do yee fall so fast?
      Your date is not so past;
   But you may stay yet here a while,
      To blush and gently smile;
      And go at last.

2.   What, were yee borne to be
      An houre or half's delight;
      And so to bid goodnight?
   'Twas pitie Nature brought yee forth
      Meerly to shew your worth,
      And lose you quite.

3.   But you are lovely Leaves, where we
      May read how soon things have
      Their end, though ne'r so brave:
   And after they have shown their pride,
      Like you a while: They glide
      Into the Grave.

Read as a meditation of the kind described, this poem gains a coherence which it might otherwise seem to lack. For the sharp transition from the second to the third stanza in particular must seem awkward in any other context than that in which the still more sudden transition of the closing lines of "The Collar" also finds its explanation. Herrick is showing us the various stages of a meditation on transience which passes from a total failure to understand the significance of the fall of the blossoms, through anger, to a complete understanding of the lesson they offer. In such a process, the pauses between each stanza become almost as meaningful as the words themselves.

The reasoning, conciliatory tone of the first stanza is that of a man who is so far from understanding the part the blossoms have in the inevitable order of things (their passing, it is worth recalling, presages the coming of fruit) that he believes their death can be delayed. The voice is one of bland incomprehension and gentle surprise, which develops in the second stanza into the voice of rebellious anger. What has happened between these two stanzas is the partial recognition, without the spiritual acceptance, of the fact of transience, a fact made all the more difficult to accept because it is the passing of beauty and innocence that is involved. The speaker no longer tries to alter the natural order by conciliatory argument; instead, he protests against it in an angry outburst heralded by the explosive "What, were yee borne to be" and concludes with a terse rejection of nature's wisdom. Then, like Donne in the ninth Holy Sonnet or Herbert in "The Collar," he moves abruptly from anger and rebellion to a harmonious understanding. Unlike the two devotional poets, however, Herrick is not able to fall back on the mercy and love of God. Instead he must be explicit: the leaves of the book must be read, the lesson which the blossoms hold for man must be spelled out and accepted.

The final stanza begins with the word that carries the weight of that acceptance, the recognition that the accusation with which the previous stanza ends is not to be considered. The word "But" leads surprisingly and decisively into the gentle rhythms and internal harmonies which are in such striking contrast to what has gone before. This new ease of movement, together with the running on of the lines in all but one instance, gives the verse something of the quality of formal prose statement. It might, indeed, seem diffuse, were it not bound together by a masterly use of internal assonances, and by the quiet dignity with which it moves—two qualities which it shares with the fine closing paragraph of George Herbert's meditation on a similar theme, "Church Monuments." Harmony and dignity work together to give the gentle restraint of Herrick's conclusion an authority that is wholly convincing. The successful conclusion of the meditation will normally involve acceptance of the order of things, a harmony between the poet and the universal laws by which he is bound. It is just such an acceptance, just such an achieved spiritual harmony, of which the closing stanza of *"To Blossoms"* convinces us. More clearly than anywhere else in *Hesperides* we see Herrick coming fully to terms with the inevitability of death, without comforting reference to any kind of immortality whatever. In that simple but profound acceptance lies the most complete victory over *"Times trans-shifting"* that *Hesperides* has to offer.

NOTES

1. All titles and quotations are from *The Complete Poetry of Robert Herrick*, ed. J. Max Patrick (New York, 1963).

2. The meditative structure of the latter poem is discussed by Roger B. Rollin, *Robert Herrick* (New York, 1966), pp. 157–60, while Herrick's treatment of death is given brief attention by Allen H. Gilbert, "Robert Herrick on Death," *MLQ*, 5 (1944), 61–67.

3. "O cruel still and strong through Venus' gifts, when the unexpected down comes on your pride, and the hair falls that now waves on your shoulders, and the complexion that now is finer than the blossoms of the crimson rose is gone, Ligurinus, changed into a bristly face, then as often as you look in your mirror you will say 'Alas, why as a boy did I not have the mind I have today, or why don't the unblemished cheeks return to this my spirit?' "

4. This was not published in *Hesperides*, but is extant in several manuscript versions; quotations are from the eclectic text in *Complete Poetry*, ed. Patrick, pp. 547–49.

5. Louis L. Martz, *The Poetry of Meditation*, rev. ed. (New Haven, 1962).

6. Cf. Stanley Stewart, *The Enclosed Garden: The Tradition and the Image in Seventeenth-Century Poetry* (Madison, Wis., 1966): "the physical garden became an emblem of meditation; its very shape and substance were understood allegorically" (p. 112).

7. "To the Courteous Reader," sigs. e–f, in *Paradisi in Sole* (London, 1629).

8. *"Anima Magica Abscondita"* in *The Works of Thomas Vaughan*, ed. A. E. Waite (London, 1919).

9. *The Arte of Divine Meditation* (London, 1606); for discussion of Hall's work, see Martz, *Poetry of Meditation*, pp. 331–52.

10. K. J. Holtgen, "Herrick, the Wheeler Family, and Quarles," *RES* (N.S.), 16 (1965), 399–405, identifies this Elizabeth Wheeler as the one who in 1613 married Simon English of the Middle Temple. If we accept this, then Herrick must have written this poem as a young man of twenty-one or less, and any question of influence by Herbert would almost certainly have to be ruled out. What is important, though, is that the treatises on meditation and at least some of the poems which were based on their disciplines, were available to both poets before this date.

11. Martz, *Poetry of Meditation*, p. 38.

12. See, e.g., *Introduction to the Devout Life* (1609), trans. Michael Day (London, 1961), p. 68: "The thoughts of men in love, with a merely natural love, are always turned towards their beloved, their hearts full of love for her, her praises always on their lips; when absent they constantly express their love in letters; they carve her name on every tree; so those who love God never stop thinking of him, longing for him, seeking him and speaking to him; if it were possible they would engrave the sacred name of Jesus on the breast of everyone in the world. Every created thing serves their love, and speaks the praise of their beloved."

13. Ibid., p. 61.

14. 2nd ed. (Oxford, 1657); from "A Preface to the Reader" (not numbered). Austen's book was first published in 1653, bound with the same author's more practical *A Treatise of Fruit Trees;* its meditations are not concerned with transience, but with simple positive lessons of conduct to be learnt from the trees.

Hesperides: Classical and Contemporary

GORDON BRADEN

Herrick's Classical Quotations

L. C. Martin's edition of Herrick's *Poetical Works* (1956) was
the culmination of a long, cooperative attempt, beginning in the
late nineteenth century, to pin down and label the numerous
scattered quotations that the poet lifted from other authors and
worked into his own writing.[1] Alfred Pollard, in 1898, proposed
that "in the final edition of his works every italicised line will
have to be traced to its original, together with numerous others,
as to the source of which his memory must have failed him when
he was seeing his book through the press."[2] This turned out to
be a major project, for the "others" far outnumber the conve-
niently italicized borrowings. Martin, adding his own researches
to those of Grosart, Pollard, Phinn, and others, produced eighty-
eight pages of annotations that make it clear how intricately Herrick's verbal texture is involved with quotations from other
writers, in an often apparently random and inconsequential way.
Pollard's sense of the italicized *sententia* as the norm is obviously
wrong, since so many borrowings are just bits of diction and
turns of phrase peripheral to the main intent of both Herrick's
poem and the original. And for this reason it seems particularly
odd that the largest class of borrowings is not from other English
poets, but from the classics. To take ideas or motifs from a foreign literature is one thing; but to take the actual nuts and bolts
of expression across a linguistic barrier as real as that between
English and Latin (or Greek) is a subtly different business, a
transaction at once more superficial and more intimate than what
we usually mean when we speak of literary "influence." And that
is the topic I want to explore here.

Almost all important English poets, of course, have had such
catalogues as Martin's made on them; the question here is how to

"place" Herrick's specific practice, both as a particular way of reading the classics, and as a particular way of writing poetry. In the former regard, this practice is a late product of the regnant style of humanistic reading in the Renaissance, a style whose importance has been stressed by Bolgar:[3] one reads one's author with, more or less literally, pen in hand and notebook open, ready to take down whatever strikes one's attention. Under such scrutiny, text fragments into smaller and smaller details: *sententiae*, phrases, words. And while the intention may be "assimilation" in the larger sense, the technique is that of an almost microscopic registration of texture. Such procedure, ignoring larger issues of content and structure, has fallen now into some disrepute, but the underlying faith might be likened to that of modern biology: that the meaning of the whole is encoded somehow in each cell, and with enough skill and patience one could clone a whole culture from any one of its *disjecta membra*.

The other question is the relevance of this style of attention to the writing of poetry, particularly to Herrick's own mode of "light" lyric. Again, his case is not isolated; and the most notorious and instructive example is a poem by another poet, whose work and techniques we know Herrick studied in some detail:

> Drinke to me, onely, with thine eyes,
>   And I will pledge with mine;
> Or leave a kisse but in the cup,
>   And Ile not looke for wine.
> The thirst, that from the soule doth rise,
>   Doth aske a drinke divine:
> But might I of *Jove's Nectar* sup,
>   I would not change for thine.
> I sent thee, late, a rosie wreath,
>   Not so much honoring thee,
> As giving it a hope, that there
>   It could not withered bee.
> But thou thereon did'st only breath,
>   And sent'st it backe to mee:
> Since when it growes, and smells, I sweare,
>   Not of it selfe, but thee.[4]

This is indeed the poem of Jonson's perhaps most completely in Herrick's vein, even to the interest in transferring bodily odors onto erotic décor. Like so many of Herrick's poems, this one concerns the deflecting of a sexual obsession away from its real object onto something that can receive such attention with less embarrassment; Herrick in fact does a miniature of Jonson's last eight lines (H-144/51.3). "Drinke to me, onely" has had a remarkable popular success for more than three centuries. Herford and Simpson call it "the one supreme success among his songs";[5] it is the one poem of Jonson's, and one of the few products of the large tradition of Elizabethan song, that everyone still recognizes. Its popularity comes from suiting everybody's ideal of what a civilized drinking song should be: graceful and trivial, neat but effortless, the inspiration (surely) of the moment—a bubble. Not until more than a century and a half after its publication did anyone note in print that the poem is virtually a cento, closely translated, of several separate bits of widely unknown Greek prose from the *Epistolai eroticai* of Philostratos: the bubble cunningly and deceitfully stitched together out of pieces from a few old inner tubes.[6]

The shock of this discovery was not exhausted by the first report, by Richard Cumberland in 1785.[7] Others have been more willing than Cumberland to see the case as testimony to Jonson's talent; but the tremor of recognition, variously displayed as amazement or outrage, remains, occasionally reported in the press, as a kind of *rite de passage* for readers of Jonson. One recent article by a classicist considers the manuscript version of the poem and determines that the later folio version represents an attempt at increased literalness. He concludes, tentatively ("This is the sort of judgement which classical scholars are often ill-equipped to appreciate—I could as easily convince myself of the reverse"), that the earlier version is superior for being "freer and more spontaneous."[8] Behind this claim lies a desire to save ground for "freedom and spontaneity" as poetic values, or perhaps, more exactly, as recognized components of poetic composition; a bubble, somehow, should not have a history. Certainly one wants some sort of term between Jonson and Philostratos, some term of "inspiration" or "revision" to account for the success of the English poem. But Jonson's intent and—one may argue—accomplishment lie in reducing the paraphrasable differences between his poem and Philostratos' prose to almost nothing.

Certainly Jonson did not, to use his own metaphor, digest Philostratos whole and then refashion him; the contours and borders of the original letters are extraordinarily clear. The first, third, and fourth groups of four lines have their exact sources in Letters 33, 2, and 46 of Philostratos respectively, like sequential entries in a commonplace book. Only two notable changes are made. An inauspicious reference to Zeus and Ganymede is suppressed in 33 and replaced by "I will pledge with mine." And 2 and 46 are deftly linked by Jonson's use of "growes" in line 15. In Letter 46 the wreath simply comes back smelling of its recipient, with no hint of the life-preserving powers adumbrated in Letter 2; Jonson unobtrusively converts the two conceits into one.

Jonson's main "creativity" is exercised in the second four lines:

> The thirst, that from the soule doth rise,
>   Doth aske a drinke divine:
> But might I of *Jove's Nectar* sup,
>   I would not change for thine.

The Philostratean sources traditionally given—Letters 32 and 60—are not exact; but they show how Jonson's "invention" works scrupulously in terms of available details: thirst and the soul (separately) from 32, nectar from 60, and Jove, with interesting economy, from the unused clause in 33. These detachable bits are fitted into a conceit difficult to distinguish in kind from those of the surrounding lines. It never seems to have been suggested that lines 5–8 represent Jonson's "real" voice breaking momentarily through the Philostratean static; and even if that might be the case, why are they medial instead of climactic? Rather, if we take the rest of the poem as in some sense "given," lines 5–8 suggest a textual critic's careful, conjectural reconstruction of a lacuna. The other major "improvisation"—

"And I will pledge with mine"—looks in retrospect like much the same thing: a reasonable and convincing extrapolation of the Greek's *men-de* texture, even though that is not the specific character of the suppressed original at this point. We may see in this a demanding literary game: punch holes in a text, and then fill them in again in such a way that nobody can guess what you have done. But all writing is a game, and in an age when textual criticism was a central cultural endeavor, this one would not seem as silly as it might today. It was the game that Spenser played (though he did not, like Jonson, punch his own holes) when he slipped two carefully made-up names into his catalogue of the Nereids;[9] the reader is not likely to guess which ones they are without consulting his Hesiod. Jonson is not "creatively transforming" the ancient text, but mastering the range of appropriate context which his *donnée* sets up: given lines 1–4 and 9–16, what would it make sense for lines 5–8 to say? It is in this peculiar Jonsonian way that the professions of scholar and writer converge.

In that convergence we have one of the few kinds of literary study that does not have to worry about being impertinent to its object, since it replies on a comparable level of literary activity. Study of the text is precisely by means of further writing: how might one, on one's own and in English, find oneself saying just these words? The goal here is the very undetectability of the source, its total effacement into the present occasion, since that is exactly the sign that a viable English literary possibility has been realized, that we now know, in at least one very specific sense, what these words mean. It is a curious but effective way of expanding English literature by lifting the burden of the past: decomposing the original in this manner, rather than trying to assimilate or answer it as a whole, converts it, at least for the moment, from *daimōn* into resource. One works this way up or back to the starting point, to the place where one begins, again, from scratch. Other relationships to one's literary past are of course possible—in fact more common and certainly easier to discuss. We may distinguish the epic style of allusion, in which a *perspective* on the past is exactly what is wanted: "Compare Milton's invocation of the Muse to Virgil's," etc. There is an important sense in which *Paradise Lost* cannot be read without knowing the *Aeneid*, or the *Aeneid* without knowing Homer. But "Drinke to me, onely" can be read without knowing Philostratos, or even who he was; most people, even professionals, do, and without missing much. The mode of allusion here—a lyric mode, perhaps—does not put the past in perspective, but makes it if anything co-present, enabling the reader to pretend that the congruences between the past and present are but happy accidents, two living minds meeting in the same words.

"Drinke to me, onely" is a limiting case in several ways—in its nearly total verbal absorption in its sources, and also in those sources' relative obscurity, which would exclude even a normally well-trained seventeenth-century reader from following the game the way he could when the source was Catullus or Ovid. But the principles involved are valid for much of Jonson's general program of classical quotation: *sententiae* and turns of phrase so adjusted to their English context, or their English context so adjusted to them, that the reader is never quite sure without checking the notes (some of them, of course, supplied by Jonson himself) what sort of ground he is walking on. And, as in the case of the famous drinking song, the reader has often complained: "the trouble [*ennui*] with Jonson is that one never knows when admiring him if one is the dupe of an innocent deception—or rather of one's own ignorance. . . . Who will tell us that certain charming verses do not come directly from Catullus or Anacreon, that the passage we admire is not simply a well-done translation or an ingenious adaptation?"[10]

If anything, the same *ennui* obtains even more extensively for Herrick; the most famous line he ever wrote is only the latest term in a clearly defined tradition that reaches back through four languages:

> "Gather ye Rose-buds"
> "Gather therefore the Rose"—Spenser
> "Cogliam la rosa"—Tasso
> "Cueillez dés aujourdhuy les roses"—Ronsard
> "Collige, uirgo, rosas"—anon.[11]

Such intermediaries, though, are relatively rare; the available evidence usually indicates a direct tracing of Latin phraseology into English. And we can often see the tracing as not just quotation, but a significant part of the way in which the poem was written. The importation is an irritant, a stimulus to establishing an appropriate English context. It is worth noting that the rules here do not require that the English context have too much to do with the Latin one:

> Goe happy Rose, and enterwove
> With other Flowers, bind my Love.   (H-238/98.2, 1–2)

> I, felix rosa, mollibusque sertis
> nostri cinge comas Apollinaris.   (Martial 7.89.1–2)
> [Go, happy rose, and with soft garlands
> bind the hair of our Apollinaris.]

The proper name, characteristically for Herrick, is glossed over, and with it the homosexuality; but otherwise the source is quite exact and unmistakable—certainly more literal than Waller's famous dealings ("lovely" instead of "happy") with the same line. After this the poems diverge:

> Tell her too, she must not be,
> Longer flowing, longer free,
> That so oft has fetter'd me.

> quas tu nectere candidas, sed olim,
> sic te semper amet Venus, memento.
> [And remember to wreathe that hair when,
> though a long time from now, it will be
> white—so may Venus always love you.]

Yet this divergence does not leave Herrick's quotation stranded. He has fixed on *cinge;* has recognized in that word an intersection with his own special concern for necklaces, bracelets, and such encircling décor; and has spun out of this juncture that very Renaissance and very un-Roman thing, a "conceit." In retrospect, one can spot the seam ("too"), but even that is consistent with the casual, paratactic way in which Herrick's "conceits" tend to proceed. The thematic issue of binding is so gracefully and unemphatically developed that it comes as something of a surprise to learn that the first two lines were written by someone else, without this particular metaphor in mind. To "change" Martial's lines this way, though, has been a matter of paying very literal attention to what they *say*, to their status as a specific verbal configuration radiating specific possibilities. Herrick shifts the emphasis to *cinge* so that, within the context of both this stanza and *Hesperides* as a whole, the borrowed lines come across with new and somewhat unexpected force: the love-gift as noose.

> The Halter was of silk, and gold,
>   That he reacht forth unto me:
> No otherwise, then if he would
>   By dainty things undo me.   (H-863/279, 5–8)

The treatment of the quotation from Martial, in Stanley Cavell's phrase, brings the words home[12]—which is to say, within the circuit of one's own *lar*.

This quotation is a relatively long one for Herrick—two complete lines of Latin and English. Most quotations of this length in *Hesperides* are unabashedly sententious, and as such are probably the least vital class of Herrick's verbal importations. In accord with what we have been saying, borrowed *sententiae* should, as indeed they do in Jonson, provoke one to a discursive aggressiveness of one's own; but poetic argument, along the lines developed in the neoclassical couplet, is simply not one of Herrick's modes. His genius was almost premental, and explicit statements of wisdom remain most viable in his work when allowed to float at the level of avuncular commonplace: "Old Time is still a flying." It is significant that several entire poems in *Hesperides* are translations of couplets from the middle of some longer Latin works; Herrick is not responding to such moments as possible stages in a larger process.

In any case, a very large class of Herrick's borrowings are not sententious at all, but much more minutely verbal. A line just quoted—"Longer flowing, longer free"—provides a good example; its phrasing and structure obviously owe a lot to Jonson: "Robes loosely flowing, haire as free."[13] Borrowing this way from Jonson is only to be expected; in the general context of contemporary writing, small gestures of diction and cadence will catch in the ear and reassert themselves. But Herrick more frequently derives such sub-sententious smatterings from the Romans than from his fellow Englishmen. The presence of these borrowings is quite difficult to detect, but the sources usually turn out to be unambiguous and often quite literal. A reference, for example, to "the old Race of mankind" (H-377/147, 38) looks perfectly innocuous, except that it could serve as an interlinear translation of Horace's "prisca gens mortalium" (*Epodes* 2.2). The "easy" gods appearing in several poems derive from an Ovidian (*Heroides* 16.282) and Martialan (1.103.4) use of *facilis*. There is often a strange reliance on cognates: "The golden pomp is come" (H-201/80.2, 4 and 5), "aurea pompa uenit" (Ovid, *Amores* 3.2.44); "Stars consenting with thy Fate" (H-106/35, 33), "consentit astrum" (Horace, *Odes* 2.17.22). This habit sometimes seems to lead to clumsy English, as in Herrick's *"supremest* kisse" (H-14/9.1, 6; also H-327/129.4, 2; H-1028/315.4, 1), which looks like a schoolboy's version of Ovid's "oscula . . . suprema" (*Metamorphoses* 6.278). But Herrick tenaciously makes "supremest" a part of his *copia uerborum* (see H-838/274.4, 6); and the borrowing is further camouflaged by the jazzy character of so much of his Latinate diction. As a neologism, "supremest" is no crazier than "circum-walk," and as a "Latinism" it is no more intrusive upon the native tongue than "liquefaction," both of which seem to be Herrick's own doing. And at any rate, this Poundian willingness to be childishly literal is part of what is meant by paying attention to the specific possibilities of specific configurations. In a similar example, Herrick writes "The Extreame Scabbe take thee" (H-6/7.1, 6) under the evident influence of Horace's recommendation, "occupet extremum scabies" (*Ars poetica* 417), "let the mange seize the hindmost." (An interesting example for several reasons; what casual reader is likely to think of "scab" as a "Latinism"?) Martin, in his note, calls this a "blurred reminiscence," but it is really a very specific reminiscence. Herrick has forgotten or ignored the grammar of the passage—*extremum*, aside from not really meaning "extreme," is not modifying *scabies*—but he has exactly remembered the way the words were arranged with respect to each other. A genuinely blurred reminiscence would get the "sense" of the passage, and maybe even some of the particular words used, but not how they went together on the page. Herrick is if anything less interested in what his poets mean than in what they say.

This last is important. Nothing in the rules of the game, as we have said, commits Herrick to the context from which his quotation is fetched. Occasionally his borrowing will seem almost to reverse the thrust that obtains in the original. "Corinna's *going a Maying*" is not, off-hand, likely to make anyone think of Persius—"So when or you or I are made / A fable, song, or fleeting shade" (H-178/69, 65–66)—but there it is: "cinis et manes et fabula fies" (5.152). Herrick is fond enough of that *locus*, in fact, to use it again, with much the same phrasing: "We must be made, / Ere long, a song, ere long, a shade" (H-336/133, 29–30). And the injunctions in the previous line of the Latin—"indulge genio, carpamus dulcia"—similarly find their places in his work: "Gratifie the *Genius*" (H-231/96.3, 6), and, probably, from the same stanza in "Corinna," "take the harmlesse follie of the time" (l. 58). Thus isolated, the Latin could serve as a two-line *précis* of *Hesperides*. But in the original the passage is all placed as part of a somewhat bitchy harangue by *sollers Luxuria*, one horn of a moral dilemma that involves a matching harangue from Avarice. Source hunting that brings context to bear can make Herrick seem rather shallow.

But such complexities of irony as those of Persius—results of literary *structure*—are of no particular use to Herrick, whose own sense of design is relatively simple, if rigorous. His response is directly to verbal *texture*, and his attention to the phrases of his originals is not effectively matched by an attention to the individual poems as wholes. There are, considering the bulk of the whole and the general ambience of classical quotation, notably few translations and imitations of complete poems in *Hesperides*. The exceptions are important and helpful— I shall be dealing with one below—but the principle remains that while Herrick seems very interested in classical poetry, he is not comparably interested in classical poems. All that we can safely say that Herrick could "get" from the classics through his style of quotation would be a certain Latinate firmness of statement—the heft or timbre of his authors' voices, but not any of their specific intentions.

Yet the prejudice persists that deeper congruences somehow obtain—a prejudice keyed by the very success of *Hesperides* as a whole: why this coherence from so much fragmentation? It is interesting that the other major tradition of nineteenth-century Herrick criticism, developing alongside the source-hunting, concerns itself with the suggestive matter of equating *Oeuvre* with *Oeuvre*. "Perhaps there is no collection of poetry in our language which, in some respects, more nearly resembles the *Carmina* of Catullus."[14] That is Nathaniel Drake in a central document of the early nineteenth-century rediscovery of Herrick. "Some respects" specifically refers only to the mixture of bitter and sweet elements in the arrangement of poems; but the suggestion activated an entire century of interest. Drake's remark found its way into S. W. Singer's preface to the 1846 Pickering edition, thence to Carew Hazlitt's edition (1869), and was widely circulated throughout nineteenth-century discussion of Herrick. By the time of James Russell Lowell, Herrick had become the "most Catullian of poets since Catullus."[15] It is certainly not an identification that seems very credible today; perhaps in the nineteenth century Catullus ("pedicabo ego uos et irrumabo") seemed much tamer (Herrick himself refers to "soft *Catullus*," H-575/206, 43), or Herrick seemed much more daring than either does today. There is in Herrick none of the vehemence that inhabits so much of Catullus's "lyricism" and for us (and for Marvell) constitutes his special character—his "intense levity," in Eliot's phrase. Yet this does not exhaust the possibilities of the approach. The first real contest to the Herrick-Catullus identification came from Edmund Gosse, who, however, instead of suggesting another approach, proposed replacing Catullus with Martial, and in so doing established the rules for much subsequent discussion. Grosart replied, defending Catullus. One scholar suggested Tibullus; Anacreon was often mentioned; and in the twentieth century the tradition died down into a general consensus for Horace.[16] That was a good conclusion, but not pushed very far; certainly the level on which most of the discussion was conducted does not inspire too much confidence. It all sounds like some parlor game: "I am a free-born *Roman*," Herrick himself says (H-713/242.1, 11), encouraging us to guess which one. But there is involved a more serious possibility, namely that the classical models as *Oeuvres* furnished Herrick with a steadying sense of his own enterprise, of how to sustain a lyric impulse until it becomes an *Oeuvre*—and in particular that the *Odes* of Horace, as a corporate entity, provided the primary example.

There are various sorts of evidence for Herrick's special regard for Horace. The number of Horatian quotations, especially of the sub-sententious class, is extraordinarily high; and the only explicitly labeled translation in *Hesperides* (H-181/70.1) is of a Horatian ode (3.9). It is intriguing that Horace is not mentioned in *"To live merrily, and to trust to Good Verses"* (H-201/80.2), the most memorable of Herrick's dealings with his classical predecessors. Moorman interprets this as evidence of Herrick's particular respect for Horace, an unwillingness to involve such a dignified and serious poet in so unseemly a bash;[17] and indeed, Horace's moralistic reputation in the Renaissance, a reputation based more on his conversation poems than on his *Odes*, should be recalled. But it may be just that reputation that Herrick is seeking to get away from when he consistently gives Anacreon to Horace as a traveling companion, as if to make the seriousness of the one continuous with the drinking habits of the other:

> Rouze *Anacreon* from the dead;
> And return him drunk to bed:
> Sing o're *Horace*; for ere long
> Death will come and mar the song. (H-111/39.3, 9–12)[18]

For someone who comes at Horace through the *Odes*, this company does not look strange at all; Herrick's "Horace," companion of Anacreon, is one part of the seventeenth-century encounter with Horace as a specifically lyric poet.[19] Alcohol is a major term in Horace's emotional economy in the *Odes*, and in fact one famous instance of it surreptitiously provides the starting point for

"To live merrily": "Now is the time for mirth," "Nunc est biben-dum" (1.37.1). It is probably an accident that the next English line ends with an echo of the Latin: "be dumbe." It is probably not an accident that the poem rounds itself off with another Ho-ratian allusion, those pyramids less durable than verse. We may agree with Moorman that Horace's absence from this poem indi-cates a particularly intimate relationship, but we may reformulate his statement of the evidence: Horace is not mentioned because, in some sense, Horace is speaking.

The matching of Herrick with Horace is really the oldest of such identifications of Herrick with a classical model, and the only one with external seventeenth-century support:

> And then *Flaccus Horace*,
> He was but a sowr-ass,
> And good for nothing but *Lyricks:*
> There's but One to be found
> In all English ground
> Writes as well; who is hight *Robert Herick.* [20]

Horace and Herrick meet specifically under the rubric of *lyric,* that title for trivial poems saved from inconsequence, it would seem, by being written well—what Auden, in his poem on Yeats, calls "this strange excuse." The ambivalent respect that the anonymous author here accords these two poets is only one entry in a millennial uncertainty about the "value" of lyric poetry, an uncertainty against which lyric poets have spent much energy insulating themselves. The semi-magical word *lyric* is itself im-portant as something of a badge or talisman. Herrick twice parades the rhyme on his own name (H-366/143.1, 3–4; H-604/213, 6 and 8); Horace's *Odes* is full of its author's aspirations to the title of *lyricus uates.* And there is to both poets a further self-consciousness about their work, particularly in their concern with the *carmen* as thematic material itself, as a factor in people's lives. This concern indeed might have made Horace's *Odes* the definitive classical lyric *Oeuvre* even if most of the others had not been mangled by time almost beyond recognition.

The chief value of the badge, for both poets, is its way of

helping them organize their image of a possible life in a given situation. The *Odes* and *Hesperides* each project a self-contained lyric "world," in which a large number of customary things go on, but not very much really *happens;* they are both attempts at realizing contentment with a set of *données*. The two "worlds" have a good deal in common: young girls, older men, herbage of various sorts, wine, music, domestic gods to be honored, a decent admixture of the grotesque, and an occasional admiring glimpse of royalty about its business—all linked by a network of *sententiae* about mortality, equanimity, and the good life. These congruences, however, are less important than the enveloping congruence of situation: two aging bachelors piddling around in their rustication, celebrating moments of pleasurable transiency while being made keenly aware of the menace of civil disruption to all such havens. The writing of lyric poetry integrates such a life, by treating thematically its emotional dynamics and by providing a career and title appropriate to both the writer's ambition and his place.

The role of Horace's example in this regard is demonstrated in a remarkable poem in which, characteristically, he is not mentioned. The opening quotation, however, is unmistakable: "Ah *Posthumus!* Our yeares hence flye" (H-336/132.3, 1). That is a fairly close translation of the opening line and a half of *Odes* 2.14: "Eheu fugaces, Postume, Postume, / labuntur anni." To this Herrick immediately gives his own special shading: "Our yeares hence flye, / And leave no sound." The insidious silence of time is one of Herrick's more personal and striking motifs, and shows up elsewhere as his addition to a source (H-62/21.6, 5–6); but instead of continuing to move away from the original, he returns to it, though similarly interleaving some more of his own contributions:

> nor piety,
> Or Prayers, or vow
> Can keepe the wrinkle from the brow   (ll. 2–4)

> nec pietas moram
> rugis et instanti senectae
> adferet.   (ll. 2–4)

Herrick's addition—"Or prayers, or vow"—again neatly excerpts. The first twelve lines of Herrick's poem constitute a telescoped translation of the first twenty-four of the original. It is arguable that nothing really crucial is left out; even the famous dying fall of the repeated name, though Herrick misses it in the first line, is caught later in a kind of miniature: "none, / None, *Posthumus*, co'd ere decline" (ll. 6–7). (The proper name is not repeated here in the original.) What is scrapped is a good deal of mythological data, in general amounting to a vision of hell here reduced to "cruell *Proserpine*" (l. 8), a slack phrase not in the original, though possibly deriving from another Horatian ode (1.28.20). But the larger arc of the Latin poem—vague regret focusing onto death—is preserved; and judicious cutting allows Herrick to realize this as a devolution onto a potent bit of funereal décor:

> no one plant found
> To follow thee,
> Save only the *Curst-Cipresse* tree. (ll. 10–12)

> neque harum quas colis arborum
> te praeter inuisas cupressos
> ulla breuem dominum sequetur. (ll. 22–24)

Herrick's repositioning of the cypress suits his own habit of ending on objects rather than thoughts. It is one way of converting a poem by Horace into a poem by Herrick.

After line 24, Horace gives, in a four-line coda, a parting glimpse of Postumus' *dignior heres* looting his predecessor's carefully preserved wine cellar; Herrick picks up from this a hint leading him out of his original:

> A merry mind
> Looks forward, scornes what's left behind:
> Let's live, my *Wickes*, then, while we may,
> And here enjoy our Holiday. (ll. 13–16)

The transformation of Postumus into Wickes signals that the translation itself is over. Still, though Herrick's sentiment here is not strictly in the original, it may be said to be implicit there, in the merry-minded heir with his own ideas on what to do with what's left behind. And the sentiment is certainly explicit in the context of the whole of the *Odes;* it is indeed the deduction that Horace might make from the presented situation, though he does not happen to do so in this particular poem. Herrick leaves *Odes* 2.14 but stays within the general Horatian context as his poem moves out from its starting point.

That poem as a whole is particularly rich in classical allusions. There are numerous bits of salient classical decoration—Iülus and Baucis, Anchus and Tullus, and Pollio's lampries—though the most memorable is as usual the least obvious: a seventeen-hundred-dred-year-old condiment dispenser fulfills something of the function of a *lar:* "we can meet, and so conferre, / Both by a shining Salt-seller" (ll. 49–50). That is, "splendet in mensa tenui salinum" (*Odes* 2.16.14). Over the next seven stanzas Herrick, in his articulation of a norm of equanimity, continually touches classical sententious bases: Catullus ("Let's live," l. 15; "the white and Luckie stone," l. 40)[21] and Persius ("Ere long, a song, ere long, a shade," l. 30), but most especially Horace. Some of the Horatian moments are exact (the waxing and waning moon, ll. 19–20), some collateral (the quotation from Persius overlaps onto "puluis et umbra sumus"—*Odes* 4.7.16—which Martin cites as the only source), and some more general and thematic: stanza 8 ("Well then, on what Seas we are tost") reads to the suspicious like a graft of *Integer uitae* onto the Ship of State, with the former's sense of humor preserved. Again, most to the point is the way that Herrick stays within Horace's orbit. The opening of stanza 4 rewrites in a major key the vision of hell slighted in the translation of 2.14–the underworld, but not Tartarus—yet does so by having recourse to another Horatian poem about death (cf. ll. 25–27 and *Odes* 4.7.14–15). And since in general nothing that Herrick says goes outside Horace's *copia sententiarum,* the first nine stanzas of the poem constitute something of an allusion to the whole of the *Odes.*

With stanza 10 the poem becomes less sententious and ("as for my selfe," l. 73) more personal and specific, as Herrick begins to visualize himself actually handling the sense of lost time in his old age. And the first nine stanzas of the poem snap into place when we realize that the primary activity that Herrick envisions for himself is reading his own poetry, some of which we have just read:

> At which I'le reare
> Mine aged limbs above my chaire:
> And hearing it,
> Flutter and crow, as in a fit
> Of fresh concupiscence, and cry,
> *No lust theres like to Poetry.* (ll. 107–12)

(The picture is very much like that of William Carlos Williams in his old age—a poet whom Herrick resembles in other ways as well.) This poem about the lost past has suddenly ceased to be a poem about memory. What Herrick is doing, first of all, is *imagining* a future act of remembering. That wife and child, Baucis and Iülus, are not serious anticipations, but blatant bits of (classical) poetic décor; Herrick postulates the assimilation in old age of all his concerns (lust, for example) to the level of imagination. And the basic statement made about his old age is that what will be remembered is not a person or object or event—these things pass—but a poetic act, one of the class of things that remain continuously available, news that stays news. Such is one of the services that poetry performs for the race as a whole; good writing is one of the few things that grow rather than decay with acquaintance and use. Herrick simply applies this lesson to his own life: the past that he will endeavor to recall, like some modern reading Homer, will be that of his imagination. Emotion is poetry recollected in excitement.

Herrick, as we have said, does not mention Horace by name. However, the central image of Herrick rereading Herrick enters the poem only after we have seen that to reread Herrick is in a certain sense to reread Horace. The tacit analogy goes something like this: old Herrick is to young Herrick as Robert Herrick, seventeenth century A.D., is to Flaccus Horace, first century B.C. Within each pairing, roughly, the latter writes and the former reads. And the special excitement in that reading probably derives from the coexistence of both parts of the analogy: it is, as

D. S. Carne-Ross has put it, exactly in a time of great contemporary poetry that all great poetry feels contemporary.[22] Or, to come at it another way, with the availability of the past, present and future open up. Certainly, a few pages earlier in *Hesperides*, the mere prospect of rereading his own poetry had provoked no enthusiasm in Herrick:

> What can I do in Poetry,
> Now the good Spirit's gone from me?
> Why nothing now, but lonely sit,
> And over-read what I have writ.   (H-334/132.1)

Because the first half of the Wickes poem makes contact with Horace's words as contemporary resource, the second half looks forward to the *use* of Herrick's own poetry; indeed, the poem is the most precise and practical of Herrick's numerous treatments of the matter of poetic immortality. Elsewhere Herrick's focus is on the marmoreal self-sufficiency of the product; here it is on the unexpected vitality that inspection of such a product—e.g., of *Odes* 2.14, in all of its Latinate, funereal rigor—can release in the beholder. And specifically the poem says that a man's life can be reintegrated across time in the same sense—no less, no more—that the race is reintegrated by occasional access to just that vitality.

Regarding Herrick's relation to Horace, there is one more layer of analogy, that of the Roman poet's own relation to the Greek lyricists in whose college he was so anxious to be enrolled. History flattens perspective, and we tend to forget that Horace faced his models across a linguistic and cultural abyss not much narrower than the one across which Herrick faced his. And enough evidence survives to show that one of Horace's strategies for bridging this void was the quickest and most obvious: the wholesale use of spot quotation, with no particular regard for context. Herrick's "Now is the time for mirth" follows Horace's example not only in sentiment, but also in being a borrowed phrase used to start a poem; for "nunc est bibendum" merely translates the opening of a poem by Alcaios: "nun chrē methusthēn."[23] That happens so often in Horace that the scholarship has a technical term for it—the borrowing of a "motto." Herrick might well have known about this example; it and several others are commonplaces of Renaissance criticism. The chapter on Horace in the elder Scaliger's book on *Imitatio* (*Poetics* 5.7), for example, is little more than an unexpanded list of four of Horace's verbatim quotations from the Greek lyricists, along with the guess that the list would be much longer if more of the Greek had survived. Four centuries of subsequent scholarship have not contradicted that guess, or turned up much evidence that such quotations are systematically controlled by context—as, say, Virgil's quotations of Homer are.[24] The respective enterprises of Horace and Herrick thus superimpose in a kind of double exposure, and suggest that this style of quotation is not incidental but central to at least a certain kind of lyric poetry. They are both songsters borrowing words to make their tunes visible. And perhaps what they have to say to us is that words are, like everything else we have, borrowed, and that the measure of our freedom and contentment is our detachment from them, and hence our awareness of them. It is only under a similar dispensation that we can hope to be at home in our lives: by training our aspirations to intersect, as though on their own, with the given. That is the opposite of the epic quest, the search for a home somewhere else, for a way to say what we mean; the lyric enterprise is, by comparison, an attempt to fulfill the obvious, to learn carefully how to mean what we say. That such poetry "of the present moment" should be so intricately linked to the past is another part of what it has to tell us: that the world has been lived in before, and may, with skill and luck, just possibly be lived in again. Bubbles have no history, but they do have precedents.

NOTES

1. Because of the special relevance to my purposes of Martin's notes, I use a double annotation for Herrick's work. References are to (1) the number of the poem in *The Complete Poetry of Robert Herrick*, ed. J. Max Patrick (New York, 1968); (2) the page and order on the page of the poem in Martin's edition, accord-

ing to his own system (explained p. vii); and (3) line numbers, except when an entire poem is meant. Unexpanded references to "sources" may be presumed to be to Martin's notes. The text throughout is Patrick's.

2. "Herrick Sources and Illustrations," *Modern Quarterly of Language and Literature*, 1 (1898), 175.

3. R. R. Bolgar, *The Classical Heritage and its Beneficiaries* (Cambridge, 1954), pp. 265–75.

4. "The Forrest," 9; text from *The Complete Poetry of Ben Jonson*, ed. William B. Hunter, Jr. (New York, 1963).

5. *Ben Jonson*, ed. C. H. Herford and Percy and Evelyn Simpson, 11 vols. (Oxford, 1925–52), II, 385.

6. For the details, see ibid., XI, 39.

7. Cumberland, *Observer*, 74, in Alexander Chalmers, ed., *The British Essayists*, 45 vols. (London, 1802–03), XLII, 205–07. For similar reports, see John F. M. Dovaston, *Monthly Magazine*, 39 (1815), 123–24; and Ernest Barker, *Spectator*, 157 (1936), 890–91.

8. A. D. Fitton Brown, "Drink to me, Celia," *MLR*, 54 (1959), 556.

9. *Faerie Queene* 4.11.48–51.

10. Maurice Castelain, *Ben Jonson: L'Homme et l'Oeuvre* (Paris and London, 1907), p. 838. For his encounter with "Drinke to me, onely," see p. 840. The translation, as with the Latin below, is mine.

11. *Faerie Queene* 2.12.75.6; *Gerusaleme Liberata* 16.117; *Sonnets pour Helene* 2.43.14 ("Quand vous serez bien vieille"); "De Rosis Nascentibus," l. 49, now most accessible in editions of the *Appendix Vergiliana*, but also, and more plausibly, attributed to Ausonius.

12. *The Senses of Walden* (New York, 1972), p. 16.

13. "Uncollected Poetry," 24.9 in Hunter, ed., *Complete Poetry*; = *Epicoene* 1.1.99.

14. *Literary Hours*, 3 vols. (London, 1804), III, 45.

15. "Lessing," in *Among My Books*, First Series (Boston, 1870), p. 341.

16. For further attacks on the Catullus identification, see Floris Delattre, *Robert Herrick: Contribution à l'Étude de la Poésie Lyrique en Angleterre au Dix-septième Siècle* (Paris, 1912), pp. 408–10n.; and James A. S. McPeek, *Catullus in Strange and Distant Britain* (Cambridge, Mass., 1939), pp. 48–49. On Martial, see Edmund Gosse, *Seventeenth Century Studies*, 4th ed. (London, 1913), pp. 152–53 (the original was in *Cornhill Magazine*, August, 1875); and the replies of Alexander B. Grosart, *The Complete Poems of Robert Herrick*, ed. Grosart, 3 vols. (London, 1876), I, ccxliii–lv, and Paul Nixon, "Herrick and Martial," *CP*, 5 (1910), 189–202. On Tibullus, see Pauline Aiken, *The Influence of the Latin Elegists in English Lyric Poetry, 1600–1650* (Orono, Me., 1932), pp. 69 ff. On Horace, see Elizabeth Hazelton Haight, "Robert Herrick: The English Horace," *CW*, 4 (1911), 178–81, 186–89; M. J. Ruggles, "Horace and Herrick," *CJ*, 31 (1936), 223–34; and (principally) Graydon W. Regenos, "The Influence of Horace on Robert Herrick," *PQ*, 26 (1947), 268–84.

17. F. W. Moorman, *Robert Herrick: A Biographical and Critical Study* (London and New York, 1910), p. 217.

18. As Chris Dahl, of the University of Michigan, Dearborn, has pointed out to me, this unannounced entrance of death into the poem is a specifically Horatian effect, very similar to the famous appearance of *pallida Mors* in *Odes* 1.4.13. For the further adventures of Horace and Anacreon in *Hesperides,* see H-128/45.1, 31, and H-544/198.1, 7–18.

19. See Valerie Edden, " 'The Best of Lyrick Poets,' " in *Horace,* ed. C. D. N. Costa (London and Boston, 1973), pp. 135–59.

20. Anon., *Naps upon Parnassus. A sleepy Muse nipt and pincht, though not awakened* (London, 1658), sig. A₃.

21. The latter is from Catullus 68.147–48; see John B. Emperor, *The Catullian Influence in English Lyric Poetry, Circa 1600–1650* (Columbia, Mo., 1928), p. 109. Martin cites only a weak parallel in Martial.

22. "T. S. Eliot: Tropheia," *Arion,* 4 (1965), 6.

23. Alcaios, fragment 332 in *Poetarum Lesborum Fragmenta,* ed. Edgar Lobel and Denys Page (Oxford, 1955).

24. The standard treatment of the issue is still that of Giorgio Pasquali, *Orazio Lirico* (1918; rpt. Florence, 1964). For his conclusions on "Nunc est bibendum," see p. 9.

JAMES S. TILLMAN

Herrick's Georgic Encomia

Readers of poetry of the English Renaissance readily recognize that distinctive type of pastoral verse in which actual persons are held up as exemplars or models. Spenser's *Colin Clout's Come Home Againe*, with its portrait of Sir Walter Raleigh, and his song to Queen Elizabeth in the April eclogue of *The Shepheardes Calender* are familiar representatives of these pastoral encomia. Customarily placed in the same category are two poems of Robert Herrick, his addresses to Endymion Porter, "*The Country life*" (H-662),[1] and to his brother Thomas Herrick, "*A Country life*" (H-106). In this essay, however, I will demonstrate that the latter two poems are not so much pastoral as georgic encomia, both in their exhortative tones and in their idealizations of the gentlemen addressed as self-restrained, laborious master husbandmen of their country estates.

The appropriation of the farmer's ethos in these poems reflects the new enthusiasm in English Renaissance literature for the celebration of country arts and labors that Dwight Durling in *The Georgic Tradition in English Poetry*[2] attributed to the influence of such Italian humanists as Vida, Pontano, and Fracastoro. Maren-Sofie Røstvig later documented the emergence of these georgic ideals in volume one of *The Happy Man: Studies in the Metamorphoses of a Classical Ideal* with her account of the repetition of Virgil's happy husbandman motif in the poetry of Ben Jonson, Mildmay Fane, Abraham Cowley, and other seventeenth-century poets.[3] In addition, John R. Cooper's recent *The Art of The Compleat Angler*[4] provides convincing evidence that even Walton's prose manual is reminiscent of traditional fishing georgics.

These English examples of the influence of the georgic, however, including the two encomia by Herrick, are not so exclusively indebted to the georgic manner and motifs that they do not also reflect the pastoral strain that was even more popular in seventeenth-century England.[5] The pastoral and georgic have always overlapped, for they differ more in emphasis and tone than in theme and setting. Since both genres oppose the simplicity and beauty of country life to the decadence of court and city life, it is misleading to insist upon rigid distinctions between the two forms. Nevertheless, a knowledge of the characteristic emphasis in georgic appreciations of country life can often illuminate works that have usually been classified as pastorals.

Georgics differ from pastorals in three characteristic concerns: they are more descriptive and instructive, providing knowledge about some country art (most often farming); they are more realistic in their presentation of the social and economic responsibilities imposed by country life; and they are more exhortative, preaching the usefulness of labor and self-restraint in particular.[6] Essentially, georgics make country *otium* and pleasure a rare reward earned by a man's painstaking labors and arts, rather than the easy prerogative of rural life and occupations that they appear to be in pastorals. That does not mean, of course, that georgic husbandmen never enjoy country pleasures. Even Hesiod's persona—hard-working peasant farmer that he is—enjoys his dog days, when no work can be done about the farm and he can stretch out in the shade, guzzling wine and offering a libation to the gods.[7] There are also occasions, of course, when the pastoral swain must submit to the constraints of exacting labors. Milon, for instance, in Theocritus's tenth idyll, called "The Reapers," berates the love-sick Busaeus with a typical georgic admonition to cut his "swath straight" and to keep time with his neighbor's reaping.[8] Yet the pleasures of the georgic husbandman are usually short, and they are always earned by labor and forethought, whereas the pastoral swain spends most of his time sitting at his ease in the shade of a tree, a spring's pleasant gurgle accompanying the music of the singing contest in which he is enthralled.

Since the bulk of Virgil's and Hesiod's georgic works is given over to instructions in farming laced with injunctions to work, descriptions of the occasional ease and pleasure granted to the husbandman are still part of a country life clearly distinct from the life of the pastoral swain. But Herrick's two short poems about country gentlemen are quite different from Virgil's and Hesiod's longer works with their consistent concern with the arts of farming. In fact, Herrick's poems more closely approximate the "rural odes" of classical and English poets in which Røstvig so often finds the happy man motif.[9] In such lyrical poetry of country life, as opposed to formal georgics, instructions in farming and consistent injunctions to work are uncommon, but a georgic ethos is still apparent in the emphasis upon a realistic portrayal of the social and economic demands of country life and upon the moral ideal of self-restraint.

One clue to the presence of this georgic ethos in Herrick's poem on country life addressed to Endymion Porter (H-662) is the realistic and exhortative presentation of Porter as a working administrator of his country estate. Much like Virgil in the second book of the *Georgics* (ll. 458–541), Herrick consistently opposes the country life of Porter as self-restrained master husbandman to the court and city life of unrestrained men. For every fruitless social and economic ambition in the city or at court, Herrick substitutes a lowly but fruitful country equivalent. Porter's travels extend no farther than his lands, but he improves the lands as he walks them (ll. 21–24); his ambitions are curtailed, but their narrower scope supports the economics of his own estate (ll. 11–14); his entertainments are merely the country holidays, but at least no one pays dearly (ll. 46–61); and his intrigues are simple country hunts, but as a consequence no falls occur beyond those of "pilfring Birds" (ll. 68–69).

By means of such contrasts the poem urges Porter to forget the exciting, but largely immoral, values and pleasures of the court and city for the sake of the mundane, but nevertheless substantial, demands and pleasures of the country estate. Moreover, the poem has Porter himself instruct the husbandmen in a lesson that merchants or courtiers might easily forget: "The Kingdoms portion *is the Plow*" (l. 28). In other words, the poem subtly reminds Porter that the microcosm of responsible order and power in the country estates of the realm provides the basis of order for the macrocosm of the state. Admittedly, supporting this georgic world of responsibility to husbandry and husbandmen does not require that Porter actually do any plowing for the sake of the estate and the kingdom, but—considering his class and position in society—he is called to a laborious, lowly, and constrained life, with no travels, with cocks to wake him at dawn, and with husbandmen as his chief companions.

There is also no doubt that this life is portrayed in the poem as remarkably happy, at times even carefree, but the very celebration of its happiness at the end of the poem is in an echo of Virgil's famous praise of the life of the husbandman in the *Georgics*,[10] not in a reminder of the implicit celebrations of the shepherd's happy life in the *Eclogues:*

> O happy life! if that their good
> The Husbandmen but understood!
> Who all the day themselves doe please,
> And Younglings, with such sports as these.
> And, lying down, have nought t'affright
> Sweet sleep, that makes more short the night.   (ll. 70–75)

Even though these lines claim that husbandmen do nothing but please themselves all day, the poem itself makes us aware that such an easy, holiday life is earned by their usual routine of daily labors. This part of the poem too, then, much like the similar passage on the husbandman's happy life in the *Georgics*, still supports the exhortative tone of the work as a whole. Herrick urges Porter here and elsewhere in the poem to realize fully, in a self-conscious manner unknown to his naive husbandmen, the special georgic values of the daily round of work and occasional holiday play in the country life of the estate. Once he achieves this philosophical appreciation of his country responsibilities, he will never neglect his restful sleep in the country, where he is at ease with his conscience and himself, for sleepless nights at court.

Certainly, the poem would be a more convincing echo of the georgic tradition if Herrick were more insistent about the need for labor, and if he lingered less upon the pleasure and ease of the holidays, but a contrast with a pastoral encomium, also addressed to Endymion Porter, does at least suggest that the georgic ethos is a more appropriate commentary on *"The Country life"* than most aspects of the pastoral ethos.

This pastoral encomium, *"An Eclogue, or Pastorall between* Endimion Porter *and* Lycidas Herrick, *set and sung"* (H-492), is similar to most poems of its kind in that it adopts the strategy of making us see the patron's grand qualities in the eyes of a naive companion who loves him for his physical beauty, his music, and his simple goodness, rather than for his position and power.[11] Herrick, as Lycidas, pleads with Porter, as Endimion, to return from the court to his former shepherd life in Latmos where Lycidas now mourns his departure so much that he even neglects his music. Lycidas reminds Endimion of the pastoral pleasures with which the court has nothing to do: those joys in love, in song, in play, in companionship, and in wine. Though Endimion, touched by Lycidas's plea, promises a return home, the promise convinces Lycidas only enough that he swears to sing again, with the hope that at least Endimion will remember him as he rises to power at court. The tone at the end is still pathetic—the simple shepherd remains behind mourning the loss of his favorite companion to higher ambitions than the songs, easy fellowship, and sensual indulgence of the pastoral life (though one should not let the pathos obscure the obvious plea of poet to patron to be remembered).

What strikes one about the poem, however, is that both the poet's persona and his patron, Porter, appear in very different roles from those in *"The Country life."* In "An Eclogue," Porter is not the responsible, working squire who rises with the cock, but the somewhat melancholy, pastoral swain with some touches of the power and beauty of the Greek god (st. 9); the poet's persona is not the omniscient, exhortative sage, but the naive pastoral singer whose greatest pain is the loss of his companion and the silencing of his song that his loss entails. As a consequence, even though both poems are appeals to give up a life at court and return to a simple country existence, the image of country life portrayed is quite different. For though pain is not absent in the pastoral encomium, the occasion for pain is not the constraint of georgic labors, but the loss of a companion. Similarly, pleasure is not absent in the georgic encomium, but the occasion is not the shepherd's daily routine of play and singing—rather it is the much less common farmer's holiday from work. Furthermore, in the pastoral encomium, Porter is called away from the court to a life of individual fulfillment and indulgence, but in the georgic encomium he is called away from the court to a life with considerably more social and economic responsibility and with more demands for self-restraint. Finally, the very nature of the rhetorical argument in the two poems is different, for Herrick's pastoral plea to Porter relies essentially upon an emotional appeal and his georgic exhortation relies essentially upon an ethical appeal.

Herrick's praise of his brother, Thomas, in his other georgic encomium (H-106) has a rhetorical appeal very similar to that of the encomium of Porter in "The Country life." Thomas's country life, like Porter's, is portrayed as more ethically rewarding than the life of city and court. It, too, is a life of labor, a painstaking endeavor for which Jove repays the laborer with blessings (ll. 55–62) such as a chaste wife (ll. 31–42) and a sweet sleep (ll. 43–54). In addition, Herrick's tone in the poem is exhortative, perhaps even more so than in the praise of Porter. His insistent pleas often solidify into moral maxims, reminiscent of Hesiod's barrage of aphorisms in his address to his brother-in-law in *Works and Days* (Hesiod, ll. 343–81). And, at one point, Herrick even pauses to exhort Thomas to prove himself worthy of the portrait that the poem paints (ll. 101–05). Yet in general this encomium is considerably more philosophical than the encomium of Porter. Indeed, Roger Rollin has called the poem the "most thoroughgoing philosophical poem of *Hesperides*,"[12] and Earl Miner in *The Cavalier Mode from Jonson to Cotton*[13] has found it useful in his exploration of a number of Cavalier values, including integrity, friendship, love, and the contemplative life. Such analyses make it clear that Thomas's portrait is obviously too richly colored by the influence of the Stoics, Epicurus, and Jonson, among others, to be a creation inspired by the georgic tradition alone. Yet the portrait of Thomas is, nevertheless, quite compatible with georgic ideals.

In fact, Thomas Herrick's self-restrained country life reflects the moral value at the heart of the georgic tradition, for georgics have always portrayed men who love a life of "discipline and foresight."[14] But, admittedly, in georgics this self-discipline is largely forced upon the husbandman by the relentless, seasonal duties of farming that are his lot in life. Unlike Thomas Herrick, the traditional husbandman does not voluntarily embrace "discipline and foresight" so much as submit to the necessity of employing them in order to survive. Nevertheless, georgic poets usually make of this necessary self-restraint a virtue in order to remind their sophisticated readers that they too can actually enjoy more blessings in life, if—like the lowly husbandman—they are content to expect less from it.

The substance of this lesson does not change when the central figure of the poem ceases to be the lowly husbandman or even when he becomes a self-knowledgeable, educated man with the philosophical convictions ascribed to Thomas Herrick by his brother. If anything, in fact, this philosophical "husbandman" provides a more impressive exemplar for the sophisticated reader, because he willingly chooses, he vows (l. 2), to accept constraints similar to those of the real husbandman. The poem transforms these constraints into blessings, but they still remain sacrifices unfamiliar to ambitious, worldly men. Hence Thomas is blessed with "Travell at the lowest price" (l. 82), because he will accept journeys by map and imagination rather than by ship; he enjoys a wife whose love is secure and enduring partly because he will not marry for beauty (l. 34); and, most importantly, he can rest at ease with his conscience, largely because he willingly exposes himself to nature's simplicity more than to the excesses of city and court (ll. 3–16). In a sense, then, Thomas actually becomes a more worthy ideal for the sophisticated reader than the lowly husbandman, because he can not only be envied for the joy of his simple country labors and pleasures, but he can be admired for his wisdom in choosing a more rewarding life than those of city or court.

Though this portrait of Thomas's ideal life has as many echoes of the pastoral strain as the encomium of Porter's,[15] especially in the description of the country landscape, it, too, is best placed in the georgic, rather than the pastoral tradition. The very fact that the tone adopted in the presentation of country life in these poems seems more austere than those that we are accustomed to in *Hesperides*[16] should warn us that a different attitude to country cares and rewards may be in control of the poems. Along with Jonson's poem to Robert Wroth[17] (which possibly inspired the encomium of Thomas Herrick in the first place), Herrick's poems are significant adaptions of the georgic ethos to the praise of gentlemen in a period when pastoral ideals still dominated most country life literature.

NOTES

1. Parenthetical references are to the line and poem numbers in *The Complete Poetry of Robert Herrick*, ed. J. Max Patrick (New York, 1968).

2. (New York, 1935), p. 7.

3. (Oslo, 1958), pp. 55–118.

4. (Durham, N.C., 1968), pp. 41–44.

5. For a discussion of Herrick's poems as "realistic pastorals," see Roger B. Rollin, *Robert Herrick* (New York, 1966), pp. 70–79.

6. See Joseph Addison, "Essay on Virgil's *Georgics*" (1697) in *Eighteenth-Century Critical Essays*, ed. Scott Elledge, 2 vols. (Ithaca, 1961), I, 2; Marie Loretto Lilly, *The Georgic* (Baltimore, 1919), pp. 19–47; Cooper, *Compleat Angler*, pp. 59–60; Røstvig, *Happy Man*, pp. 46–47; and Thomas G. Rosenmeyer, *The Green Cabinet: Theocritus and the European Pastoral Lyric* (Berkeley, 1969), pp. 20–29.

7. *Works and Days*, in *Hesiod, The Homeric Hymns and Homerica*, trans. Hugh G. Evelyn-White, Loeb Classical Library (Cambridge, Mass., 1914, rev. 1936), ll. 582–95, pp. 46–47.

8. *The Poems of Theocritus*, in *The Greek Bucolic Poets*, trans. J. M. Edmonds, Loeb Classical Library (Cambridge, Mass, 1912, rev. 1937), ll. 2–3, pp. 130–31.

9. Røstvig describes the "rural ode" as an "original creation along lines suggested by Horatian rural lyric" in which the "main difficulty" is to "reconcile the claims of philosophy with those of the lyric poem" (p. 46). A. C. Partridge includes "*The Country life*" (to Porter) among the Horatian odes in *The Tribe of Ben: Pre-Augustan Classical Verse in English* (London, 1966), p. 93.

10. *Georgics*, in *Eclogues, Georgics, Aeneid*, trans. H. Rushton Fairclough, in *Virgil with an English Translation*, Loeb Classical Library, 2 vols. (New York, 1916), I, bk. 2, ll. 458–74, pp. 149–50. There is also a close parallel between the figure of the master living on his lands that Virgil describes (ll. 493–532) and Porter, since both of them are shown to be appreciative of the abundance, the animals, the

country folk, and the holidays encountered in a rural existence. See also Horace's second Epode on the happy man, as well as Røstvig's chapter on the classical happy man tradition (pp. 13–52).

11. See the chapter on "Pastoral and Techniques of Flattery" in Calvin W. Truesdale, "English Pastoral Verse from Spenser to Marvell: A Critical Revaluation" (Ph.D. diss., Univ. of Washington, 1956), pp. 42–71, especially p. 46.

12. Rollin, *Herrick,* p. 75.

13. (Princeton, 1971), pp. 151–53, 278–81.

14. Rosenmeyer, *Green Cabinet,* p. 21.

15. Rollin, *Herrick,* p. 71.

16. *"The Hock-cart"* (H-250) immediately comes to mind as a poem with at least a touch of this austere tone, especially in its portrayal of the husbandman's "tough labours," the praise of the plow as "Commonwealth," and the Lord's parting words on the pain of plowing that will "spring againe" (ll. 3, 39, and 55). But the happy harvest occasion with its pleasant abundance of food and drink and its easy companionship of Lord and husbandmen largely vitiates the georgic austerity.

17. Røstvig notes the influence of the *Georgics* on Jonson, pp. 63–64.

Herrick's Epigrams of Praise

Although Herrick was an ardent disciple of Ben Jonson, he never published a volume resembling his master's *Epigrammes* (1616). *Epigrammes* is a collection confined to one genre, a "Theater"[1] of contemporary society which concentrates on aristocratic and urban subjects. *Hesperides* includes several genres; it is a "mixed garden"[2] of short forms dominated by lyric and pastoral poems. Yet in his satiric, moral, and occasional verses Herrick is clearly a social poet[3] and often an epigrammatist. Among the occasional poems in *Hesperides* are a number of brief encomia—addresses to royalty, statesmen, writers, patrons, and friends of the poet—which may be called epigrams of praise. Like Herrick's epitaphs, these epigrams derive from the standards established in Jonson's work and develop the Jonsonian epigram to suit Herrick's own designs.

Along with other forms of encomia, the epigram of praise may be viewed today as a tedious sort of poem: conventional, dutiful, probably insincere, and certainly limited to the circumstances of its occasion. Renaissance literary theory, however, assigned to praise the important task of commemorating and encouraging virtuous action.[4] The moral value ascribed to epideictic literature, whether commendatory address or panegyric, is apparent in the ethical stress of Jonson's compliments. As instruction and commemoration, then, the verse compliment may transcend the vices of flattery and the limitations of the merely topical. In *Hesperides*, furthermore, the epigram of praise assumes meanings particularly related to the conventions of its genre. Herrick's eulogies indicate that he saw his collection as containing "A City . . . of Heroes" (H-365), a *"white Temple* of my *Heroes"* (H-496), an "Endsse-Kalendar" (H-444), and a "Testament" (H-977).[5] These civic

and religious metaphors suggest that Herrick has made specia
use of his brief compliments; the Hesperidean garden encom
passes both a city and a temple, figured in the epigrams or "in
scriptions"[6] to particular persons.

Both as inscriptions and as social gestures, the epigrams o
praise are important to the diverse motifs of *Hesperides*. As in
scriptions, they balance the lyrics on fragility and transience b
offering instances of the transformation of ephemeral life int
enduring art. The compliments are also social poems dealin
with contemporary people and events, and ranging in tone fron
urbane friendship to ceremonious invocation. The epigrams c
praise are not the "real toads" in the pastoral garden (the satiri
epigrams must claim that honor), but they bring the resonance c
particular people and events into Herrick's grove.[7] Yet as Her
rick's own metaphors imply, the epigrams confront real occasion
only to transform them through the techniques of naming an
identifying. Their subjects become lasting images in verse.

The epigrams in *Hesperides* are representatives of a long tradi
tion which includes the *Greek Anthology*, the epigrams of Martia
and numerous Latin and vernacular imitations of these model
By the end of the sixteenth century, the epigram was a forr
available for personal or public praise as well as for satire.
might be paired with the madrigal or emblem, and it was ofte
seen as an "ancient" kind of sonnet.[8] English epigrammatist
developed the satiric branch of the genre, with which the
whipped and scourged their way through the heyday of epigran
at the turn of the century; their salty collections contain onl
scattered compliments. Jonson's collection is noteworthy for i
full use of the possibilities of the genre: *Epigrammes* balanc
praise against blame, and devotes as much space to complimer
as to satire in its survey of men and manners. The use of th
epigram for dignified praise is thus an outstanding feature of th
collection, and Jonson's example undoubtedly recommended th
form to Herrick.

Jonson sometimes uses the epigram for a brief personal ac
dress, as in the poem "Inviting a Friend to Supper" (*Epig.* ci
His most characteristic epigrams of praise, however, are publ

utterances with the memorable terseness of inscriptions. True to the pointedness of epigram, Jonson usually presents himself as the frank judge, as well as the advocate, of those he praises. His subjects become exemplars or epitomes of virtue whom the poet—ordinarily a satirist, with a satirist's eye for weakness— has chosen for their value as models to posterity. The full range of this technique, from the poet's discriminating judgment to the discovery of his subject's exemplary power, can be seen in the epigram to William, Earl of Pembroke, the patron of Jonson's collection (*Epig.* cii):

> I doe but name thee PEMBROKE, and I find
>   It is an *Epigramme,* on all man-kind;
> Against the bad, but of, and to the good:
>   Both which are ask'd, to have thee understood.
> Nor could the age have mist thee, in this strife
>   Of vice, and vertue; wherein all great life
> Almost, is exercis'd: and scarse one knowes,
>   To which, yet, of the sides himselfe he owes.
> They follow vertue, for reward, to day;
>   To morrow vice, if shee give better pay:
> And are so good, and bad, just at a price,
>   As nothing else discernes the vertue' or vice.
> But thou, whose noblêsse keeps one stature still,
>   And one true posture, though besieg'd with ill
> Of what ambition, faction, pride can raise;
>   Whose life, ev'n they, that envie it, must praise;
> That art so reverenc'd, as thy comming in,
>   But in the view, doth interrupt their sinne;
> Thou must draw more: and they, that hope to see
>   The common-wealth still safe, must studie thee.

Jonson's address unites the gesture owed by a poet to his patron with the larger aims of *Epigrammes.* It singles out Pembroke for his virtue, justifies the poet's choice, and preserves his image of Pembroke for posterity. The opening conceit, which identifies Pembroke's "name" with the powers of epigram, is central to this process, for it connects Pembroke with Jonson's art. In his prefatory epistle, Jonson claims that his book not only exposes vice but leads forth "good, and great names . . . to their remembrance with posteritie." Since Pembroke's behavior works "Against the bad, but of, and to the good," he shares the double force of the epigram; and his power for ethical discrimination is mirrored in the language of the poem, which stresses the distinction between "Vice, and vertue," "good, and bad." Jonson's epideictic conception of the genre is thus applied to his patron and pursued in the argument of his praise.

The concept of "Name," which may denote title or reputation as well as a given name, is an important element in *Epigrammes*, where "good, and great names" are preserved for posterity. When Jonson suggests that we "studie" Pembroke, he reminds us that this naming is both an inscriptional commemoration of fame and a portrait of a man whose virtue is exemplary. Thus, while Jonson's epigrams are hortatory, pointing to ethical distinctions and encouraging their subjects to "stand" firm in the "one posture" of virtue, they are also images or portraits which represent the poet's ideals to the reader. The epigram's associations with type portraits and with emblem make it particularly accessible to this technique. Readers of Jonson have noted his treatment of the epigram as a "name poem" or portrait, and some have suggested that *Epigrammes* be viewed as a portrait gallery, commonwealth, or "directory of good and evil,"[9] as well as a theater of social poems.

Unlike *Epigrammes, Hesperides* is not an epideictic collection. That is, it is not governed by a dialectic of praise and satire or by systematic ethical distinctions. It is a grove of short poems, not an *epigrammata* but a mixture of kinds. Yet Herrick's debt to Jonson is evident in the epigrams of praise. These compliments are more carefully developed than their counterparts, the satiric type portraits; they strive for Jonson's terse civility and poised social address, and even echo some of Jonson's phrases. Most significant is Herrick's adaptation of Jonson's emphasis on names; a number of compliments, stressing poetic fame, develop the epigram as image and as inscription.

Herrick's love for the Tribe and for literary society in general informs a number of epigrams to writers and patrons. Here, Jonson's bluff manner can be adapted to Herrick's own enthusiasms,

as when the poet interrupts his praise of "Cooper's Hill" to ex-
claim, "by *Apollo!* as I worship wit, / (Where I have cause to burn
perfumes to it:)" (H-673). Similarly, Endymion Porter is exuber-
antly thanked for his "Oyle of Maintenance" in a poem with the
unusual opening, "Let there be Patrons" (H-117). An address to
the Bishop of Exeter (H-168) which plays with ecclesiastical terms
illustrates Herrick's feeling for the puns and the pointed wit of
epigram. Less exuberant poems reflect Jonson's habit of using
the epigram to make judgments of value: Herrick's praise of the
military or civic virtues of Sir John Berkeley, governor of Exeter
(H-745), John Weare, Counsellor (H-557), and the alderman Sir
Thomas Soame (H-466) draws terse distinctions between good
and bad conduct. An epigram *"Upon Master* Ben. Johnson." (H-
382) praises the departed "Arch-Poet" by castigating the current
ignorance and degeneration of the theater.

Jonson's habit of perceiving his subjects as epitomes or sum-
mations of virtue provided Herrick with a number of complimentary topics. The Earl of Dorset is addressed in terms which recall
Jonson's "theater":

> If I dare write to You, my Lord, who are,
> Of your own selfe, a *Publick Theater.*
> And sitting, see the wiles, wayes, walks of wit,
> And give a righteous judgment upon it.
> What need I care, though some dislike me sho'd,
> If *Dorset* say, what *Herrick* writes, is good?   (H-506)

A similar conceit, that of the man as a volume of virtues, opens
Herrick's tribute to his kinsman Sir William Soame (H-331).
Here, however, Herrick moves away from the ethical concerns of
Jonson and more toward celebration:

> I can but name thee, and methinks I call
> All that have been, or are canonicall
> For love and bountie, to come neare, and see,
> Their many vertues volum'd up in thee;
> In thee Brave Man! Whose incorrupted fame,
> Casts forth a light like to a Virgin flame:
> And as it shines, it throwes a scent about,

As when a Rain-bow in perfumes goes out.
So vanish hence, but leave a name, as sweet,
As *Benjamin,* and *Storax,* when they meet.

The emphasis on name and reputation, like the "volume" conceit, will recall Jonson. However, Herrick does not contrast Soame with the foolish or vicious; he develops his feeling of admiration in the images of the rainbow and perfumes, metaphors for Soame's fame. The poem concludes, not with a moral sentence, but with a sensuous benediction.

In general, Herrick uses the epigram, not to expose the conflicts of good and evil, but to realize the power of art and fame in evocative, often sensuous, images. Many compliments center on an image or a series of images and exploit the epigram's affinities with emblem and portrait; in Herrick's less rigorous moral atmosphere, Jonson's technique of "naming" can be expanded to include larger figurative identifications. The address to Soame, for example, develops a synaesthetic image composed of color, light, and scent. The aromatic flame, a kind of incense, becomes the emblem of Soame's reputation. Similarly, Herrick's address to another Soame, the alderman Sir Thomas (H-466), imagines a portrait of the "Goodly man" as a *"Patrician"* in his robes of office. On other occasions Herrick uses the epigram to create representative images of public events. He hails King Charles's victory at Leicester by describing an emblem or triumph in which Charles holds Fortune his captive: "other Kings / Hold but her hands; You hold both hands and wings" (H-823). In the voice of the *"Oke"* or oracle, he prophesies an end to the *"unhappy distances"* of the King and Queen: they are like separated streams which will flow together, when "C. and M. shall meet, / Treading on *Amber,* with their silver-feet" (H-79). Charles, the "Prince of Cavaliers," is imagined as a spring bridegroom when he arrives, with the sun and rains, to awaken the widowed and "Drooping West" (H-77). In these court poems Herrick amplifies his subjects and events by "naming" them metaphorically; each epigram centers on a figurative rendering of its occasion.

Herrick's stress on image in these poems joins epigrammatic wit with the techniques of emblem. Elsewhere, he conceives of his "inscriptions" as memorials to friends or patrons, poems which preserve worthy names. And as many epigrams are inscriptions, so Herrick sees his book as including an assemblage of monuments or a poetic record devoted to the poet's chosen few. *Hesperides* contains several epigrams which offer metaphoric names for imagined groups of poems. The Queen, for example, is welcomed as *"Goddesse of Youth, and Lady of the Spring,"* to *"This Sacred Grove"* (H-265). Herrick's reference to her as *"Poetresse"* suggests that the grove is a group of poems as well as the scene of a court ceremony; and a companion poem to the King (H-264) clearly alludes to the poet's book when it asks Charles to name *"The Heire to This great Realme of Poetry."* Herrick's prefatory poem plays on the stellar imagery associated with Prince Charles: the Prince is the *"Creator," "Flame,"* and *"Expansion"* of the poet's little stars, or hesperides.[10] The grove, the realm, and the stars are figures which give individual compliments their wit and coherence, and which draw attention to larger patterns within *Hesperides.*

We are accustomed to the association of *Hesperides* with gardens and with constellations. In a number of epigrams, however, Herrick also imagines his book as a repository of worthy names, and he identifies this imagined text through Roman, biblical, or liturgical images.[11] These images amplify the ancient and sacred connotations of Herrick's praise, and lend it the overtones of ceremony; each compliment is an inscription offered as a gift, a gesture which writes a name in the list of the "elect." A brief verse to Arthur Bartly promises that "Thou shalt thy Name have, and thy Fames best trust, / Here with the Generation of my Just" (H-664). Reference to the Chosen People recurs in an address to Stephen Soame (H-545) which imagines both a list of the elect and a canonization. Herrick will "inscribe" Soame among his "righteous Tribe," a tribe of "One / Civil Behaviour, and Religion." The civil tribe is also "A stock of Saints" in an "eternall Calender," while Soame is both "Canonized" and (in a Roman allusion) "markt out with the whiter stone." All of this rather eclectic wit centers on Herrick's presentation of his compliments as a sacred text of names, and of this poem as the inscription of a friend's name in that book. The imagery of lists and inscriptions in these poems stresses the commemorative functions of art and identifies a portion of *Hesperides* as a permanent record of worthy names.

Herrick's sense of his book as a "Calender" or a "Testament" (H-977) differs from the theater metaphor Jonson applies to *Epigrammes*, and the difference is instructive. While Jonson does develop the epigram as a "name poem," his collection is dramatic in its opposition of good and evil, and in its stress on the active power of goodness in a corrupt world. *Hesperides* does not imitate Jonson's ethical focus, and Herrick's compliments present his book in terms of written lists and designed or engraved artifacts. Thus, Herrick carries the notion of the epigram as name or inscription into larger areas of his collection; *Hesperides* includes a text or testament which is an assemblage of inscriptions. Herrick's metaphors for his book of compliments are usually static images, which stress the enduring and commemorative rather than the reforming powers of praise. Where Jonson's praise stresses action, conflict, and testing, Herrick perceives his subjects and his collection of compliments in terms of engraving or pictorial image.[12]

Herrick's treatment of the epigram as artifact is most obvious in the compliments which employ architectural and sculptural images. An address to Thomas Shapcott, noting that the actions of *"Brave men"* are "Writ in the Poets Endlesse-Kalendar," offers itself as a verse which will "Arch-like, hold up, *Thy Name's Inscription"* (H-444). Herrick introduces Richard Stone—not without a pun on his name—into the *"white Temple* of my *Heroes,"* a hall of "stately Figures" (H-496). The "Figures" are statues, but also the images or literary "figures" preserved in other compliments; both the commemorated subjects and Herrick's poems are seen as fixed works of art. The point of contact between the person and the poem occurs in the poem's naming or identification of its subject, a fusion for which the epigram, essentially an inscription, is obviously suited.

Through these epigrammatic images of sculpture and inscription, Herrick's compliments not only mimic their genre but allude to a larger work, a text or a hall of monuments, formed of poems. These images require us to adjust our notion of *Hesperides* as a garden of pastoral verses. The pastoral mode tends to dominate the collection, as the responses of readers testify and as Herrick's title suggests. But while the garden, the grove, and the heaven of little stars are appropriate figures for the book, there are sequences of poems in *Hesperides* which Herrick identifies in other terms. The complimentary epigrams form such a sequence, variously named in the images of portrait, sculpture, and inscription. Thus Herrick uses the epigram's association with engraving to create a significant pattern—an imagined collection—within the larger book, *Hesperides.*

Complimentary epigrams are social gestures as well as inscriptions, and the focus on image and artifact does not prevent Herrick from observing the civilities due on such occasions. The learned John Selden, for example, is of such rare capacity that he can bestow laurel on the poet: "I Who have favour'd many, come to be / Grac't (now at last) or glorifi'd by thee." Returning the honors, Herrick the "Lyric Prophet" will place Selden in an eternal city:

> A City here of *Heroes* I have made,
> Upon the rock, whose firm foundation laid,
> Shall never shrink, where making thine abode,
> Live thou a *Selden*, that's a Demi-god.   (H-365)

The "City" is an ambitious image for Herrick's collection of compliments, and may surprise those who think of *Hesperides* in terms of gardens. Yet like the pastoral garden, the city on the rock suggests the ideals of permanence and perfection, while it preserves the sacred connotations Herrick often gives to praise. The epigram is both gesture and inscription: its offer of an exchange of honors is a tribute to Selden, realized in the image of the eternal city and in the repetition of Selden's name.

Near the end of *Hesperides*, Herrick promises Michael Oldisworth that his name will be followed by "Fame's rear'd Pillar," and "Held up by Fames *eternall Pedestall*" (H-1092). Such an obvious play on the design of his book suggests that Herrick attached some importance to his role as the preserver of names, and to those epigrams which are monuments to fame. *"The pillar of Fame,"* like the city of heroes, stands on a "Firme and well fixt foundation" (H-1129), and as a shaped poem it shares the iconic functions of many of Herrick's epigrams. Thus, it may remind us that the epigrams of praise are not only social and occasional verses, but a significant part of the design of *Hesperides.*

The choice of engraving and artifice as metaphors for praise confirms Herrick's trust in the permanence of art, whether pictorial art or good verses. Furthermore, the fusion of literary praise with visual art in these images indicates that Herrick perceived virtue, goodness, and fame as essentially timeless and static ideals. Here again he resembles Jonson, whose poems praise a virtue which is ideal, if embattled, and which can be "named" with certainty by the poet-judge. The compliments of both poets differ in this respect from the grandiloquent and politically complex panegyrics of Waller and Dryden. For Herrick as for Jonson, praise and the fame it embodies have the clarity of outline, the certainty, and the fixity of true inscription.

NOTES

1. Jonson calls his book *"my* Theater, *where* CATO, *if he liv'd, might enter without scandall,"* in the dedicatory epistle to *Epigrammes. Ben Jonson,* ed. C. H. Herford and Percy and Evelyn Simpson, 11 vols. (Oxford, 1954), viii, 26. Subsequent references to Jonson's work cite this edition.

2. Rosalie Colie, *The Resources of Kind: Genre-Theory in the Renaissance* (Berkeley, 1973), p. 26, discusses *Hesperides* "(that mixed garden)" and finds Herrick "choosing the epigram as his major poetic form."

3. Floris Delattre, *Robert Herrick* (Paris, 1912), pp. 123–47, offers a survey of Herrick's social verse; many of the occasional poems are discussed by A. Leigh DeNeef, *'This Poetick Liturgie': Robert Herrick's Ceremonial Mode* (Durham, 1974).

4. See O. B. Hardison, *The Enduring Monument: A Study of the Idea of Praise in Renaissance Literary Theory and Practice* (Chapel Hill, 1962).

5. Herrick's poems are cited by number from *The Complete Poetry of Robert Herrick,* ed. J. Max Patrick (New York, 1968).

6. The derivation of "Epigram" from inscription is a commonplace of the genre; see, for example, George Puttenham, *The Arte of English Poesie,* ed. E. Arber (London, 1906), bk. 1, ch. 27, p. 68.

7. I have borrowed the notion of resonance and the use of Marianne Moore's phrase from William V. Spanos, "The Real Toad in the Jonsonian Garden: Resonance in the Nondramatic Poetry," *JEGP*, 68 (1969), 1–23.

8. On the English epigram, see T. K. Whipple, "Martial and the English Epigram from Sir Thomas Wyatt to Ben Jonson," *University of California Publications in Modern Philology*, 10 (Berkeley, 1925), 279–414; and H. H. Hudson, *The Epigram in the English Renaissance* (Princeton, 1947). The development of the epigram is treated by James Hutton, *The Greek Anthology in Italy to the Year 1800* (Ithaca, 1935). An important Renaissance account is J. C. Scaliger, *Poetices Libri Septem* (1561), ed. A. Buck (Stuttgart, 1964), p. 170. On the relationship of epigram to other genres, see Rosalie L. Colie, *Shakespeare's Living Art* (Princeton, 1974), ch. 2.

9. David Sykes, "Ben Jonson's 'Chast Book'—The *Epigrammes*," *Renaissance and Modern Studies*, 13 (1969), 76–87; Edward Partridge, "Jonson's *Epigrammes*: The Named and the Nameless," *Studies in the Literary Imagination*, 4 (1973), 153–98; Anthony Mortimer, "The Feigned Commonwealth in the Poetry of Ben Jonson," *SEL*, 13 (1973), 69–79; and Bruce R. Smith, "Ben Jonson's *Epigrammes*: Portrait-Gallery, Theater, Commonwealth," *SEL*, 14 (1974), 91–109.

10. See the notes to this poem and to H-265 in *Complete Poetry*, ed. Patrick, pp. 9, 148.

11. See also Heather Asals, "King Solomon in the Land of the *Hesperides*," *TSLL*, 18 (Fall 1976), 362–80.

12. See also Norman K. Farmer, Jr., "Herrick's Hesperidean Garden: *ut pictura poesis* Applied," in this volume.

CLAUDE J. SUMMERS

Herrick's Political Poetry: The Strategies of His Art

One of the consequences of the persistent belief that Herrick "in a troubled age is largely content to create a timeless Arcadia"[1] has been the neglect of his political poetry. But throughout *Hesperides,* Herrick repeatedly responds to the political turbulence of his era. In epigrammatic couplets, in poems addressed to members of the royal family, in occasional verse prompted by specific events of the Civil War, and in intimate reflections on the "Times most bad," he reveals an awareness of current events and a political sophistication which both extend and modify the celebration of eternal cycles of work and play, love and decay, which *Hesperides* as a whole is often seen to embody.[2]

Although far from reaching unanimity concerning its precise nature, recent critics agree that the totality of *Hesperides* equals something more than the sum of its parts. The world of Herrick's book is complex and various, and one dimension of that world is political. The political poems often point the contrast between "the world as it actually is, and the '*Sacred grove,*' the world as it might be."[3] They help to provide an immediacy to the poet's recurrent longing for an older, more stable society,[4] and establish a context for Herrick's conservative ideal. And quite apart from their function as a significant aspect of the total world of *Hesperides,* some of the political poems are important in their own right. The best of these works illustrate some of Herrick's most characteristic tendencies, especially his instinct for ritualizing specific events into transcendent patterns. As a political poet, Herrick is very seldom merely topical. His ability to incorporate topical issues into a richly complex vision makes several of his poems examples of political discourse of a very high order. The strategies of his art in these poems entitle Herrick to recognition as a political poet.

Before these strategies are examined, it may be useful to discuss briefly Herrick's political point of view. Although his epigrams are not his best poetry, they express most explicitly the poet's conservative political temper and thus establish an important field of reference in which to read *Hesperides*. As the epigrams repeatedly illustrate, Herrick's most consistent and most important political position is his extreme royalist attitude.[5] *"The Difference Betwixt Kings and Subjects"* (H-25)[6] presents a conventional religious concept of kingship, a view under increasingly violent attack in the seventeenth century: "Twixt Kings and Subjects ther's this mighty odds, / Subjects are taught by *Men*; Kings by the *Gods*." In *"Obedience in Subjects"* (H-269), the poet, paraphrasing Tacitus, presents an ultra-conservative view of the respective responsibilities of kings and their subjects, one that only the most dedicated royalists in the seventeenth century would endorse: *"The Gods to Kings the Judgement give to sway: / The Subjects onely glory to obay."* And in *"Duty to Tyrants"* (H-97), he espouses the familiar doctrine of passive obedience: the Christian's duty of obedience extends even to bad kings, whom God uses to scourge his people; worse than the tyrant is the rebel. In all three of these epigrams Herrick refers to *the Gods* rather than to God. But this mixture of the classical and the Christian should not obscure the fact that Herrick's political vision is an orthodox conservative one, rooted in the conventional religious claims of the Stuart monarchy.[7]

These theoretical epigrams, which stress traditional political relationships, are supplemented by more practical ones, which illustrate the dangers in abandoning divinely sanctioned order. *"Dangers wait on Kings"* (H-80) may be a sardonic comment on the struggle for power among the Parliamentary leaders: "As oft as Night is banish'd by the Morne, / So oft, we'll think, we see a King new born." And *"The power in the people"* (H-345) revealingly characterizes the discrepancy between theory and practice: "Let Kings Command, and doe the best they may, / The saucie Subjects still will beare the sway." Herrick's distrust of the common people and his fear of the mob pervade the political epigrams. He defines *"Ill Government"* (H-536) as that

"Preposterous" condition "When Kings obey the wilder Multitude." His advice to the King to be merciful and moderate, to eschew flatterers, and to seek the love of his people may be largely culled from classical sources, but much of this advice rings with political realism. The people are *"prone to discontent"* (H-921) and the King is beset on all sides by currish subjects and ungrateful opportunists.

These epigrams establish clearly Herrick's political conventionality. As a social thinker, he is, as one critic states, "tiresomely orthodox, quite immersed in the views of the ruling classes of his day."[8] The theoretical and practical conservatism of the epigrams permeates *Hesperides* and underlies such apparently nonpolitical works as *"The Hock-cart"* (H-250) and *"The Country life"* (H-662). The recurrent espousal of traditional political relationships and the often-repeated doctrine of obedience help generate in *Hesperides* a tension between the ideal and its decay. His basic distrust of the common people, which he shares with most political thinkers of the century, may help to explain one part of his conservatism and should remind us of the need to qualify the romantic picture of the country vicar shepherding his faithful flock. The affection expressed for the country people in *Hesperides* is not naive. It results from a paternalistic rather than an egalitarian attitude. And, finally, the dominant political position asserted in the epigrams, extreme royalism, is in other poems translated into art of a complex and subtle orchestration.

As might be expected, Herrick's poems addressed to members of the royal family affirm this extreme royalism. Although written in a well-established tradition which permits—perhaps requires—unrealistic praise, even the most conventional of the verse compliments to the royal family must have been seen as politically significant when they were published in 1648. And several of these poems are clearly, though not simply, topical in their intentions. Most important of all, the best of these poems shape conventional attitudes into celebrations of sacred kingship, portraying the King and his heir as poets, healers, shadows of Christ.

One of the most compelling aspects of Herrick's emphasis on the divine aspect of kingship is the connection he makes between the political and the poetical worlds. In a succinct and penetrating analysis, Roger Rollin has observed the correspondences between these realms in three companion poems, addressed respectively to King Charles (H-264), Queen Henrietta Maria (H-265), and their son James, Duke of York (H-266).[9] In these poems, Herrick unites a poetic vision and a political scheme in which King Charles determines the succession to "This *great Realme of Poetry*"; Henrietta Maria is invited to rest in Herrick's "*Sacred Grove*" and "be both *Princesse* here, and *Poetresse*"; and the young Duke of York is confirmed by the Muses as "Prince of *Hellicon*." These poems simultaneously establish, on the one hand, the poetic ideal of the pastoral and, on the other, the political ideal of Edenic kingship. In the poem dedicating *Hesperides* to Prince Charles, Herrick stresses an even closer relationship between the political and poetical realms. He declares that Charles, whose birth in 1630 corresponded with the appearance of Hesperus in the midday sky, is "my Works *Creator*, and alone / The *Flame* of it, and the *Expansion*." Creator of and light-giver to Herrick's hesperides (or little stars), the Prince also translates them into indestructible bodies, safe from mutability and decay: "Full is my Book of Glories; but all These / By You become *Immortall Substances*." Herrick's attribution of sacred, creative powers to the Prince points up the intimate link between poetry and kingship, an intimacy intensified by the passionate love for poetry and the trust in the immortalizing power of good verses which pervade *Hesperides*.

The sacred quality of kingship is apparent in many poems. In "*A Pastorall upon the birth of Prince* Charles" (H-213A), the identification of Charles with Christ is inescapable. The future Charles II is prince and shepherd, his birth announced by an Eastern star and greeted by a trio bearing gifts. In "*To the King*" (H-685), Herrick describes Charles I as a star whose light dims all others in the poet's "ample Orbe." Charles as King is god-like; and in the conclusion, Herrick describes the King in terms which echo God's reply to Moses when asked to see his glory ("Thou canst not see my face: for there shall no man see me and live" [Exodus 33:20]):

> *Princes, and such like Publike Lights as these,*
> *Must not be lookt on, but at distances:*
> *For, if we gaze on These brave Lamps too neer,*
> *Our eyes they'l blind, or if not blind, they'l bleer.*

The allusion to the divinity of kingship in the context of a poetic universe elevates topical considerations from the mundane to the ideal, while at the same time it emphasizes an implicit contrast between that ideal of the King as God's anointed and the very real troubles experienced by Charles during the Civil War.

"TO THE KING, To cure the Evill" (H-161), one of Herrick's most important political poems, celebrates divine kingship by reference to a ceremony which itself asserted that the King's authority derived from God. The poem is based on the belief that the King's touch could cure scrofula.[10] The practice of "touching" was a very old one, but during the Civil War this ceremony of healing acquired increasingly greater importance as evidence of the King's divine right, as proof that he ruled by grace of God and not by the will of his subjects. On one level, the poem, with moving simplicity, sings of the King's mysterious power to heal. On a more important level, it is a prayer asking the King, as a shadow of Christ, to heal the national affliction of civil war and disobedience.[11] The poem illustrates the appropriate attitude the nation should assume, a posture of submission and faith; for it is only with such a stance that the King's Christ-like powers can be effective.

The poem begins by announcing the object of the speaker's (and the nation's) quest:

> To find that Tree of Life, whose Fruits did feed,
> And Leaves did heale, all sick of humane seed:
> To find *Bethesda*, and an Angel there,
> Stirring the waters, I am come.

At Bethesda Christ demonstrated that his power of healing was a divine imitation of God's: "Verily, verily, I say unto you, The Son can do nothing of himself, but what he seeth the Father do" (John 5:19). He made whole a man whose infirmity precluded his taking advantage of the pool whose waters, troubled by an Angel, could effect cures. The leaves of the Tree of Life "were for the healing of the nations" (Revelation 22:2). In Herrick's poem, the speaker finds (as the nation can) "The Tree, Bethesda, and the Angel too: / And all in Your Blest Hand." Charles as Christ has within himself the power to heal. The King's hand, "the Branch of Heavens faire Tree," is capable of healing "all sick of humane seed" if one but submits "To that soft *Charm*, that *Spell*, that *Magick Bough*, / That high Enchantment" embodied in the sacred institution of kingship. Through faith in "Adored *Cesar*," the speaker will be (and the nation can be) cured as the afflicted man at Bethesda was healed by Jesus.

Just as Herrick celebrates the sacred mystery of kingship and the powers of healing therein, he also hints that the nation may not have faith enough to avail itself of the much needed cure. There is precedent for this fear. Christ's healing was frequently greeted by doubt and derision. During one of his healing miracles, he observes: "A prophet is not without honour, but in his own country and among his own kin, and in his own house" (Mark 6:4).[12] And significantly, one of the symptoms of scrofula as it was diagnosed in the seventeenth century was blindness.[13] Unless the nation is able to "see" the King as a type of Christ the healer, it cannot be cured. Having registered these fears, Herrick concludes the poem with a moral which has topical implications: "The Evill is not Yours: my sorrow sings, / Mine is the Evill, but the Cure, the KINGS." The evil of discord and disobedience, of national blindness, can be cured only when England submits itself to the healing ritual of kingship, acknowledging the source of her disease and pleading for her Christ-King's cure.

"TO THE KING, To cure the Evill" is important not only for the extremity of its royalist point of view, but also for its discovery of political hope in a mysterious ritual. To Herrick, the King is not simply a monarch but a type of Christ whose enchanting spells can cure the spiritual evil of national disease. The poem does not explicitly refer to the Civil War, yet the absence of such topicality actually strengthens its significance. To discover in the King the cure for national blindness is to transcend the merely political. And the involved personal tone, with its veiled pessimism singing its sorrow as well as its transcendent joy, establishes the realism necessary to make the poem a serious comment on national affairs and not simply an encomium to the King.

Several other poems characterize the Civil War as a disease. In *"To Prince* Charles *upon his coming to Exeter"* (H-756), Herrick declares that the Prince's arrival has renovated the West and has robbed the heat from "That Preternaturall Fever, which did threat / Death to our Countrey." When Prince Charles journeyed to Exeter in August 1645, it appeared, even to most Royalists, that the King's cause was lost. The gentry at Exeter urged the Prince to open negotiations for peace.[14] Herrick's poem, rather than advising peace, argues for a continuation of the war: "Something there yet remaines for Thee to do; / Then reach those ends that thou wast destin'd to." Herrick enjoins the Prince's Fate to make Charles like Sulla, who in a civil war had defeated a popular party formed of the dregs of society. He invokes Apollo, significantly the patron of medicine as well as of poetry, to bless the Prince's war "with white successe."

The poem concludes with a beautiful vision of peace achieved through victory. When Charles wins the day, "our smooth-pac't Poems all shall be / Sung in the high *Doxologie* of Thee." The phrase "high *Doxologie*" probably refers to the Greater Doxology, that praise to the Almighty which begins "Glory to God in the highest, and on earth peace among men of good will."[15] Herrick's celebration of the Prince characterizes him as healer and warrior, a divinely guided savior of his country. When his "discreetly made" war has succeeded, he will be praised through poetry and religious rites: "Then maids shall strew Thee, and thy Curles from them / Receive (with Songs) a flowrie Diadem." In curing the unnatural disease which has almost killed England, Charles will himself become a poet and rule an idyllic realm of poetry.

The curious parenthetical description of the Prince's projected war may illustrate how well Herrick incorporates informed topicality into his celebration of the ideal. The term "discreetly made" may have been prompted by the public revelation in August 1645 that King Charles had commanded his son to leave the country should he be exposed to danger.[16] The King's fear for his son's safety was interpreted as a confession that further resistance was hopeless. In so curiously qualifying the kind of war that must be waged, Herrick may be attempting to establish his credibility in the face of widespread despair. He is not urging the Prince to be foolhardy, but at the same time he does wish him to remain in England and to fight ("discreetly") to a satisfactory conclusion. But this poem, which is so thoroughly grounded in the particular circumstances of political crisis, finally goes beyond the specific to celebrate the ideal of divinely fated kingship. That this political ideal is linked inextricably with a poetic ideal is characteristic of Herrick's vision.

"TO THE KING, *Upon his welcome to* Hampton-Court" (H-961) again compares the Civil War to illness and the King to "a still protecting Deitie." Although the King's actual return to Hampton Court in August 1647 may have been seen by many as a hopeful event, it was not the triumphal entry Herrick celebrates.[17] A prisoner of the Army, Charles was caught in the rivalry between Parliament and the Army and was himself attempting to play off various factions against each other. Herrick goes beyond the actual circumstances, ambiguous at best, to celebrate the King as "Our *Fate,* our *Fortune,* and our *Genius.*" The King's return signals the renewal of peace, the end of "our long, and peevish sicknesses." But beneath the poem's celebratory tone is an implicit awareness of political reality. The poem's insistence on viewing Charles as a returning conqueror ("*Great Cesar,*" "*Great Augustus*") is touchingly undercut by a hint of possible disaster. The King's celebrants look for auspicious signs before committing themselves to a permanent temple. They resolve, "That sho'd you stirre, we and our Altars too / May (*Great Augustus*) *goe along with You.*" This statement reflects the widespread uncertainty which existed on all sides in 1647. It is also evidence of a cautious attitude toward the hopes for real peace in a precarious situation. The phrase "sho'd you stirre" may ironically betray the poet's awareness that, in the real circumstances of the King's return, he is a prisoner. The celebration of Charles's arrival at Hampton Court attempts to interpret his dire circumstances in the best light possible. But the tension in the poem between the celebratory ritual and the uncertainty concerning "our safeties new foundation" makes the conventional conclusion ("Long live the King; and to accomplish this, / We'l from our owne, adde far more years to his") seem more than simply conventional. The vulnerability beneath the surface of the insistent celebration intensifies the emotional response when we discover how thin is the veneer of triumph. The poem is a fine example of public poetry: informed with topical knowledge, it subtly exploits the contrast between the actual and the ideal.

Most of the poems addressed to royalty and others occasioned by specific events in the Civil War (*"A Dirge upon the Death of the Right Valiant Lord,* Bernard Stuart," H-219, and *"To Sir* John Berkley, *Governour of Exeter,"* H-745, for example) are written in what has been termed a "ceremonial mode." Leigh DeNeef describes this mode as one "whose purpose is to transform literal action into meaningful, celebratory ritual and whose form is designed specifically to achieve this end. Furthermore, the permanence of the artistic rendering is itself the ultimate ceremonial act, for in elevating any given action, the poem removes that action from the realm of literal mundane existence into a realm peculiar to art itself."[18] Herrick's choice of this mode in many of his political poems accounts for the optimistic, festive tone the speaker assumes even when the actual occasion is less than literally festive, as in the poems discussed above. These poems assert, rather than argue, a political point of view, confidently singing of Royalist triumphs even in inauspicious circumstances—perhaps especially in inauspicious circumstances. Choosing to celebrate events which might seem more appropriately mourned is not false optimism or misinformed confidence on the poet's part. Rather, the choice results from a carefully devised poetic strategy which utilizes the literal, mundane world as a telling contrast with the celebrated world. By subtly betraying his awareness of topical reality even as he transforms the literal through ritual, Herrick simultaneously provides a glimpse of the ideal and condemns by contrast the real.

Herrick responds to political situations in several poems more intimate than those addressed to royalty. Although these are "personal" works in the sense that they record subjective reactions to often unspecified public events, they are firmly rooted in external political conditions. In them, Herrick's technique differs from that characteristic of his more obviously public poems. In the occasional verse, he attempts to subsume the particular in a larger vision, usually implying rather than stating the contrast between the idyllic and the real. In these more intimate poems, however, his strategy is to recount in concrete terms the tangible effects of political strife, offering the ideal as an antidote to the actual.

The notion that adverse political fortunes affect poetry adversely occurs frequently in *Hesperides*. It is the reverse side of Herrick's connection between ideal poetry and ideal kingship. In *"The bad season makes the Poet sad"* (H-612), the speaker's poetic voice has been stopped:

> Lost to all Musick now; since every thing
> Puts on the semblance here of sorrowing.
> Sick is the Land to'th'heart; and doth endure
> More dangerous faintings by her desp'rate cure.

The poet can be revived only by a fervent hope:

> But if that golden Age wo'd come again,
> And *Charles* here Rule, as he before did Raign;
> If smooth and unperplext the Seasons were,
> As when the *Sweet Maria* lived here;
> I sho'd delight to have my Curles halfe drown'd
> In *Tyrian Dewes,* and Head with Roses crown'd.

The idyllic world of poetry can be restored only when an Edenic kingship ushers in a golden age. The personal effects of the unnatural public sickness intensify the vision of public health that the return of the golden age could bring.

In these confrontations with the private experience of war, the personae alternate between hope and despair. In *"Upon the troublesome times"* (H-596), the speaker can discover no hope at all: no place is secure "In this our wasting Warre." In contrast to this despair, *"Farwell Frost, or welcome the Spring"* (H-642) finds comfort in the prospect of ultimate peace. As spring reappears after the destructive horrors of winter, so too must peace finally replace "this War (which tempest-like doth spoil / Our salt, our Corn, our Honie, Wine, and Oile)." The poet is consoled by the hope that at last "The gentle Dove may, when these turmoils cease, / Bring in her Bill, once more, *the Branch of Peace.*" The homeliness of the poem's imagery and the consistently powerful contrasts between spring and winter emphasize in tangible, humanly felt terms the speaker's desire for an end to war. The persona's sincerity is convincing, but the hope for peace he expresses is not simply a private emotion.

In *Hesperides*, then, Herrick responds to the political turmoil of his day in poems of wide range and scope. The political poems record the genial royalist's political attitudes, hopes, and fears. These poems, in more than negligible ways, enrich the texture of *Hesperides* as a whole. But they do more: they exemplify modes of talking about political issues which incorporate politics into a broad vision of life and art. The connection between the poetic and the political worlds which Herrick envisions is symptomatic of this tendency to see political issues in terms far larger and far more important than mere politics; so also is the recounting in personal, often homely, terms of the tangible effects of civil war in order to intensify a vision of idyllic government. The best of the political poems are informed and sophisticated, employing the mundane to emphasize the ideal. Rather than simply creating a "timeless Arcadia," Herrick complexly integrates a sensitive awareness of the real with an imaginative apprehension of the transcendent.

Admittedly, Herrick's conservative political temper does not speak to our awakened sympathies as it did to those of many of his contemporaries. His poems are not argumentative and, in any case, are not likely to convert modern readers to his political point of view. But they have an essential integrity to which we can respond. If we are no longer capable of perceiving Charles I as a shadow of Christ, we can at least appreciate the intense vision which did, and we can understand the enormous political implications of such a vision. We may no longer share Herrick's rage for traditional order, but we can still respond to the harmonious beauty of his pastoral world which embodies that order. And, finally, though the political events which moved Herrick to celebrate his king and mourn his nation's sickness no longer interest us with a passion comparable to his own, the strategies of his art have an abiding interest. The subtlety and sureness of these strategies, as well as the essential integrity of the vision, can excite admiration for Herrick as a political poet. More than that, they merit for him recognition as an important public poet, one who rendered transient and partisan political concerns in the universal form of art.

NOTES

1. Douglas Bush, *English Literature in the Earlier Seventeenth Century*, rev. ed. (New York, 1962), p. 115. The fullest account of Herrick's political concerns is Roger B. Rollin, *Robert Herrick* (New York, 1966), especially pp. 165–69.

2. As in, e.g., S. Musgrove, *The Universe of Robert Herrick*, Auckland University College Bulletin No. 38, English Series No. 4 (1950); Thomas R. Whitaker, "Herrick and the Fruits of the Garden," *JEGP*, 22 (1955), 16–33; and Bush, *English Literature*, pp. 115–19.

3. Rollin, *Herrick*, p. 165.

4. On this point, see, e.g., Musgrove, *Universe*, pp. 26–28; and Robert H. Deming, "Robert Herrick's Classical Ceremony," *ELH*, 34 (1967), 327–48.

5. A few poems (H-780 and H-826, for instance) may appear to criticize specific policies of the King. See F. W. Moorman, *Robert Herrick: A Biographical and Critical Study* (1910; rpt. New York, 1962), p. 128. But this kind of poem is very rare and is usually general and proverbial in nature.

6. All titles and quotations are from *The Complete Poetry of Robert Herrick*, ed. J. Max Patrick (New York, 1963).

7. See chapters 7 and 8 of John Neville Figgis, *The Divine Right of Kings* (1896; rpt. New York, 1965), pp. 137–218; the survey of English political attitudes in J. W. Allen, *English Political Thought 1603–1644* (London, 1938); and Musgrove's comments on Herrick's royalism, *Universe*, p. 26.

8. Roger B. Rollin, "Missing 'The Hock-Cart': An Explication Re-explicated," *SCN*, 24 (1966), 40. See also A. Leigh DeNeef, "The Ceremonial Mode of Poetic Expression in Robert Herrick's *Hesperides*" (Ph.D. diss., Pennsylvania State University, 1969), pp. 239–43.

9. *Herrick*, pp. 28–30.

10. A useful history of this belief is Raymond Crawfurd, *The King's Evil* (Oxford, 1911).

11. Cf. Herrick's poem with Ben Jonson's "An Epigram. To K. Charles for a 100. Pounds He Sent Me in My Sicknesse" (*Underwood* LXII), which concludes: "What can the *Poet* wish his *King* may doe, / But, that he cure the Peoples Evill too?" See *Ben Jonson*, ed. C. H. Herford and Percy and Evelyn Simpson, 11 vols. (Oxford, 1925–1952), VIII, 235.

12. In the two Gospel passages which were part of King Charles's healing ceremony, similar statements appear. In Mark 16:14, Jesus upbraids his apostles "with their unbelief and hardness of heart"; and in the first chapter of John, Jesus is described as being "in the world, and the world was made by him, and the world knew him not" (vs. 10). Crawfurd reproduces the ceremony on pp. 85–86.

13. Crawfurd, *King's Evil*, p. 99.

14. Samuel R. Gardiner, *History of the Great Civil War 1642–1649*, rev. ed., 4 vols. (1893; rpt. New York, 1965), II, 337–38.

15. In the service of Holy Communion in the Book of Common Prayer, to be said or sung after receiving the elements of bread and wine.

16. Gardiner, *Civil War*, II, 338. Clarendon, in *History of the Rebellion*, ed. W. D. Macray, 6 vols. (Oxford, 1888), reproduces the letter (Bk. IX, par. 74).

17. Gardiner, III, 355.

18. "Herrick's 'Corinna' and the Ceremonial Mode," *SAQ*, 70 (1971), 533–34. See also DeNeef's *"This Poetick Liturgie": Robert Herrick's Ceremonial Mode* (Durham, N.C., 1974). Although I am persuaded by much of Professor DeNeef's explanation of the ceremonial mode in Herrick, I do not agree with his assertion that "in the ceremonial mode the reader is not referred to elements outside the poem and is not expected to commit further action on the basis of what is given in the poem. The poem simply does not lead beyond itself" ("Herrick's 'Corinna,' " p. 534). Clearly the political poems refer to events in the real world. By the subtle rhetorical strategy explained below, the occasional poems also urge action, though the exhortation is implicit rather than explicit.

Hesperides: Parallelism and Integration

SHONOSUKE ISHII

Herrick and Japanese
Classical Poetry: A Comparison

In *A History of English Literature*[1] Emile Legouis has suggested that Herrick's singing of beautiful flowers and lamenting their ephemerality recalls the poets of Japan or China. This view coincides with the opinion of some Japanese scholars and readers of Herrick who find interesting similarities between the works of the English poet-priest and those of the composers of *waka* and *haiku* of older Japan, among which the short verse form and the note of pathos are most remarkable. It may be added—though at the risk of some oversimplification—that resemblances are to be found between two notable qualities of Japanese classical poetry, *aware* (associated with the type of poetry known as *waka*) and *okashi* (more characteristic of *haiku*), and the poems of *Hesperides.*

Waka has two meanings. In its broad sense it can be translated simply as "Japanese song," especially with reference to several different types of older lyrics having seven and five syllables as their basic units; in its narrower sense, *waka* denotes a special verse form consisting of thirty-one syllables, usually divided into smaller units of 5, 7, 5 and 7, 7 syllables. (The latter form is sometimes called *tanka,* but that term usually applies to modern works.) Devised much later than *waka, haiku* (or *haikai*) is a shorter verse form, divided into units of 5, 7, 5 syllables.

Of the two qualities noted above, *aware* is more difficult to describe than *okashi. Aware* is sometimes represented as *mono-no-aware* or "the pathos of things"—having reference to a mood in which an impression of beauty, perceived in some object, is flooded with private emotion. Less ambiguously, some scholars translate *aware* simply as "sensitivity to beauty." This quality was elevated to an ideal by Ki no Tsurayuki (868?–945?), compiler of the first "Imperial" anthology, *Kokin-waka-shu* (905), which followed by a century and a half the first great anthology of Japanese poems, *Man-yo-shu* (759).[2]

The concept of *aware* went through various modifications in the following seven "Imperial" anthologies (usually called *Hachi-dai-shu*—eight anthologies of eight different ages). Except the last, *Shin-kokin-waku-shu* (1201), these collections appeared during the Heian period (794–1192), when Japanese court poetry, and *waka* especially, most flourished. Two of these modifications of *aware*, *yugen* and *ushin*, were advocated by Fujiwara Shunzei (1114–1204) and his son Teika (1162–1241), and were variously interpreted by different schools of poets.[3] *Waka* which exhibited these qualities, it was held, embodied mental impressions faithfully and gracefully expressed in ethereally beautiful yet mysterious and profound language. In such poetry Japanese readers achieve empathy with natural scenes, with natural objects such as birds, flowers, and dew, with the changing seasons, with lovers, with those who suffer untimely deaths, and so forth. This note of pathos is sounded even in the poems of the *Man-yo-shu*, for all of their plain, rustic, strong tones, and in such poems of *Hesperides* as "To Daffadills" (H-316),[4] "To Violets" (H-116), "To Blossoms" (H-467), and "To Meddowes" (H-151).

To some extent after the Heian period, the composition of *waka* gradually gave place to that of *haiku* or *haikai*. Literary activity was taken up by the common people, with consequent greater emphasis upon the quality of *okashi* than *aware*.[5] *Okashi* literally means "funny," but in fact implies a state of mind which is at once sober and sensible of stern reality. *Okashi*, it should be noted, was not absent even from the poems of the *Man-yo-shu*, for the Japanese were continually aware that laughter and realism are not antithetical. This quality, however, was more conspicuous in other genres of classical Japanese poetry such as *kagura*, *saibara*, *azuma-asobi*, and *fuzoku*.

As the composing of *waka* became a widespread practice, among not only the nobility and the courtiers but even the warriors and the priests, it gradually became stereotyped, losing the spontaneity and vitality given it by the master poets of previous ages. Moreover, with the introduction of Zen Buddhism during the Kamakura period (1192–1333), the Japanese, especially those among the learned classes, began to feel more keenly than ever a sense of the mutability and transitoriness of life, and they sought to ease their fear and despair by severing their strong attachments to worldly pleasure and fame. They were thus led to observe the world more objectively and to place more importance upon an intellectualized response to it. Such a tendency had been present in earlier *waka*, but it received more emphasis in *haikai* as that literary form increased in popularity.

The quality of *okashi* can of course be associated with humor and satire, and here again resemblances to Herrick appear. *Haikai*, having approximately half the thirty-one syllables of *waka*, calls to mind the epigrams of *Hesperides* and Herrick's poems on himself, above all in their tone, and even some of the poet's longer works contain passages which Japanese readers can readily associate with the scenes, moods, and attitudes to be found in *haiku*. What follows then are some examples of Japanese classical poems in which the ideals of *aware* and *okashi* are present and which therefore can be related to the poetry of Robert Herrick.

The first selections are taken from the works of Saigyo (1118–1190), called Sato Norikiyo as a layman, a Buddhist priest who wrote during the twelfth century, nearly at the end of the Heian period. His favorite themes involve the love of nature, of beautiful flowers, and of beautiful women, and the sorrow of old age. It will also be noted that Saigyo, like Herrick, is not without a sense of humor.

> I will try to find some older cherry-trees
> whose flowers look listless and weary;
> how many more springs can they meet after this?
> [Wakite mimu / oiki wa hana mo / aware nari /
> ima ikutabi ka / haru ni oobeki.]

> Where are those scenes once so beautiful,
> when spring was here, at Naniwa, in the county of Tsu?
> They are like dreams; the cold wind of autumn
> blows over the withered reeds.
> [Tsu-no-kuni no / Naniwa no haru wa / yume nareya /
> ashi no kereha ni / kaze wataru nari.]

Water is now let, for the planting season,
into the highland fields, among the sedges;
how happily sing the frogs and paddocks,
thus given the pool to jump and swim in!
[Masuge ouru / yamada ni mizu o / makasureba /
ureshigao ni mo / naku kawazu kana.]

How can I ever forget your gentle look
so faintly shining out of the reach
of the silver beams of the waning moon?
[Yumihari no / tsuki ni hazurete / mishi kage no /
yasashikarishi wa / itsuka wasuremu.]

Whenever I look back upon my life long past,
how vainly vain it seems to me,
just as those dewdrops on morning glories
exhaled to heaven after their brief sojourn.
[Hakanakute / suginishi kata o / omou ni mo /
ima mo sakoso wa / asagao no tsuyu.]

To show instances of representative court poems, the following
selection from Saigyo's contemporaries and some earlier poets is
added:[6]

Hunting for cherry-flowers,
I have been caught in this sudden shower.
I prefer to be drenched, if I must,
sheltered beneath these flowering boughs.
[Sakura-gari / ame wa furikinu / onajiku wa /
nuru to mo hana no / kage ni kakuremu.]   (Anonymous)

On this radiant day of spring
when the sky is so calm and serene,
why should the cherry-flowers hurry to fall
with unsettled heart to earth?
[Hisakata no / hikari nodokeki / haru no hi ni /
shizugokoro naku / hana no chiruramu.]   (Ki no Tomonori)

Although I had heard from the first
that to meet can only mean to part,
I gave myself to love for you
Unconscious of the approaching dawn.

[Hajime yori / au wa wakare to / kiki nagara /
akatsuki shirade / hito o koikeri.]   (Fujiwara Teika)

Weary of living among people,
I had thought of retreating here
in the mountain village.
However, the bright moon in the clear midnight sky
does cast too clear a sheen.
[Sumiwabiba / mi o kakusubeki / yamazato ni /
amari kuma naki / yowa no tsuki kana.]   (Fujiwara Shunzei)

Although these are examples of Japanese court poetry which flourished five centuries before Herrick's time, the similarities in fancy and sentiment are clear. Such is also the case, however, with certain *haiku* of Matsuo Basho (1644–1694) in Herrick's own century and of Yosa Buson in the next. The former elevated *haiku*, transforming it from what was almost a pastime to a form with content of true literary value, in the process founding a distinctive new school of his own:

Spring is with us now;
even a low hill without a name
wears a veil in the morning mist.
[Haru nareya / namo naki yama no / usugasumi.]

To make the memory of her old age happier,
the cherry-tree is doing her best
to put on as gorgeous flowers as possible.
[Ubazakura / sakuya rogo no / omoide ni.]

The winding mountain path—
a violet blooming cool in the shade.
What a relief, its humble form and color!
[Yamaji kite / naniyara yukashi / sumire-gusa.]

Sympathizing with the frail flowers of a pink,
dew falls like tears from the leaves
of a camphor-tree near by.
[Nadeshiko ni / kakaru namida ya / kusu no tsuyu.]

In the field of grape blossoms
sparrows are gathering
to enjoy looking at the dappled yellow and green.
[Nabatake ni / hanami gao naru / suzume kana.]

No flower remains now;
only some seeds of grass are sprinkled,
lamenting over the withered field.
[Hana mina karete / aware o kobosu / kusa no tane.]

Yosa Buson (1716–1783) was a painter and poet, famous for his romantic and sensitive brushwork and his sensuous descriptions.

Endless expanse of young green leaves
in variety of colors—
above them towers Mt. Fuji, unburied.
[Fuji hitotsu / uzumi nokoshite / wakaba kana.]

Full of sorrow I go up the hill
to find sweet eglantine
blooming all around on the top.
[Urei tsutsu / oka ni noboreba / hana-ubara.]

In the old deserted garden
a warbler keeps on singing of spring
all day long.
[Furuniwa ni / uguisu nakinu / himosugara.]

Since the plum-blossoms are gone,
the willow looks so lonely,
drooping and shaking its head.
[Ume chirite / sabishiku narishi / yanagi kana.]

A *haiku* poet, Kobayashi Issa (1763–1827), and a *waka* poet, Tachibana Akemi (1812–1868),[7] resemble in many ways Matsuo Basho and Yosa Buson:

The snow has melted away.
In every vacant lot of the village,
a swarm of children in their games.
[Yuki tokete / mura ippai no / kodomo kana.]   (Issa)

You, thin wretched frog,
fight it out! Never say die!
I, Issa, will back you up.
[Yase-gaeru / makeruna Issa / koreni ari.]   (Issa)

On the gatepost settles a butterfly.
The baby creeps, it flies away.

Again she creeps, it flies away.
[Mon no cho / ko ga haeba tobi / haeba tobi.]   (Issa)

What a delight it is
when, of a morning, I get up
and go out to find in full bloom
a flower that yesterday was not there.
[Tanoshimi wa / asa okiidete / kinoo made /
nakarishi hana no / sakeru miru toki.]   (Akemi)

What a delight it is
when on the straw matting
in my grass-thatched hut,
all on my own,
I make myself at ease.
[Tanoshimi wa / kusa-no-iori-no / mushirojiki /
hitori kokoro o / shizume oru toki.]   (Akemi)

The similarities between the examples of *waka* and *haiku* given above and Herrick's poems may be summarized as follows. First, the short poem as a characteristic mode. Not only in *waka* and *haiku* but in other types of songs and lyrics in the classical tradition, Japanese poets preferred the briefer verse forms, as Herrick so often does. In such deliberately limited forms neither the poem's topic nor its fancy or sentiment is given full logical development; much is left unstated so as to bring into play the reader's imaginative appreciation. Such suggestiveness is the soul of Japanese classical poetry. Sometimes, however, it is taken for thinness of substance—a charge also leveled against Herrick. The latter's *"To the Virgins, to make much of Time"* (H-208), for example, has been regarded as less substantial than Marvell's "To his Coy Mistress," although both express a *carpe diem* theme. For Japanese classical poets, however, saying too much when a little suffices is considered vulgar or impolite, contrary to decorum, a sign of ignorance or lack of refinement. Japanese readers are not certain as to how far this Eastern standard can be applied to Western poets, but this much can be said: Herrick's fewer words are often more pleasing to the Japanese sensibility than other poets' eloquence or verbosity. Although even Herrick is considerably more loquacious than those Japanese poets who work with only seventeen or thirty-one syllables, to the Japanese he does seem to appreciate the virtues of modesty and restraint. Perhaps the problem is how to discriminate between genuine suggestiveness and mere thinness, and here opinions will, of course, differ.

Herrick learned his style from Greek and Latin poets as well as from his mentor, Ben Jonson, and thus mastered the technique of using a simple, refined language which is clear and lucid yet not devoid of an impression of spontaneity, owing to the short verse form and the singleness of theme. This refinement is reminiscent of the *aware* (*yugen, ushin,* or *yoen*) of Japanese *waka* poets, as well as the *soboku* (simplicity) of the *Man-yo* poets and the *shadatsu* (elegant detachment) of the *haiku* poets. Here again Japanese readers sense a slight but important difference. Both Herrick and Japanese classical poets seem to write simple and spontaneous verse, but these qualities are actually the result of repeated effort at improvement. For the Japanese poets such polishing was essential, demanded by the strict number of syllables which their verse form prescribed. Herrick is also a careful reviser, but he sometimes seems satisfied with a piece not fully finished, as if he lacked the creative energy to fix an impression or sentiment in a hard, bright jewel of a poem.

Japanese readers, however, feel that Herrick seems to sing more freely and more at his ease when he employs units of verse that are considerably longer than those used by Japanese classical poets. His lyrics of more than ten or twenty lines evoke in the Eastern reader a sense of the fundamental difference between traditional Japanese poetry and Western poetry, with the latter's closer attachment to reality, its stronger aspiration toward the construction of a logical whole, a microcosm of thought and feeling. The Japanese technique is rather to mine reality for single gems, without thought of setting them in some organic whole.

As noted above, Herrick and the Japanese classical poets can treat similar topics. Both are accustomed to writing occasional verse—poems of congratulation, lament, grief, or parting; both sing of love and death; and both meditate upon the frailty of human life and contemplate life in another world. Many of these topics are, of course, also treated by other English poets. Characteristic of Herrick, however, is his reiterative presentation of the theme of the transiency of happiness, beauty, and love in poems dealing with little or young things such as flowers or maidens. This continuous interaction between the appreciation of the beauty of life and the keen awareness of its passing provides an emotional link between the poems of the Japanese classical poets and those in *Hesperides*. Likewise, Herrick's emphasis on love—in his addresses to his dainty mistresses, in his solicitations of their compassion, in his complaints of their neglect—affords a comparison with Japanese court poets, many of whose lyrics were of this type.

There are some interesting differences in the characteristic images employed by Herrick and by the poets of *waka* and *haiku*. For example, in Herrick's poetry the sun appears as an image more often than the moon, while the reverse is true in Japanese classical poetry. In the latter, autumn, with the opportunities it affords for sounding an elegiac tone, is the preferred season, followed by spring as the season of plum blossoms and cherry flowers, whereas in *Hesperides* poems of spring and summer predominate and only one is set in autumn. Furthermore, the range of Herrick's images is, generally speaking, both broader and deeper than that of the *haiku* and *waka* poets. Finally, Herrick seems a more robust and "physical" poet than the Japanese traditional poets, doubtless owing partly to their emphasis upon the spiritual life and partly to the impressionistic qualities of their verse and their employment of highly restricted forms.

In conclusion, it should be pointed out that the observations set forth here must perforce omit other considerations such as technical matters, parallels between Herrick and modern Japanese poetry, especially recent *waka* and *haiku*, and other examples (of which there are many) of traditional poems which resemble those of Herrick.[8] Nonetheless, this essay has succeeded in its aim if it has suggested, at least, how the twain, West and East, can and do meet in poetry, and come to that meeting similarly appareled in grace, in dignity, and in felicity.

NOTES

1. Emile Legouis and Louis Caziman, *A History of English Literature*, rev. ed. (London, 1933), p. 546.

2. More exactly, "an anthology of poems collected by Imperial command."

3. Both Shunzei and Teika were among the compilers of the eight anthologies and were also distinguished theorists and practitioners of *waka* poetry.

4. Herrick's poems are cited by number from *The Complete Poetry of Robert Herrick*, ed. J. Max Patrick (New York, 1968).

5. In *haiku*, this element of *aware* was later subdivided and developed into *sabi* (tranquillity), *shiori* (sympathy), and *hosomi* (profundity), all of which were regarded as important as the element of *okashi*. (*Okashi* was also given, in certain contexts, subtle shades of meaning, to be translated as something like "gracefully charming.")

6. The poems are taken from Fujiwara Teika's *Hyakunin-isshu* and *Kindai-shuka*, two well-known anthologies of *waka* masterpieces. For the four English versions that follow I am much indebted to Robert H. Brower and Earl Miner, *Fujiwara Teika's Superior Poems of Our Time* (Tokyo, 1967).

7. The two English versions of Akemi's *waka* have been borrowed with admiration and thanks from Geoffrey Bownas and Anthony Thwaite, *The Penguin Book of Japanese Verse* (Harmondsworth, 1964).

8. What has been said of Japanese classical poetry in contrast with Herrick's work is to some extent applicable to modern *waka* and *haiku*, since the fundamental lyrical quality, with its refined emotional coloring, cannot after all be quite effaced from the core of these two genres, in spite of their gradually developed tendency toward more intellectual themes and topics.

VIRGINIA RAMEY MOLLENKOTT

Herrick and the Cleansing of Perception

In *The Marriage of Heaven and Hell,* William Blake wrote, "If the doors of perception were cleansed, everything would appear to man as it is, infinite." Robert Herrick's poetry can be viewed as expressing concern with a similar cleansing of human perception and with the spiritual consequences of such cleansing. If we are willing to call a transcendental integrative vision by the name of religion, then Herrick is a religious poet, not only in *Noble Numbers* but especially in *Hesperides.* One implication of his art is that Herrick knows how to perceive the finite in terms of infinity and to perform finite actions in an infinite manner. Thus, even what has been termed Herrick's "paganism" may be part of his comprehensive vision and purpose, an essential element of his divine comedy.

There are, of course, differing concepts of religion. One, an all-inclusive, organic, and holistic perception of reality, had some currency in the seventeenth century. It occurs, for example, in John Donne's Sermon XXIII from the 1640 Folio. Speaking on 1 Corinthians 13:12, "For now we see through a glass darkly, but then face to face," Donne distinguishes between two attitudes or perceptions of earthly reality: "The naturall man sees Beauty, and Riches, and Honour, but yet it is a question whether he sees them or no, because he sees them, but as a snare. But he that sees God in them, sees them to be beames and evidences of that Beauty, that Wealth, that Honour, that is in God, that is God himselfe." On the basis of this holistic vision, Donne counsels his auditors to "see God in every thing, and then thou needst not take off thine eye from Beauty, from Riches, from Honour, from any thing."[1] Later in the century, Thomas Traherne expressed a similarly holistic attitude toward experience:

197

> What wondrous things upon the Earth are don
> Beneath, and yet abov, the Sun?
> Deeds all appear again
> In higher Spheres.[2]

No action, then, can be deemed inconsequential. Similarly, George Herbert made clear in "The Elixir" that the difference between secular and sacred is not external, but stems from inner attitudes or perceptions. The drudgery of sweeping a floor becomes "divine" to the person who does it for God's sake and thus perceives the opportunity to worship God even in the mundane. The Cambridge Platonists also held an all-embracing view of human experience and therefore of religion. As C. A. Patrides has written, "All that the Cambridge Platonists ever uttered reverts in the end to Whichcote's refusal to oppose the spiritual to the rational, the supernatural to the natural, Grace to Nature."[3]

It is my contention that within this holistic concept of religion, Herrick is more entitled to be called a religious poet than has previously been admitted. I will attempt to demonstrate that in Donne's sense of seeing God in everything, Herrick is a religious poet, even in some poems which seem quite secular from a more traditional religious viewpoint.

Sensitive readers of Herrick have often noticed that "Corinna's going a Maying" (H-178) has a "religious" dimension, that it synthesizes and closes the gap between Herrick's "natural religion" and his more orthodox religious impulses. The poem seems to embody the principle which Herrick stated at the very end of *Noble Numbers:* "Of all the good things whatsoe're we do, / God is the Alpha, and the Omega too."[4] Herrick's persona is careful to say that going Maying is such a good thing that it is "sin" and "profanation" slothfully to postpone joining the fun, even if the postponement is lengthened by traditional religious observances: "Few Beads are best, when once we goe a Maying."

Comparison with the probable source of "Corinna," a lyric drawn from Thomas Bateson's *First Set of English Madrigals* (1604), shows that by holistic standards, Herrick's genius is essentially religious:

Sister, awake! close not your eyes!
  The day her light discloses,
And the bright morning doth arise
  Out of her bed of roses.

See, the clear sun, the world's bright eye,
  In at our window peeping:
Lo! how he blusheth to espy
  Us idle wenches sleeping.

Therefore awake! make haste, I say,
  And let us, without staying,
All in our gowns of green so gay
  Into the park a-maying.[5]

Herrick's poem makes the situation considerably more dramatic: a man calls a woman to rise and join the revelers, as opposed to the much more static situation of one sister speaking to another from the bed they share. But the real power of Herrick's version comes from the pulsing religious awareness that nature is alive with personality, alive with worship. The sun is a god unshorn, dawn is a busy domestic, the flowers have bowed toward the East, the birds have said their matins and sung their thankful hymns. As the budding boys and girls enjoy themselves, they too will become part of nature, sweet as Flora, wearing their foliage, giving and getting their green gowns, turning houses into arks and tabernacles by their devotion to the joyous May Day celebration. Pleasure, then, can be sacramental, an act of worship. Whereas the apocryphal Wisdom of Solomon puts its *carpe diem* sentiments into the mouth of "the wicked," Herrick's persona takes pains to say that this is a "harmlesse follie" which must be enjoyed while "we are but decaying," before the night of death. And whereas the traditional religious perception is "Work, for the night is coming," Herrick's implication is "Play, for the night is coming"—but that play is set in such a natural rhythm, and so surrounded with imagery of natural worship, that there is no tone of defiance. They also serve who only go a-Maying.

A comparison of Herrick's *"Meat without mirth"* (H-541) with its source in Plutarch's *Symposiacs*,[6] translated by Holland in 1603, reveals once again that Herrick's genius is to add the religious dimension. Plutarch tells of a pleasant man who used to say, "Eaten I have this day, but not supped." Plutarch interpreted this to mean that meals should never be "without mirth and good companie, to season the same, and to give a pleasant taste to the viands." Out of this Herrick creates the following:

> Eaten I have; and though I had good cheere,
> I did not sup, because no friends were there.
> Where Mirth and Friends are absent when we Dine
> Or Sup, there wants the Incense and the Wine.

Here again we may see the concept of pleasure as sacrament. Eating with friends and mirth is transfigured by the words "Incense" and "Wine" into a type of Eucharistic feast, a celebration of oneness between God and humanity through friendship between human beings. Thus the mundane world is suffused with meaning, transformed into a world of mystery and wonder.

When Herrick turns to doctrinal matters, as in *"His Creed"* (N-78), he seems childlike in his simplicity. He begins with the fact of his own death ("I do believe, that die I must") and proceeds from this existential groundwork to only the most clear-cut and basic of Christian doctrines. This is not necessarily a sign of religious naiveté; it may signify an instinctual awareness that "He who knows does not speak, and he who speaks does not know."[7] Herrick does not seem to find the essence of religion in lengthy creeds, since even the wisest and holiest of words cannot release mankind from clouded and delusory perceptions. True religion apparently consists, rather, of having ears to hear, eyes to see, and a heart to accept the reality of "what is," including the fact of one's own death. Such acceptance leads to equanimity: "Whatever comes, let's be content withall: / Among Gods Blessings, there is no one small" (N-55).

Submission to God's will (or *dharma*, or *Tao*) has been termed "saying yes to the inevitability of happenings."[8] When one is thus enlightened, when the doors of perception are cleansed, it is said that one may enter the blissful state of indifference to external fortune by means of the perception that during life's vicissitudes, the deepest or cosmic Self remains infinite and untouched. The *Bhagavad-Gita* says that "A serene spirit accepts pleasure and pain with an even mind, and is unmoved by either."[9] In "*To Fortune*" (H-677), Herrick puts it this way:

> Tumble me down, and I will sit
> Upon my ruines (smiling yet:)
> Teare me to tatters; yet I'le be
> Patient in my necessitie.
> Laugh at my scraps of cloaths, and shun
> Me, as a fear'd infection:
> Yet scarre-crow-like I'le walk, as one,
> Neglecting thy derision.

In "*Upon God*" (N-87) Herrick explains the reason for his detachment:

> God when He takes my goods and chattels hence,
> Gives me a portion, giving patience:
> What is in God is God; if so it be,
> He patience gives: He gives himselfe to me.

Examples could be multiplied of Herrick's universal and profoundly integrative insights, in *Hesperides* no less than in *Noble Numbers*. In fact, *Noble Numbers* often provides a valuable gloss upon the poems in *Hesperides*. For instance, in *Noble Numbers* Herrick recognizes that God is literally everywhere and in everything, acknowledging that he has derived this concept from Judaism: "God, in the *holy Tongue*, they call / The Place that filleth *All in all*" (N-185). God is therefore the Ground of all Being:

> God's present ev'ry where; but most of all
> Present by Union *Hypostaticall:*
> God, He is there, where's nothing else (Schooles say)
> And nothing else is there, *where He's away.*   (N-207)

Because God unites Himself with His creation in a very personal and individual (hypostatical) way, Herrick is able to say that "God is *all-present* to what e're we do, / And as *all-present*, so *all-filling* too" (N-237).

Because God fills all and is *"present to what e're we do,"* love to Herrick can be sacred, and success in love may be celebrated in joyful and natural worship. To the lark he cries out a cheerful

> Good speed, for I this day
> Betimes my Mattens say:
>   Because I doe
>   Begin to wooe:
>   Sweet singing Lark,
>   Be thou the Clark,
>   And know thy when
> To say, *Amen.*
>   And if I prove
>   Blest in my love;
>   Then thou shalt be
>   High-Priest to me,
>   At my returne,
>   To Incense burne;
> And so to solemnize
> Love's, and my Sacrifice.   (H-214)

As in "Corinna's *Going a Maying*," there is a sense of organic union with nature and a collapsing of any distinctions between what is natural, what is pleasurable, and what is worshipful: the lark will be the high priest presiding over the joyful offering of thanks should the wooing prove successful.

And the beloved woman herself can be a manifestation of God, for whereas the poet recognizes that he will put on "immortall clothing" after he has gone to his mansion in eternity, Julia is already, while human and alive in the mundane world, "Cloth'd all with incorrupted light" (H-819). Although the light is only a "counterfeit" of the full splendor she will achieve in eternity, nevertheless the reference to the "uncorrupt light" of Wisdom of Solomon 18:4 constitutes a handsome compliment. Repeatedly and skillfully Herrick utilizes religious imagery in his love poetry, at least partially in order to show that because everything is holy, women are holy; that love-making can be a sacred activity; and that physical pleasure can be sacramental.

Even an ordinary house is full of the One Spirit of God and

cannot be rightly regarded as an exclusively secular object. Herrick prays to the tutelary spirit of his house in unmistakably scriptural terms:

> Command the Roofe great *Genius*, and from thence
> Into this house powre downe thy influence,
> That through each room a golden pipe may run
> Of living water by thy *Benizon*.
> Fulfill the Larders, and with strengthning bread
> Be evermore these Bynns replenished.
> Next, like a Bishop consecrate my ground,
> That luckie Fairies here may dance their Round:
> And after that, lay downe some silver pence,
> The Masters charge and care to recompence. (H-723)

Recognizing that when Milton speaks of "the mighty Pan" he is not "expressing paganism" but is picturing Christ as the omnipotent good shepherd and that Spenser's prayer to "glad Genius" in *Epithalamion* is a poeticized Christian appeal for God's blessing on the reproductive and creative aspects of the marriage, the reader is alerted to the possibility that although Herrick addresses Genius he may be expressing not "paganism," but a sense of a guardian angel in his home (Matthew 18:10) and of God in all things. Herrick gives us several hints in that direction, alluding to the "living water" identified with Christ in John 4:10, and comparing Genius to a Bishop and even to the Good Samaritan who, when he had rescued the man fallen among thieves, took him to an inn and left him in the charge of the innkeeper, laying down two "silver pence / The Masters charge and care to recompence" (cf. Luke 10:30–35).

Not only does Herrick make clear that the presence of the One Spirit will bless the house of any inhabitant willing to be so blessed, but he also shows that a religious perception of nature transforms the mundane into the miraculous:

> First offer Incense, then thy field and meads
> Shall smile and smell the better by thy beads.
> The spangling Dew dreg'd o're the grasse shall be
> Turn'd all to Mell, and Manna there for thee.
> Butter of *Amber*, *Cream*, and *Wine*, and *Oile*

> Shall run, as rivers, all throughout thy soyl.
> Wod'st thou to sincere-silver turn thy mold?
> Pray once, twice pray; and turn thy ground to gold. (H-370)

The title of this poem, *"Pray and prosper,"* might lead one at first to believe that Herrick is offering rather dismal priestly encouragement to act godly in order to garner material blessings in return. But the first four lines suggest that what Herrick is referring to is a cleansing of perception: if one prays, the fields and meads will look and smell better than they did before, and the dew on the grass will be transformed into honey and manna. By changing the attitude of the beholder, prayer performs the alchemical miracle: ordinary earth becomes pure silver, ordinary ground turns to gold.

Herrick speaks of another cleansing of perception in *"To Julia in the Temple"* (H-445):

> Besides us two, i'th'Temple here's not one
> To make up now a Congregation.
> Let's to the *Altar of perfumes* then go,
> And say short Prayers; and when we have done so,
> Then we shall see, how in a little space,
> *Saints* will come in to fill each Pew and Place.

Is the reader to believe that because the speaker and Julia pray briefly at the altar, when they are finished they will look up and find that, without being summoned, the good parishioners of Dean Prior have filed softly into the church and filled every single seat? Hardly. Instead, after they have prayed the scales will fall from their eyes: they will be able to perceive that they are surrounded by the saints of God, "compassed about" with the "great cloud of witnesses" mentioned in Hebrews 12:1, observed by a congregation of spiritual creatures who walk the earth invisible to ordinary sight but are aware of human affairs. Herrick would not have laughed at Blake for seeing a tree full of angels.

In the holistic context that God is *"all-present* to what e're we do,"* Herrick even pictures his writing as a sacred activity, with himself as a Priest for the Muses (H-778); and he sees his epithalamia and his lyrics as valid responses to the love of God. Asking

God to lay his "stately terrours by, / To talke with me familiarly," Herrick promises fitting responses:

> Speake thou of love and I'le reply
> By way of *Epithalamie*,
> Or sing of *mercy*, and I'le suit
> To it my Violl and my Lute.   (N-232)

In his address to the son of George Villiers (H-245), Herrick compares the Villiers name to the Shekinah glory of God, coming in that poem to dwell within the tabernacle known as *Hesperides:* "a Cloud of Glory fills my Book" (cf. Exodus 40:34–38). And inside that tabernacle, Herrick's poems are the liturgies. He promises that "Saint *Ben*" shall be "Writ in my *Psalter*" (H-604), that his "smooth-pac't Poems" shall be the "high *Doxologie*" of Prince Charles (H-756), and that Stephen Soame will, by being "Canonized" in a Herrick poem, join the "Holies" in the "eternall Calender" of *Hesperides* (H-545). Though sometimes used playfully, the religious images sprinkled thickly throughout *Hesperides* need not be regarded as merely facetious; they can entail the sort of significant playfulness which strikes through to ultimate matters, and they imply that Herrick could have been conscious of a religious dimension in much of his ostensibly secular writing.

The famous *"Argument of his Book"* identifies one basic topic of Herrick's verse: "I sing (and ever shall) / Of *Heaven*, and hope to have it after all." Remembering that Herrick sees God as "The Place that filleth *All in all*"—and what is Heaven, if not the presence of God?—we can take seriously his claim that Heaven is a basic topic in *Hesperides*. Herrick may in fact be telling us that even in this poem about brooks and bridal cakes and "cleanly-*Wantonnesse*," he is singing about Heaven, and he always *will* be singing about Heaven.

The overall effect of the seven introductory poems which follow the Argument is to assert the purity of *Hesperides* for those who have pure minds. H-5 and H-6, which rain appropriate curses on those who dislike the poet's works, imply that "all seems infected that the infected spy," while H-7 urges his book to avoid men who are like bread with too much leaven. Since leaven is usually a symbol of sin and evil desires in the Bible and rabbinical literature (cf. Exodus 12:19; 1 Corinthians 5:6–8), Herrick now implies that "to the pure all things are pure" by warning his book to avoid people with impure attitudes. In the last of his introductory poems (H-8), Herrick speaks of his poems as "Enchantments" and "holy incantation[s]," and instructs that they be read during Bacchanalian pleasantries rather than on sober mornings. Like Spenser, who celebrated the holiness of his wedding day by exhorting not only the people but even the walls and doorposts to be soused with bellyfuls of wine, Herrick associates holiness with hilarity and human pleasure. He wants his poems read "when the *Rose* raigns"—and the rose is a symbol of pleasure. Herrick's blend of religious terminology ("holy incantation") with Bacchanalian revelry implies that for him pleasure and piety are not mutually exclusive.

The multiplicity of *Hesperides* recalls a Zen saying from the fourth century B.C.: "The perfect man uses his mind as a mirror. It grasps nothing, it refuses nothing. It receives but does not keep."[10] Or, in the words of a twentieth-century Zen thinker, "Through the multiplicity of forms and appearances the Structure of Reality [is] mirrored, and disclose[s] itself, unconfused by concepts, opinions, labels, and prejudices."[11] Like certain Zen-artists and like anyone who can describe various phenomena realistically, Herrick has been accused of lacking humanity and good manners, especially in some of his epigrams about foul breath, rotten teeth, and the like. But these too are part of the Structure of Reality which Herrick describes and mirrors.

H. R. Swardson rightly recognizes that Herrick's poem beginning *"Pardon me God"* (N-113) is one of the most problematic for any reading of Herrick as a religious poet. Swardson sees the poem as unequivocal evidence of a conflict between Christian and classical traditions:[12] thus, he views Herrick in this poem as taking the extreme Christian stance whereas in his "undiluted eroticism" the poet is regarded as taking an equally extreme classical-pagan stance. However, it is also possible to read *"To God"* as an exercise in becoming aware that God is not only immanent but transcendent. In the eyes of a transcendent and perfect

Other, surely all things mortal (including Herrick's poetic output) must seem low and imperfect:

> Pardon me God, (once more I Thee intreat)
> That I have plac'd Thee in so meane a seat,
> Where round about Thou seest but all things vaine,
> Uncircumcis'd, unseason'd, and prophane.
> But as Heavens publike and immortall Eye
> Looks on the filth, but is not soil'd thereby;
> So Thou, my God, may'st on this impure look,
> But take no tincture from my sinfull Book:
> Let but one beame of Glory on it shine,
> And that will make me, and my Work divine.

Two factors dispute the thesis that this represents a rejection of Herrick's classical-pagan writings: first, the "sinfull Book" in which this poem occurs is not *Hesperides* but *Noble Numbers*. And second, should God choose to let the beam of His glory shine on Herrick's book, both the poet and his poems will become "divine." Herrick usually writes as if God were immanent within His Creation as well as outside and above it; but in this poem he presents God as Other and expresses a different kind of immanence. It is not a matter of rejecting one segment of his poetic output in favor of another; the *entire* output stands or falls depending upon whether or not God chooses to be present within it. Thus the poem is perfectly in tune with the one that follows it and has the same title:

> Lord, I am like to *Mistletoe*,
> Which has no root, and cannot grow,
> Or prosper, but by that same tree
> It clings about; so I by Thee.
> What need I then to feare at all,
> So long as I about Thee craule?
> But if that Tree sho'd fall, and die,
> Tumble shall heav'n, and down will I.   (N-114)

This perception of a natural and organic relationship between the dependent creature and the Creator by whom "all things consist" (Colossians 1:17), between the personal spirit and the Spirit that is "deeply interfused" and "rolls through all things" (Wordsworth), between the individual self and the universal or cosmic Self, seems to me as profound as anything in seventeenth-century literature.

Roger B. Rollin has shown us that Herrick, even more than other seventeenth-century artists, makes a religion of his art.[13] Several twentieth-century psychologists have demonstrated the similarities between various forms of meditation, aesthetic experience, human empathy, and the holistic religious attitude;[14] as the contemporary artist, Frederick Franck, declares, "There is no split between a man's being, his art and what one might call his 'religion,' unless there is a split in the man. These three are inextricably interwoven: they are one."[15] In Robert Herrick there was no split: the man was one, and he practiced his art as an act of worship.

Herrick's reputation as a religious poet has suffered from a concept of religion oriented toward doctrine, theory, and organization. Western religious and philosophical dualism has led to dichotomized views of Herrick. Is he trivial or profound? Is he religious or secular? Is he pagan or Christian? But if one is willing to broaden the definition of religious faith to include a cleansing of perception which enables one to perceive the sacredness of everything that lives, Herrick's stature appears impressive, his contributions solid and significant.

From one perspective, it is valid to argue that if *everything* is religious and holy, *nothing* is either religious or holy; but Herrick's poetry seems to indicate that he would disagree. Like Paul the Apostle, who instructs that "whatsoever ye do" should be done as an act of worship (1 Corinthians 10:31), like some of his seventeenth-century contemporaries, and like Blake, who perceives everything as infinite, Herrick expands religion beyond the walls of the church and into every aspect of life.

NOTES

1. *The Sermons of John Donne*, ed. E. M. Simpson and G. R. Potter, 10 vols. (Berkeley, 1962), VIII, 221.

2. "On Leaping Over the Moon," in *Thomas Traherne: Centuries, Poems, and Thanksgivings*, ed. H. M. Margoliouth, 2 vols. (Oxford, 1958), II, 131.

3. *The Cambridge Platonists* (Cambridge, 1970), p. 10.

4. *The Complete Poetry of Robert Herrick*, ed. J. Max Patrick (New York, 1963), p. 534. All subsequent Herrick quotations are from this edition.

5. Quoted by F. W. Moorman, *Robert Herrick: A Biographical and Critical Study* (1910; rpt. New York, 1962), p. 227.

6. Cited in *The Poetical Works of Robert Herrick*, ed. L. C. Martin (Oxford, 1956), pp. 540–41.

7. A Taoist and Zen aphorism. See "The Tao-Te-King, LXXXI" and "The Works of Chuang Tze" in *The Bible of the World*, ed. Robert O. Ballou et al. (New York, 1973), pp. 505 and 529.

8. Claudio Naranjo, *The One Quest* (New York, 1972), p. 180.

9. As quoted by Claudio Naranjo and Robert Ornstein, *On the Psychology of Meditation* (New York, 1971), p. 26.

10. Chuang Tze, as cited by Frederick Franck, *The Zen of Seeing* (New York, 1973), p. 125.

11. Franck, *Zen of Seeing*, p. 121.

12. *Poetry and the Fountain of Light: Observations on the Conflict between Christian and Classical Traditions in Seventeenth-Century Poetry* (Columbia, Mo., 1962), p. 44.

13. *Robert Herrick* (New York, 1966), p. 164.

14. Naranjo and Ornstein, *Psychology of Meditation*, p. 29.

15. Franck, *Zen of Seeing*, pp. 8–9.

WILLIAM ORAM

Herrick's Use of Sacred Materials

"Corinna's *going a Maying*" (H-178) is a poem about the pagan revelry of May Day and it celebrates the cyclical renewal of nature; it ends echoing Catullus and Horace on the brevity of life and the consequent need to seize the present time. Yet the last stanza also echoes the Wisdom of Solomon, and the first three stanzas of the poem make use of the language of Christian belief: "sin," "devotion," "tabernacle," "ark." The coexistence of these elements in the poem dramatizes the uncertain role that religion plays in *Hesperides*. Is divine worship the central concern of the book, giving purpose and direction to its heterogeneous and secular materials? Or is it more usually a dutiful afterthought, as seems the case with many of the less inspired *Noble Numbers*? Certain facts are clear: *Noble Numbers* presents Herrick as a believing and pious Christian and many of the poems in *Hesperides* contain religious language, imagery, and allusion. Matters become less clear when the critic has to evaluate the role such religious materials play in the individual poems, and in the book as a whole. The scope of the problem goes well beyond this essay, but here, by looking at three of Herrick's minor poems, I shall indicate some of the ways in which he used the religious materials he incorporated into his work. I shall stress two aspects of his poetry: his use of religious reference and of ceremony. Both suggest the same conclusion: when Herrick incorporates sacred materials into his work he changes them radically. They serve the purposes of an ordering that is more artistic than religious.

Herrick's knowledge of the Bible appears throughout his poems. He repeatedly echoes biblical phrases, often in unlikely places. It is, in fact, the unlikeliness of his references—their far-fetched quality—that is most striking. The whimsical envoy, "*To his Booke*" (H-3), will serve as an example:[1]

> While thou didst keep thy *Candor* undefil'd,
> Deerely I lov'd thee; as my first-borne child:
> But when I saw thee wantonly to roame
> From house to house, and never stay at home;
> I brake my bonds of Love, and bad thee goe,
> Regardless whether well thou sped'st, or no.
> On with thy fortunes then, what e're they be;
> If good I'le smile, if bad I'le sigh for Thee.

Herrick's poem plays wittily with a theme made familiar by the silver-age Latin poets, the farewell of the author to his book. The manuscript, which has passed from hand to hand, perhaps appearing in corrupt copies, is like a child who has evaded parental authority, "wantonly" leaving home. Herrick plays with the idea of his child's "sinfulness" by echoing several biblical passages. Three of the most noticeable follow.[2]

Blessed are the undefiled in the way, who walk in the law of the Lord. (Psalm 119:1)

When Israel was a child, then I loved him, and called my son out of Egypt. As they called them, so they went from them: they sacrificed unto Baalim, and burned incense to graven images. I taught Ephraim also to go, taking them by their arms; but they knew not that I healed them. I drew them with cords of a man, with bands of love. (Hosea 11:1–4)

And in the same house remain, eating and drinking such things as they give: for the laborer is worthy of his hire. Go not from house to house. (Luke 10:7)

The religious reference in the poem is surprising and witty, but it lacks any deeper resonance. When Milton invokes a biblical passage, its context frequently comments on his statement and gives a sacred weight to his verses; Herrick, on the contrary, invokes these passages in a spirit of fun. They further the idea of "sin" in the poem, but sin is here no more than a playful (and slightly perverse) metaphor for the manuscript's passage from hand to hand. If one dislikes the poem, one accuses Herrick of trivializing the biblical passages. If one finds pleasure in it, one praises his witty play with the biblical texts. But both judgments meet in the observation that Herrick places a serious religious text in a playfully blasphemous secular context. The wit of the poem consists in its ability to invoke, with mock seriousness, religious concepts that have no true relevance to its subject. Although I have termed this procedure "blasphemous," the word is too weighty for Herrick's poem. Ben Jonson might grumble about Donne's "First Anniversary," where the religious language invests Elizabeth Drury with a quasi-religious status, but here Herrick cancels any such potential for religious shock. The Bible becomes a text one can toy with, in somewhat the same way as one would toy with Horace or Catullus; its words are no more than words and their misuse will cause no blasphemy. In this context it becomes a literary source, not a sacred text. Sin is a metaphor, but not a metaphor to be taken seriously.

Much of the most interesting recent work on Herrick has stressed the importance of the ceremonies that appear so frequently in his poems. These ceremonies often appear in connection with crucial stages in the life of the individual or with the course of the year—marriages and funerals, May Day, and harvest. Can they be understood as religious or at least "proto-religious" rites, looking toward or implying a "dependence on a higher order"?[3] If Herrick associates ritual with the worship of a transcendent being, one place to look for confirmation of such an association is *Noble Numbers*. The poems that fill this section of Herrick's book do not, however, establish such a connection. Since *Noble Numbers* is composed largely of personal prayers and sacred epigrams, few of its poems contain the public rituals so noticeable in the rest of *Hesperides*. There are epigrams on the meaning of certain church rituals, some songs composed for specific religious occasions, and two funeral dirges which come as close to classical lament as nominally Christian songs can come.[4] But these are few in comparison with the largely private pieties of the section. There are none of the meditated funerals so prominent in the earlier part of the book. By contrast with the work of a devotional poet like George Herbert, Herrick's specifically religious poetry is not, on the whole, much concerned with Christian ritual. In the absence of such explicit connections between ritual and Christian worship, one may hypothesize that Herrick is attracted by ritual less because of its religious potential than because it holds some other value for him.

What this value might be can be inferred from a study of one of the famous miniatures of *Hesperides*, in which a rose dies like a sainted nun:

> The Rose was sick, and smiling di'd;
> And (being to be sanctifi'd)
> About the Bed, there sighing stood
> The sweet, and flowrie Sisterhood.
> Some hung the head, while some did bring
> (To wash her) water from the Spring.
> Some laid her forth, while other wept,
> But all a solemne Fast there kept.
> The holy Sisters some among
> The sacred *Dirge* and *Trentall* sung.
> But ah! what sweets smelt every where,
> As Heaven had spent all perfumes there,
> At last, when prayers for the dead,
> And Rites were all accomplished;
> They, weeping, spread a Lawnie Loome,
> And clos'd her up, as in a Tombe. (H-686)

The poem plays with the rites of Christian burial just as the envoy *"To his Booke"* plays with the idea of Christian sin. The little scene, with its flowery sisterhood and its ceremonial acts, never loses its whimsy. Most commentators stress the ways in which the poem reflects Christian worship, but what seems more obvious is the way in which that reflection avoids Christian piety. Here one does not find the rose of the virgin soul, but an actual rose, and the "Sisterhood" is merely one of flowers. Herrick does not let the reader forget that they are flowers: he chooses attitudes and attributes for the sisters that are appropriate to flowers, making a series of visual puns. The flowers hang their heads like sisters; the sisters scatter flowery "sweets" in all directions. The final line stresses that the sisters close up the

Rose "*as* in a Tombe"; it reminds us that the flowers are only *like* sisters. As often in Herrick, the reader sees a sort of double exposure in which maidens are superimposed on blossoms: now he imagines the figures as women; now he remembers they are flowers. The alternation is pleasing: one of the pleasures of the poem lies in its fleeting animism, its capacity to give the reader a glimpse of a sentient, sympathetic natural world.

Still, the serious reader looks for something more. Is there not a higher symbolism, a vision which is ultimately Christian or which *looks* at least toward some higher order? I think not; but there is something in the poem that gives it a greater resonance than its delicate if slightly saccharine imagery would suggest. This is the theme of death. The poem, like so many of the poems of *Hesperides*, treats death and reactions to death, but it does so in a way that is "screened" or mediated. Death in itself is too frightening, too repulsive for direct confrontation: what poems like these do, finally, is to give it a playful, orderly, and hence an acceptable form. The fact of death is "sweetened" when it is transferred from human beings to roses, and sweetened again by the forms of ceremony which human beings use to make the unknown acceptable.

Herrick's attitude toward these sweetening ceremonies is complex. One way to understand it more clearly and to judge its relation to true religious ceremony is to look at another of the funeral poems, the fine "*To* Perilla" (H-14), in which the speaker imagines his own decease. These lines are not an actual set of directions for burial nor are they primarily an attempt to comfort the imagined Perilla, though the poem makes use of both these fictive situations. Rather, the poem attempts to confront and minimize the fearfulness of death, through the speaker's dramatized calmness and the orderly rites of burial.

> Ah my Perilla! do'st thou grieve to see
> Me, day by day, to steale away from thee?
> Age cals me hence, and my gray haires bid come
> And haste away to mine eternal home;
> 'Twill not be long (Perilla) after this,
> That I must give thee the *supremest* kisse.

The opening lines establish the character of the speaker and his relation to the faithful Perilla. The tone is grave, easy, almost fatherly: the speaker seems less anxious about his own death than about his Perilla's grief. He explains to her that his gray hairs bid him "haste away" to his "eternal home," and he has the equanimity to pun on the word "supremest": his last breath will be his last and his greatest kiss, an ultimate farewell.[5] The pun dramatizes better than any direct assertion his lack of fear.

Having established the speaker's ability to face death with equanimity, the poem continues with instructions for the funeral:

> Dead when I am, first cast in salt, and bring
> Part of the creame from that *Religious Spring;*
> With which (*Perilla*) wash my hands and feet;
> That done, then wind me in that very sheet
> Which wrapt thy smooth limbs (when thou didst implore
> The Gods protection, but the night before)
> Follow me weeping to my Turfe, and there
> Let fall a Primrose, and with it a teare:
> Then lastly, let some weekly-strewings bee
> Devoted to the memory of me:
> Then shall my *Ghost* not walk about, but keep
> Still in the coole, and silent shades of sleep.

If one looks for religious feeling in the poem, one comes up against several obstacles. The first is the *"Religious Spring"* of Perilla's eyes. This is an elaborate and courtly compliment to the weeper, and its function as compliment tends to cast doubt on the seriousness of the other "religious" references in the poem. The reminiscence of Perilla's "smooth limbs" further dilutes the specifically otherworldly content of the poem. The secular emphasis is the more apparent because the burial rites the speaker mentions are, as Robert Deming points out, largely classical.[6] The mention of Herrick's "eternal home" sounds Christian, but the "coole, and silent shades of sleep" call up an image of Hades, not heaven. To argue that this is essentially an exercise of Renaissance syncretism would be to miss the direction of the poem, which is turned toward Perilla, not Christ. If there is religion here, it is the slightly whimsical religion of *"The Funerall Rites of the Rose."*

If Herrick does not stress the religious significance of the rites he does elaborate on their orderly performance. We are given, in proper succession, the casting of salt, the lamentation, the washing and wrapping of the body, the following of the corpse, and the strewing of flowers. All these images avoid the actual ugliness of death; they clothe the physical facts of decay which a poet like Skelton delights in:

> Our days be datyd
> To be chekmatyd,
> With drawttys of deth
> Stoppyng oure breth;
> Our eyen synking,
> Our bodys stynking,
> Our guyymys grynning
> Our soules brynning.[7]

Nothing could be further from Herrick's funeral poems than the grotesque detail of "Uppon a Deedmans Hed." Where Skelton pictures with some gusto the body's dissolution, Herrick lends death the beauty of aesthetic form. Death is ceremonialized— wrapped, so to speak, in a covering of ordered language. Even the last lines about the ghost, with their carefully patterned long and short vowels and their repetitions of "s" and "l," suggest an ordered reserve, a "coolness" about the spirit world.

Both *"To* Perilla" and "Uppon a Deedmans Hed" are among the vast number of Renaissance meditations on death: the looking forward to the crucial moment when man must bid farewell to the world. The function of such a meditation is usually to ready the Christian for the afterlife and reaffirm his ties with the world of the spirit. But Herrick's poem differs from most such meditations in its refusal to stress the afterlife. Instead, it substitutes an imaginary burial service, dwelling on a set of earthly ceremonies. The divine meditation is secularized while the funeral loses most of its religious significance: it is changed into an aesthetic or at most a communal form. The rites establish a bond between this death and earlier deaths; they order, dignify and commemorate the speaker's passing. They do not bring heaven closer to earth. It is significant that instead of addressing himself to God or to his own soul, the speaker addresses himself to another human being—although Perilla herself may be an imagined mistress, an aesthetic creation. In this poem death appears less the concern of God than of men and women.

I do not mean to suggest that Herrick was an agnostic or atheist. He seems to have been a conventionally pious minister of the Church of England, as *Noble Numbers* dutifully attests. But his imagination tended more toward the transient, the sensuous, and the social than toward the absolute. He may at times appear the last of the Elizabethans, but as a recent critic has pointed out,[8] he can be seen more accurately as a poet whose concern with immediate sensuous experience (and, I would add, whose lack of religious fervor) anticipates the later seventeenth century. Herrick makes considerable use of the sacred in his work, but it usually undergoes a transformation in the process. It often supplies form but rarely direction for his greatest verse.

NOTES

1. All quotations follow J. Max Patrick, ed., *The Complete Poetry of Robert Herrick* (New York, 1963).

2. Patrick (p. 13) also cites Deuteronomy 21:15.

3. Robert Deming, "Robert Herrick's Classical Ceremony," *ELH*, 34 (1967), 347 uses this phrase to argue that Herrick's poems are "not incompatible with Christianity."

4. See, for example, N-65, N-83, N-96–98, N-123, and N-155. "*The Dirge of* Jepthahs *Daughter*" (N-83) is particularly interesting: here, as elsewhere, Herrick makes the religious tree bear secular fruit.

5. See Robert Deming, "Herrick's Funeral Poems," *SEL* 9 (1969) for a commentary on the last kiss. "*To* Perilla" is finely discussed in A. Leigh DeNeef's "*This Poetick Liturgie*": *Robert Herrick's Ceremonial Mode* (Durham, 1974), pp. 145–47. DeNeef's conclusion that the ceremony of the poem attempts an "artistic transcendence" of death anticipates my own conclusion.

6. Deming, "Herrick's Funeral Poems," p. 158.

7. "Uppon a Deedmans Hed," quoted from John Skelton, *Poems*, ed. Robert S. Kinsman (Oxford, 1969), p. 9.

8. Paul Jenkins, "Rethinking What Moderation Means to Robert Herrick," *ELH*, 39 (1972), 32–52.

Herrick and His Public

J. MAX PATRICK

"*Poetry perpetuates the Poet*": Richard James and the Growth of Herrick's Reputation

In H-3, "*To his Booke*," Robert Herrick sends forth *Hesperides* to an uncertain reception in the world: "On with thy fortunes then, what e're they be; / If good I'le smile, if bad I'le sigh for thee." But in more serious moments he had no doubt that ultimately the greatness of his poems would be recognized. Thus in H-82, "*To the reverend shade of his religious Father*," Herrick tells his long-neglected parent to "take a life immortal from my verse." And to the living, Herrick's message is that of H-201, "*To live merrily, and to trust to Good Verses*":

> Trust to good Verses then;
>   They onely will aspire,
> When Pyramids, as men,
>   Are lost, i'th'funerall fire.
>
> And when all Bodies meet
>   In *Lethe* to be drown'd;
> Then onely Numbers sweet,
>   With endless life are crown'd.

Similarly in H-211, "*His Poetrie his Pillar*," he reiterates the certain immortality of his poems:

> Behold this living stone
>   I reare for me,
>   Ne'r to be thrown
> Downe, envious Time by thee.
> Pillars let some set up,
>   (If so they please)
>   Here is my hope,
> And my *Pyramides*.

This volume of essays based on papers delivered at the Herrick Memorial Conference reveals that his confidence was justified, that each of his lyrics is truly "a Legacie / Left to all posterity" (H-218, *"Lyrick for Legacies"*). Nevertheless, it has taken a long time for his just fame to be recognized—longer than his editor, L. C. Martin, was willing to admit; for he overestimated the earliest-known tribute to Herrick and claimed that the poet's reputation peaked before 1630 and then declined to a low for more than two centuries. My purpose is to counter Martin's contention with a more realistic survey of Herrick's slow rise toward the fame that he now enjoys. From the beginning he had some recognition, though the evidence for it is slight. But what is well evidenced—not only by this present volume but by other tercentenary tributes—is the truth of his own observation in H-721, *"Fame"*: *"Tis still observ'd, that Fame ne're sings / The order, but the Sum of things."* In other words, it is not the *"order"* or progress whereby a reputation grows, but the *"Sum"*—the long-run outcome—that constitutes true fame. Lack of immediate reputation is of no real importance, for, in the words of H-654, *"Long lookt for comes at last,"* "Though long it be, yeeres may repay the debt; / None loseth that, which he in time may get."

It was odd of L. C. Martin to go out of his way to belittle most of the comments printed about Robert Herrick in the seventeenth and eighteenth centuries. Editors usually give their authors the benefit of doubts when evidence is inconclusive. But Martin variously disparaged those comments as unconvincing, "broken-backed," "inglorious," or possibly ill-informed, and he neglected to indicate how far constructions more favorable to Herrick could be put on them.[1] However, he made one exception. It was for "Some *Johnson, Drayton,* or some *Herick,*" which is part of a line in *The Muses Dirge* (1625) by Richard James. Overimpressed by this remarkably early reference to poets such as Herrick as possible alternatives to poets like Ben Jonson and Michael Drayton, Martin went to the opposite extreme from his belittling and read into that rather vague mention amazingly favorable implications about Herrick's reputation in the 1620s. They are amazing because none of his poetry had reached print by 1625 and because its manuscript circulation can hardly have extended much, if at all, beyond a limited coterie. Moreoever, instead of quoting the full context of the line, Martin partly glossed over and partly misrepresented the passage in which it occurs. He did not identify Richard James or check his reliability and seriousness; and he did not consider how far credence could be placed in such a brief mention within a highly artificial, hyperbolic memorial dirge for King James I. Furthermore, it apparently did not occur to Martin that the passage was open to a quite different, less flattering, and more credible interpretation.

According to Martin, "Richard James, in *The Muses Dirge* (on the death of James I), tries to explain why the King had not been praised while he lived by some really well-known poet: 'Some *Johnson, Drayton,* or some *Herick.*' " Having thus given the false impression that Richard James refers to Herrick as a "really well-known poet," Martin transmogrified the bathos of the line, alleging (1) that it is the "most flattering public compliment that Herrick is known to have received" in the seventeenth century; (2) that it takes Herrick's abilities "for proven"; (3) that it puts him "on a footing with two of the most distinguished of Elizabethan veterans"; and (4) that it "is also part of the evidence that his contemporary reputation never stood higher than in the 1620's before he went into Devonshire." This is indeed a heavy load of significance to pile on one petty partial line! I will scrutinize it in context, detail various objections, present a more plausible interpretation, and reassess the evidence concerning Herrick's reputation and his contemporaries' reception of his work.

The Muses Dirge, Consecrated to the Remembrance of the High and Mightie Monarch, Iames. . . . Written by Richard Iames, Master of Arts and Preacher of Gods Word at Stoke Newington was composed and published in 1625 in the months that followed the king's death late in March of that year.[2] As my quotations will reveal, it is a pretentiously erudite, exhibitionistically witty, eulogistic profession of mourning that drags variants on conventional memorial sentiments through twelve pages of often awkward iambic pentameter couplets. To them the author appended a series of anagrams such as "King Iames: I am seeking." Obviously, a tribute to Herrick amid the hyperboles and extravagances of such an effusion may lack the reliability of sober prose statement. But Martin did not approach "Some *Johnson, Drayton,* or some *Herick*" with the skeptical attitude that led him to declare John Harmar's calling Herrick "second only to Apollo" "the kind of praise that convinces no one." Nevertheless, James's line needed such scrutiny. For in 1625, if anyone entertained the possibility that the line put Herrick "on a footing" with Jonson and Drayton, the notion must have seemed "the kind of praise that convinces no one." And if such a contemporary had recognized Herrick's name at all (which is unlikely), he could hardly have regarded the elevation of an obscure, unprinted Cambridge poet-priest to the level of such eminent authors as anything but incredible flattery or licentious poetic fantasy or simple irony.

However, Martin viewed the line as a sincere, credible, and representative opinion about Herrick's reputation in the 1620s. He not only interpreted it to mean that Herrick was "well-known" in 1625 but upheld it as only "part of the evidence" that Herrick's reputation was high—indeed at its lifetime peak—before he went to Devonshire. But the "evidence" Martin gave (on pages xxxiv–xl of his edition) for a high reputation before 1630 is exiguous and largely conjectural. What it adds up to is that by 1630, before he went to Devonshire, Herrick had written a considerable body of excellent poetry—perhaps his best—and that the existence today of a few manuscript copies shows it had some currency. All this may be granted; but at this point Martin's reasoning becomes circular, amounting to this: that the manuscript circulation must have been extensive because otherwise James's line could not mean that Herrick was "well-known" in 1625! In any case, Martin's argument can refer only to circulation up to about 1625. And other objections may be raised: only seven of Herrick's extant poems are datable by 1625;[3] no other references to this allegedly well-known poet are extant before 1648 apart from an abortive 1640 entry in the Stationers' Register and a few manuscript attributions; and if Herrick was so well known, one may well wonder why his poems did not reach print in the 1620s or soon thereafter. The conclusion that emerges is that

Richard James's allusion did not, as Martin claimed, voice a general opinion about Herrick's reputation. It is best regarded as a significantly early mention by an Oxford man who greatly admired and possibly knew Ben Jonson and who had probably become acquainted with Herrick or his works in that connection.

A critical opinion soberly voiced by Richard James probably deserves some respect.[4] He was the nephew of Bodley's first librarian, Thomas James, and in 1608 became a Scholar of Corpus Christi College, Oxford. He graduated M.A. in 1615 and in the following year was elected a Probationer Fellow of Corpus. In 1618, after taking holy orders, he traveled widely in Great Britain, visited Greenland, and went to Russia as chaplain to Sir Dudley Digges. Proficient in Hebrew, Latin, Greek, French, Spanish, and Italian, he also compiled an Anglo-Saxon dictionary and a Russian vocabulary. His extensive historical and theological writings include an erudite life of Thomas Becket and a defense of Sir John Oldcastle. He composed numerous poems in English and Latin. About 1624, when he became a Bachelor of Divinity, he and Patrick Young, the royal librarian, helped John Selden examine the Earl of Arundel's marble statues in preparation for Selden's *Marmora Arundeliana* (1628). Anthony à Wood describes him as "a very good Grecian, poet, an excellent critic, antiquary, divine, and admirably well skill'd in the Saxon and Gothic languages," but adds that he was "humorous"—that is, eccentric. Sir Simonds D'Ewes terms him an "atheistical, profane scholar, but otherwise witty, and moderately learned," and accuses him of betraying Sir Robert Cotton's trust in him. The fact that he describes himself on the title page of *The Muses Dirge* as "Preacher of God's Word at Stoke Newington" also arouses some suspicion, for he never held any cure of souls there. However, he seems to have been generally esteemed as a scholar, and Wood's commending him as an excellent critic was probably sound. Accordingly, if Richard James expressed a clear critical judgment of Herrick in a serious context, it would have some authority.

But the panegyric, hyperbolic, witty nature of *The Muses Dirge* makes one hesitate to accept any statement in it as valid documentary evidence. Moreover, the phrase that Martin found so significant occurs in a context of extreme poetic fantasy. Referring to the death of the king, Richard James asks,

> Shall no *Plebeian* Verse
> Adorne the Shrine of his diuiner Hearse?
> Shall not the Muses learned Pensill raise
> Some Monument to his immortal praise?

The poem then lauds the king's own writings and asks if *"Apolloes* Laureat Conclaue" will be too envious to bring "tributary Layes" in his praise. The answer is "Not so, nor so," for "Fames Vestall flames" will burn before the king's consecrated urn "Till Times last period." But why did not poets eulogize the king while he was still alive? Richard James gives no proper explanation, but he fantasizes conjectural reasons in a series of rhetorical questions: was it not because the Muses were stunned by the king's sun-like refulgence? Was it not because they were fearful that they could not do justice to his perfections?

> For wast not that the Muses stood at gaze
> Vpon that Sunne, whose splendor did amaze
> Their dazeled senses? Wast not that his life
> Within their doubtfull Iudgements rais'd a strife,
> And made their Consort to demurre at large,
> Before they durst to vndergoe this charge,
> Thinking their outward Varnish might deface
> His inward worth, perfection, forme, and grace[?]

Failing to understand this passage correctly, the typesetter put a semicolon after "grace" where I have supplied a question mark. Then, mistaking the next two couplets for questions, he put an interrogation mark after each of them. But as the syntax clearly requires commas in those positions, I have substituted them below in brackets after "liue" and "Mortalitie." In the first of these lines, "their" refers to the Muses, and "Had it not been," rather than beginning a question, is a laconism for *If it had not been for the fact that.*

> Had it not been their candor scornes to giue
> Fames Funeralls to Princes whilst they liue[,]
> Or that their Synode did desire to see

> The final Act of his Mortalitie[,]
> Some *Johnson, Drayton,* or some *Herick* would
> Before this time haue charactred the Mould
> Of his perfections; and in liuing Lines,
> Haue made them knowne before these mourning times.

In other words, if the Muses' high standards of purity and honesty
had not made them disdain to give living princes the tributes that
properly belong to the dead, or if the Muses had not wanted to see
the king's life fully acted out (so that it could be fittingly glorified
in verse), some Jonson or Drayton, or some Herick, would have
delineated the king's perfections and would have made them
known before these times of lamentation for his death.

The passage does not say that the king would have been
praised by "some really well-known poet" and then, as if to
elaborate that point, add "Some *Johnson, Drayton,* or some *Herick.*" That is Martin's interpretation. Because Jonson and Drayton
were indeed "well-known," he assumed that Richard James was
thinking only of well-known poets. And that is why Martin read
the line as putting Herrick "on a footing" with them and also as
partial evidence that Herrick had a peak reputation in the 1620s.
But a more obvious interpretation, and one more consonant with
other known facts, is that Richard James was making a contrast
between the two famous major poets and an obscure minor
one—just as, earlier, he had contrasted *"Plebeian* Verse" and
"the Muses learned Pensill." The meaning then is that, had it not
been for the Muses' scruples, some great and illustrious poets
such as Jonson and Drayton would have praised the living king
in living lines or at least some unknown minor poet such as
Herrick would have done so. In oral delivery this contrast would
be brought out by emphasizing the strong caesural pauses after
"Drayton" and *"Herick"* and by lowering the voice for "or some
Herick." In modern punctuation and spelling the passage might
read that, but for the Muses' scruples about the king,

> Some Jonson, Drayton—or some Herrick—would,
> Before this time, have charactered the mould
> Of his perfections, and, in living lines,
> Have made them known before these mourning times.

Though Martin greatly exaggerated Herrick's early reputation, he rightly recognized that Richard James pays a generous tribute to Herrick's competence as a poet. The passage explicitly credits not only Jonson and Drayton but also Herrick with ability to represent the royal perfections "in liuing lines." Surprisingly enough, Martin glossed over this, failing to quote it. However, it is noteworthy that the eulogist did not say that all three would have done equally well or put Herrick "on a footing" with the other two: such implications are possible but far from definite. Nevertheless, Richard James seems to have felt that, at least in some measure, the talents of the obscure Herrick were comparable to those of Jonson and Drayton. Obviously a eulogist of the king would never suggest that if great poets failed to praise him, hack writers or poetasters would have done so. Anyone who penned the royal perfections would have to be suitably talented. The implication is that Herrick had the necessary genius.

Accordingly it may be concluded that Richard James voices a personal laudatory judgment of Herrick. Though this private opinion, thus made public, is neither adequate nor partial evidence that in 1625 Herrick was well known or at his reputation's peak, it is evidence that a versatile, generally respected scholar, himself an able author, recognized Herrick's proficiency and promise as a poet. Thus rescued from Martin's extravagance, Richard James's passage is significant as a remarkably early perception of the competence of a little-known unprinted poet.

Even as Martin overinterpreted the importance of this earliest printed reference to Herrick, so he overly disparaged later ones. He could have conceded that beneath the hyperbole of Harmar's unconvincing "second only to Apollo" there was a recognition that Herrick had some claim to greatness. When *Naps upon Parnassus* (1658) declared Herrick the only Englishman (then alive) who "writes as well" as that "sour-ass" Horace, the compliment was indeed "broken-backed"; nevertheless the implication, though wry, is that Herrick could stand comparison with Horace. Edward Phillips undoubtedly mentioned Herrick "ingloriously" when he ranked him with Robert Heath and grudgingly granted that *Hesperides* had some merits despite "trivial passages." But

Martin could have noted that Phillips viewed Herrick as important enough to deserve a place in *Theatrum Poetarum*. Anthony à Wood's misclaiming Herrick for Oxford suggests what other sources indicate—that little was accurately known about the author of *Hesperides* and that its poems were more widely known than the name of the man who wrote them. Moreover, it must have been some awareness of the merits of the poetry that led Wood to try to add Herrick's luster to Oxford—as he also did in the case of Milton. Certainly Wood states with confidence that Herrick's poems "made him much admired in the time when they were published, especially by the generous and boon loyalists." Martin tried to cast doubt on this statement. But the fact that Wood was inaccurate about what college Herrick attended—information not readily gained in the seventeenth century—does not mean that he was also inaccurate about a matter on which he probably had direct knowledge—the reception of *Hesperides*.

Moreover, though the paucity of *printed* references to Herrick before the nineteenth century indicates that he was not well known, his reputation should not be confused with the reception of his poetry. The distinction is important because there is considerable evidence that many of Herrick's poems, usually without his name attached, did have attractions for his contemporaries in the 1650s, 1660s, and 1670s. As Earl Miner points out, "*Witts Recreations* included above sixty of his poems in editions of 1654, 1663, and 1667," and later.[5] And Martin himself records almost a hundred of Herrick's poems that were reprinted in twenty-eight collections between 1649 and 1674.[6] Moreover, Martin also records forty poems that occur in seventeenth-century manuscripts, one of them as many as twenty-four times;[7] and my own edition adds further instances.

All this is sufficient evidence to disprove allegations that *Hesperides* and *Noble Numbers* met with general indifference, that Herrick's reputation was higher in the 1620s than later in his life, and that his poetry found few readers and was generally neglected during the Restoration period. Martin's dictum, that much of what Herrick published in 1648 belonged to an earlier time and was not in tune with tastes then and later, is also open to some question. Obviously the end of the civil wars, just before the execution of Charles I and the setting up of the Commonwealth, was not a period when poetry was likely to meet with large sales and a warm reception. But there is no reason to believe that other verse that appeared in 1648 and 1649 sold better or was more timely—Beaumont's *Psyche*, Denham's *Cato Major* translation, John Hall's *Emblems* and *Satire against Presbytery*, Wither's *Prosopopeia Britannia*, Dryden's *Upon the Death of the Lord Hastings*, and Lovelace's *Lucasta*. Likewise, poetry published in the years 1650 through 1655 was hardly more attuned than Herrick's to Martin's notion of the then-prevalent taste; for example, Heath's *Clarastella*, Vaughan's *Silex Scintillans*, Cleveland's *Poems*, Davenant's *Gondibert*, Sherburne's *Salamacis*, Benlowes's *Theophila*, Basse's *Pastorals*, the Duchess of Newcastle's *Poems and Fancies*, and William Hammond's *Poems*.

However, there is a further argument on which Martin hinged his contentions that *Hesperides* was poorly received and that Herrick's poetry was neglected: "apparently," he asserted, "the edition of 1648 had not been sold out some twenty years after, when Peter Parker advertised *Hesperides* in a list of 'Books Printed and Sould' by him (under 'Books of Divinity')." But, for all we know, Parker may have had only one leftover copy. If there were more, they were not necessarily new ones: the loss of booksellers' stocks in the Great Fire of 1666 had been considerable; and it may well be that Peter Parker made up for his losses by purchasing the libraries of needy county gentlemen, or that he took the trouble to acquire a few leftover copies of *Hesperides* from the issue sold by "Thomas Hunt, Bookseller in Exon"—copies that perhaps were hidden away in Exeter after the defeat of the Royalists in that area and which might now find eager buyers in London. It is also possible that during the Interregnum some booksellers, fearful that they would be accused as Monarchists, had hidden copies of *Hesperides* and gradually brought them out for sale in the Restoration period. Indeed, the advertising, instead of indicating that the book was "neglected," may be proof that it was still in demand. Certainly in a period of revolution, restoration, fire, and plague, sales must have been erratic—especially sales of a volume so sympathetic to Royalism. With the return of the Royalists to power, it probably had a selling potential that was lacking when possible purchasers were in the countryside or exiled abroad, deprived of revenues and properties. Accordingly, it seems wisest to accept Wood's statement that the volume met with popularity on publication, especially among Royalists, and to conclude that it was no more "neglected" than other volumes of verse published in the late 1640s and in the 1650s. Moreover, the fact that a surprising number of copies survived the turbulent times and the Great Fire and are extant today suggests that the two issues in 1648 were large. In short, Martin went too far on exiguous evidence in claiming a high reputation for Herrick in the 1620s; too far in alleging that *Hesperides* met with unqualified "neglect"; too far in undervaluing his own demonstration that Herrick's poems were often copied and were frequently printed and reprinted in collections throughout his lifetime; and too far in belittling the admittedly infrequent comments on Herrick in the seventeenth century.

Though "neglected" is too strong a term for the reception of Herrick's poetry by his contemporaries, its greatness was inadequately recognized while he lived and for more than two hundred years after his death. The simplest explanation is that he published too late—in the middle of a revolutionary period when it was difficult for literary compositions to find an audience. (Controversial tracts were another matter.) When *Hesperides* reached the London bookstalls, "literary circles" hardly existed to provide discussions and to disseminate a reputation; such groups had been broken up by the Revolution. If, like Herbert, Cowley, Carew, Waller, Davenant, and Quarles, Herrick had come into print in the 1630s or early 1640s, his verse could have been better appreciated. But publication at an inopportune time does not afford the full explanation: other poets seem to have fared better during the revolutionary years. For example, Sir John Denham's *Coopers Hill* was published in 1642, 1643, 1650, 1655, and 1709—as well as being latinized in 1675. Volumes of poetry by Henry Vaughan reached print in 1646, 1650, 1651, 1652, 1655, and 1679. And works by Edward Benlowes appeared variously in

1636, 1645, 1649, 1652, 1657, 1672, and 1673. These facts suggest that, for a poet who desired fame, Herrick made three major but related mistakes: his reputation would have fared better if he had begun to publish in the 1630s; if, instead of crowding almost fourteen-hundred poems into one volume, he had issued a series of thinner books; and if he had been more selective about what he put into print and had placed his best work more prominently. It seems probable that if in the 1630s he had published about a hundred and fifty of his best lyrics, that volume would have met with acclaim and would have laid the foundations for a reputation that would have grown as three or four other volumes appeared at intervals. Instead, Herrick put all of his literary eggs into one basket and took it to market at the worst possible time. Moreover, the poems in *Hesperides* are unequal and so arranged that the merits of the better ones are not immediately visible. *"The Argument of his Book"* (H-1) could impress a bookstore browser, but not many of the poems that immediately follow it would arouse an urge to buy or read further: H-2 (*"To his Muse"*), the four poems H-3, H-4, H-5, and H-7 (*"To his Booke"*), and H-6 (*"To the soure Reader"*) are tongue-in-cheek compositions without beauty or notable distinction. Although quality improves thereafter, there is much that is trivial and shallow: excellence is only intermittent in the sequence. It is not hard to see that Edward Phillips cursorily examined the volume and was led to couple Herrick with Heath and to object to "trivial passages." It is also not hard to conceive that the volume would have been better received if the *Argument* had been followed with H-83, *"Delight in Disorder"*; H-90, *"His Cavalier"*; H-106, *"A Country life: To his Brother"*; H-128, *"His fare-well to Sack"*; H-133, *"The Eye"*; H-149, *"An Epithalamie to Sir* Thomas Southwell *and his Ladie"*; H-178, *"Corinna's going a Maying"*; and the like. Herrick's merits might well have overcome the unfortunate circumstances of his publication date and would have been more justly recognized thereafter if he had presented his materials more attractively. Even today, one gains a better sense of Herrick's greatness from a good anthology than one does initially from trying to cope with the 1648 volume. This does not mean, of course, that a reader who gains a fuller familiarity will not change his mind. For then he may come to recognize a grand design in *Hesperides* and that what at first seemed trivia or bathos has a function within its total excellence. Had the volume appeared in a peaceful, prosperous period when readers had time to savor it, the barriers of seeming trivialities, bathos, and hodgepodge arrangement would probably have been surmounted; then Herrick would not have had to wait almost three centuries to gain the high esteem he expected and so richly deserved.

This dictum gives rise to a final question. Despite his reiterated confidence in future fame, was Herrick disheartened by lukewarm reception of his volume? The fact that no later poetry by him is known to be extant does suggest that his disappointed muse stopped singing. But that seems unlikely. It may be that weak eyesight and health hindered him from writing down his new inventions. Perhaps he continued to compose lyrics but, like Marvell, made no effort to get them into print. His later verse may have ended as kindling for fires or wrapping for fish. But further manuscripts may still turn up; and remembering how brilliantly Milton wrote in his old age, we may hope that a *New Hesperides* will be among them. And if we also remember that Milton retained works from his earlier years and published them much later, we may also remember what no one seems to have mentioned—that Herrick must have been a capable Latin scholar who, inevitably in the seventeenth century, composed Latin poems, probably many of them. Indeed, it is not impossible that it was some of those Latin poems that were known to Richard James and led him to assert that if some Jonson or Drayton had not sung the praises of King James I, Herrick could have done so, in living lines—of Latin!

NOTES

1. *The Poetical Works of Robert Herrick*, ed. L. C. Martin (Oxford, 1956), "Introduction," pp. xvii–xix. Unless otherwise noted, all quotations below are taken from these pages. However, quotations from Herrick and the key numbers attached to them derive from *The Complete Poetry of Robert Herrick*, ed. J. Max

Patrick (New York, 1963); the pagination and key numbers are the same in the paperback editions of this text published by Anchor Books and by W. W. Norton and Co.

2. It was printed by A. M[atthews] and J. N[orton] for J. Browne. *The Muses Dirge* consists of 278 lines on pp. 1–12, and it is followed by three pages of anagrams, in Latin and English, on "King James" and "Jacobus Rex." My quotations are from the original edition.

3. In approximate chronological order they are H-106, "*A Country Life* . . . "; H-818, "*To my dearest Sister* . . . "; S-12, "Parkinson's *shade* . . . "; H-140, "*An Epithalamie* . . . "; H-590, "*To his Brother in Law* . . . "; S-4, "*Master Herrick's Farewell* . . . "; and H-319, "*A New-yeares gift*. . . . " (In the footnote to H-245, "*To the High and Noble Prince, Duke, Marquesse, and Earle of* Buckingham," I erred in identifying the duke as George Villiers rather than as his son. Accordingly the poem is a late composition.)

4. Biographical information about James is available in the *Dictionary of National Biography*, in the introduction to his *Iter Lancastrense*, edited by Thomas Corser for the Chetham Society in 1845, and in A. B. Grosart's edition of *The Poems of Richard James* (London, 1880). The information and quotations in the following paragraph derive from Corser's introduction.

5. *The Cavalier Mode from Jonson to Cotton* (Princeton, 1971), p. 161.

6. Pp. xxiv–xxvii.

7. Pp. xxvii–xxxi.

TED-LARRY PEBWORTH
with A. Leigh DeNeef, Dorothy Lee, James E. Siemon,
and Claude J. Summers

Selected and Annotated Bibliography

Herrick scholarship has reached such impressive dimensions that there is now need for an annotated, selective bibliography. Although useful in various ways, the three most recent bibliographical efforts are, for differing reasons, all unsatisfactory. The Tannenbaum bibliography is unannotated, indiscriminately arranged, often enigmatic, and frequently inaccurate.[1] Guffey's supplement to it, also unannotated, is incomplete and omits reviews. Hageman's study, valuable for its discussion of recent criticism, occasionally misleads in its annotations; and its unannotated lists include works containing only passing references to Herrick or—in a few instances—no mention of him at all.

The present bibliographers have tried to avoid such shortcomings. They have carefully checked all previous bibliographies of Herrick and have attempted to locate, examine, and annotate each book, dissertation, article, and note containing Herrick materials. In addition, they have made every effort to discover items overlooked by previous bibliographers. From the resulting master list,[2] the compiling editor has selected the entries to be included here. Space limitations have necessitated the exclusion of certain kinds of works: manuscript miscellanies containing Herrick poems; anthologized selections; M.A. theses; poetic tributes to Herrick; Herrick listings in standard bibliographies of English literature; brief notices in literary histories, dictionaries, and encyclopedias; and unanswered periodical queries which do not themselves contain significant information. Other categories have been restricted. The only editions included (Section I) are those of particular textual or historical interest, and the only bibliographies included (Section II) are those which have not been entirely superseded by later lists.

In the area of scholarship and criticism, much more selectivity has been exercised among those items written prior to 1910 (Section IIIA) than among those works written since that year (Section IIIB). With a

237

few notable exceptions (as indicated in the annotations), the studies of the earlier period are primarily of historical interest, charting the vicissitudes of Herrick's reputation—and of popular taste—during the seventeenth, eighteenth, and nineteenth centuries. Only in the second decade of the twentieth century did important scholarship begin to appear in quantity, heralded by the critical studies of Delattre and Moorman and spurred by the latter's scholarly edition; and in the last thirty years, Herrick scholarship and criticism have noticeably quickened in pace and deepened in perception. Their way pointed by Brooks and Musgrove and their task aided immeasurably by the editions of Martin and Patrick, scholar-critics of the present generation have made major contributions to an identification of Herrick's complex achievement and an understanding of it. Section IIIB is, consequently, the most inclusive and the most fully annotated part of this bibliography. Even some insignificant works, if they appear in obscure books or periodicals, have been included, in order to save scholars the effort of locating copies only to find the items disappointing.

In addition to producing books and articles, scholar-critics during the last several decades have also written notes explicating individual poems, discussing their texts, and identifying their sources. For convenience these separately published notes on individual poems are grouped together, by poem title, as Section IV; and to conserve space, only those items with enigmatic titles are annotated. It should be stressed, however, that commentaries on individual poems and *explications de texte* are also to be found in the books and essays of Section III.

For book-length works exclusively or largely devoted to Herrick, selected reviews are cited. Although space limitations prohibit their annotation here, many of these reviews make important critical statements and should be consulted. Critical and scholarly controversies are cross-referenced. The abbreviations used are those sanctioned in the *MLA International Bibliography* "Master List and Table of Abbreviations."

The editors thank Professors Paul Crapo and Michael Palencia-Roth, The University of Michigan–Dearborn, and Mrs. Nina Orr, Farmington, Michigan, for their aid in the translation of items in foreign languages. The assistance of the following libraries is also gratefully acknowledged: The University of Michigan Libraries, Dearborn and Ann Arbor; Wayne State University Library; University of Detroit Library; University of Washington Library; the Libraries of the University of California at Los Angeles, including The Clark Library; Duke University Library; University of North Carolina Library; North Carolina State University Library;

the Regenstein Library of The University of Chicago; The Newberry Library, Chicago; and The Folger Shakespeare Library, Washington, D.C.

NOTES

1. Instances of erroneous publication information are too numerous to detail here, but it should be noted that items 375 and 844 refer to works on the American novelist Robert Herrick. The Tannenbaums are not the only bibliographers who have made that error, however; one finds it in the *MHRA* bibliography for 1955–56 (item 5025), the *PMLA* bibliography for 1965 (item 4461), the *SP* bibliography for 1965 (item E867), and Guffey's supplement to Tannenbaum (item 058).

2. A bound xerographic copy of all items annotated by the present bibliographers is available through interlibrary loan from The University of Michigan–Dearborn Library, 4901 Evergreen Road, Dearborn, Michigan 48128. Request Pebworth et al., *An Annotated Bibliography of Robert Herrick: Master List*.

I. Significant Editions
(Arranged Chronologically)

Hesperides: or, The Works Both Humane & Divine of Robert Herrick Esq. London: for John Williams and Francis Eglesfield, 1648. [A variant title page adds "and are to be sold by *Tho: Hunt*, Book-seller in *Exon*."]

Rpt. in facsimile, Menston, England: Scolar, 1969.

Contains 1,130 unnumbered poems in the *Hesperides* section; 272 unnumbered poems in the *Noble Numbers* section, the latter separately paged and bearing a title page dated 1647. Copies described in several modern editions of Herrick, but see also J. P. Collier, *A Bibliographical and Critical Account of the Rarest Books in the English Language.* London: Joseph Lilly, 1865, II, 129–30; Thomas Corser, *Collectanea Anglo-Poetica.* London: for the Chetham Society, 1877, Pt. 7, pp. 200–08; C. P. Phinn and Alfred W. Pollard, *The Library*, NS 4 (1903), 206–12, 328–31; W. F. Prideaux, *N&Q*, 10th Ser. 4 (1905), 482–83; and Thomas J. Wise, *The Ashley Library.* London: privately printed, 1922, II, 179–80.

Select Poems from the Hesperides or Works both Human and Divine of Robert Herrick, Esq. Ed. J. N[ott]. Bristol: J. M. Gutch; London: Longman and I. Miller, [1810].

First independent publication of Herrick after 1648. Contains 284 poems.

Review: [Barron Field], *Quarterly Review*, 4 (1810), 165–76. On the authorship of this review, see Peter Cunningham, "Herrick and Southey," *N&Q*, 1st Ser. 10 (1854), 27.

The Works of Robert Herrick. Ed. with a Biographical Notice by Thomas Maitland (Lord Dundrennan). 2 vols. Edinburgh: W. and C. Tait, 1823.

First "complete" edition of Herrick after 1648.

Hesperides, or Works both Human and Divine by Robert Herrick, Esq. With a Biographical Notice by S[amuel] W[eller] S[inger]. 2 vols. London: Pickering, 1846.

Rpt. Boston: Little Brown; New York: J. S. Dickerson et al., 1856.

A poor edition with a memoir paraphrased from Maitland's edition, above; but the reprint constitutes the first American edition of Herrick.

Review (of the reprint): F. M. Hubbard, *North American Review*, 84 (1857), 484–501.

Hesperides: The Poems and Other Remains of Robert Herrick Now First Collected. Ed. W. Carew Hazlitt. Library of Old Authors. 2 vols. London: John Russell Smith, 1869.

First edition to include uncollected MS and early printed poems; prints fourteen letters by Herrick to his uncle William (written between 1613 and 1617).

Review: *Every Saturday*, 8 (1869), 378–80.

The Complete Poems of Robert Herrick. Ed. Alexander B. Grosart. Early English Poets. 3 vols. London: Chatto and Windus, 1876.

Dedicated to Swinburne. Biographical and critical introductions; text of 1647–48 with original italics, capitalization, and punctuation. An influential edition, but careless in detail and occasionally misleading in the biographical information.

Reviews: *Saturday Review*, 42 (1876), 576–77; Edmund Gosse, *The Academy*, 10 (1876), 513–15; *Athenaeum*, 7 July 1877, pp. 7–9.

The Hesperides and Noble Numbers. Ed. Alfred Pollard with a preface by A. C. Swinburne. The Muses' Library. 2 vols. London: Lawrence and Bullen; New York: Scribner's, 1891. Rev. ed., 1898.

Contains some commentary and a few variants from early printed texts; first edition to number the poems (*Hesperides* and *Noble Numbers* separately) according to their order of appearance in 1647–48; some of the epigrams moved to the end of vol. 2. W. F. Prideaux suggested textual corrections in *N&Q*, 8th Ser. 1 (1892), 290. Swinburne's impressionistic preface, calling Herrick "the greatest song-writer—as surely as Shakespeare is the greatest dramatist—ever born of English race," is rpt. in his *Studies in Prose and Poetry*. London: Chatto and Windus, 1894, pp. 44–48 (see J. M. Robertson, Section IIIA).

Reviews: A. T. Q[uiller] C[ouch], *Speaker*, 16 January 1892, pp. 82–84; *Spectator*, 68 (1892), 238–40; *Athenaeum*, 23 July 1892, pp. 124–25; *Nation*, 54 (1892), 217; *Saturday Review*, 100 (1905), 560–61.

The Poetical Works of Robert Herrick. Ed. George Saintsbury. The Aldine Edition of the British Poets. 2 vols. London: G. Bell and Sons, 1893.

Contains a biography and a critical introduction; numbers the poems consecutively through *Hesperides* and *Noble Numbers;* lists variants and appends poems attributed to Herrick but not in the 1647–48 edition. Introduction rpt. as "Robert Herrick" in *The Literary Era*, 1 (1894), 25.

Review: *Saturday Review*, 77 (1894), 50–51.

The Poetical Works of Robert Herrick. Ed. F. W. Moorman. Oxford English Texts. 2 vols. Oxford: Clarendon Press, 1915.

Rpt., with a prefatory note by Percy Simpson, but without textual notes, as a single volume edition in the Oxford English Poets series, London and New York: Oxford University Press, 1921.

Introduction surveys the MS and early printed versions of Herrick's poems; text contains poems not found in *Hesperides* or *Noble Numbers;* does not number the poems. The standard edition for forty years. O. W. F. Lodge calls attention to a misprint, *TLS*, 17 June 1915, p. 206; and Moorman agrees, *TLS*, 24 June 1915, p. 214.

Reviews: *Nation*, 101 (1915), 206; *Living Age*, 286 (1915), 802–07; F. S. Boas, *MLR*, 12 (1917), 89–93; Solomon Eagle (pseud. for J. C. Squire), *Books in General*. 1st Ser. New York: Knopf, 1919, pp. 121–26; [Edmund C. Blunden], *TLS*, 18 August 1921, p. 528, rpt. in Blunden's *Votive Tablets*. London: Cobden-Sanderson, 1931, pp. 70–76; *The Observer*, 4 September 1921, p. 4.

The Poetical Works of Robert Herrick. Ed. L. C. Martin. Oxford English Texts. Oxford: Clarendon Press, 1956.

Rpt., without commentary and with only a few textual notes, as *The Poems of Robert Herrick*. Oxford Standard Authors. London and New York: Oxford University Press, 1965.

Informative introduction in the fuller version surveying the textual problems; poems not numbered, but paged exactly as in Moorman's edition; elaborate critical notes and commentary. A definitive edition, but too uncritical in assigning several MS poems to Herrick (see Ditsky, Section IIIB), and occasionally faulty in the text.

Reviews: Harold Nicholson, *The Observer*, 25 March 1956, p. 16; *The Listener*, 55 (1956), 727; Ray L. Armstrong, *SCN*, 14 (1956), 7–8; Pierre Legouis, *EA*, 10 (1957), 152–54; Vivian de Sola Pinto, *MLR*, 52 (1957), 259–60; Frank Kermode, *RES*, NS 9 (1958), 78–82; Rhodes Dunlap, *MP*, 56 (1958), 65–67.

The Complete Poetry of Robert Herrick. Ed. J. Max Patrick. The Anchor Seventeenth-Century Series. Garden City, N. Y.: Doubleday, 1963.

Rpt. in the Stuart Editions. New York: New York University Press, 1963. Rpt., with a new foreword, New York: Norton, 1968.

Excellent brief introduction; copious explanatory notes, in each case following the text of the poem; textual notes; the poems of *Hesperides* and *Noble Numbers* numbered separately. An excellent edition for both the general reader and the serious scholar.

Reviews: Ray L. Armstrong, *SCN*, 21 (1963), 13–14; *TLS*, 30 August 1963, p. 658; Karl Josef Höltgen, *Anglia*, 84 (1966), 232–33.

II. Bibliographies and Concordances
(Arranged Chronologically)

Thomson, John. "Indexes to the First Lines and to the Subjects of the Poems of Robert Herrick." *Bulletin of the Free Library of Philadelphia,* No. 3 (August 1901).

May be used only with the 1856 Little Brown edition of *Hesperides* (Section I). Contains little in the subject index that cannot be found in MacLeod's concordance.

Cox, E. Marion. "Notes on the Bibliography of Herrick." *The Library,* 3rd Ser. 8 (1917), 105–19.

Describes the two states of the 1647–48 volume and the extant copies; lists the publication data on those poems which appeared separately; tabulates the editions of Herrick which have appeared since 1648. The lists are incomplete.

MacLeod, Malcolm. *A Concordance to the Poems of Robert Herrick.* New York: Oxford University Press, 1936.

Originally done as a Ph.D. dissertation, University of Virginia. Based on Moorman's 1915 edition, but may be used with Martin's and Patrick's editions. Contains an analysis of Herrick's vocabulary and a tabulation of word usage in the poems.

Tannenbaum, Samuel A. and Dorothy R. *Robert Herrick (A Concise Bibliography).* Elizabethan Bibliographies No. 40. New York: Elizabethan Bibliographies, 1949.

Rpt. in *Elizabethan Bibliographies*, III. Port Washington, N.Y.: Kennikat, 1967.

Carelessly compiled; incomplete information in several entries; some unverifiable items; erroneous details throughout; no annotations.

Guffey, George Robert. "Robert Herrick: 1949–1965." *Elizabethan Bibliographies Supplements*, III. London: Nether Press, 1968.

Items listed by year of publication; incomplete and unannotated; does not list reviews.

Hageman, Elizabeth H. "Recent Studies in Herrick." *ELR*, 3 (1973), 462–71.

A bibliographical article surveying editions and biographical, scholarly, and critical studies. Incomplete and occasionally misleading; errors of fact in a few of the annotations, but an important and useful compilation.

III. Scholarship and Criticism

A. BEFORE 1910

Aldrich, Thomas B. "Robert Herrick, the Man and the Poet." *Century Magazine*, 59 (1900), 678–88.

Excerpted in *Current Literature*, 28 (1900), 151–53. Expanded in *Ponkapog Papers*. Boston: Houghton Mifflin, 1903, pp. 153–95.

Questions the depth of Herrick's religious verse; sees the best secular lyrics as faultless in form but lacking in passion and insight; notes a paradoxical combination of remoteness and nearness in his best poems.

Anon. "Dii Minorum Gentium, No. 1: Carew and Herrick." *Blackwood's Magazine*, 45 (1839), 782–94.

A general comparative article concluding that Carew is the better poet. Notes Herrick's "strange sensuality" and his want of refinement; charges that his poems lack emotion.

———. "A Poet of Spring." *Temple Bar*, 111 (1897), 26–41.

Follows Swinburne in calling Herrick the greatest Elizabethan song-writer; relates his poetry to the school of Jonson and to classical authors; notes a persistent sense of loss and time.

————. "Robert Herrick." *Edinburgh Review*, 199 (1904), 109–27.

A review article on four editions of Herrick. A major early statement on Herrick's polish, erudition, and seriousness. Tannenbaum (item 850) identifies the author as C. F. Warre.

Ashe, T. "Robert Herrick." *Temple Bar*, 68 (1883), 120–32.

Rpt. in *Living Age*, 157 (1883), 485–91.

A general "appreciation" which sees the poems as both delicate and disgusting. Discusses Herrick's naive simplicity, his "manly honesty," and his interweaving of humor and melancholy.

Beeching, H. C. "The Poetry of Herrick." *National Review*, 40 (1903), 788–99.

Argues that the best of Herrick's secular verse was written before 1629. Disagrees with Gosse's disparagement of *Noble Numbers,* seeing in the sacred poetry a sincere, practical religion, though one devoid of rapture.

B[ullen], A[rthur] H. "Robert Herrick." *Dictionary of National Biography*. London: Smith, Elder and Company, 1891.

Incomplete, but basic. Contains general critical comments, a bibliography of editions, and some account of separately published poems.

De la Mare, Walter. "Robert Herrick." *Bookman* (London), 34 (May 1908), 51–56.

Biography and critical comment, noting a lack of profundity in Herrick but recognizing delicacy and grace in the poems. Illustrated with photographs and drawings.

Deshler, Charles D. *Afternoons with the Poets*. New York: Harper, 1879, pp. 133–37.

Calls Herrick the best lyricist of the Jacobean era, remarkable for his perfect structures, his airy thought, graceful expression, brevity, joy, and variety.

Drake, Nathan. "On the Life, Writings and Genius of Robert Herrick." *Literary Hours; or, Sketches, Critical, Narrative, and Poetical.* London: for T. Cadell and W. Davies, 1804, III, 25–88.

The first important scholarly evaluation of Herrick. Attributes the neglect of the poet to his unevenness. Praises Herrick as a master of language and versification. Still valuable.

Gosse, Edmund W. "Robert Herrick." *Cornhill Magazine,* 32 (August 1875), 176–91.

Rpt. in *Living Age,* 127 (1875), 285–94, and in Gosse's *Seventeenth-Century Studies.* London: Kegan Paul, Trench, 1883, pp. 111–40.

Critical biography stressing Herrick's wit, imagination, and variety in meter. Argues the influence of Martial and Jonson. Still a worthwhile study, but see Beeching.

Granger, J. *A Biographical History of England.* London: for T. Davies, 1769, I, 496.

A catalogue of engraved British heads giving locations of the portraits and biographical details. Notes the 1648 *Hesperides* frontispiece and comments briefly and in general terms on Herrick's poetry.

Hale, Edward Everett, Jr. *Die Chronologische Anordnung der Dichtungen Robert Herricks.* Halle: Kaemmerer, 1892.

An inaugural dissertation. Takes issue with Grosart's chronology of Herrick's poems and offers a slightly different one. Concerned with the underlying principles of dating lyric poetry.

Hearn, Lafcadio. "Notes on Robert Herrick." *Interpretations of Literature.* Ed. John Erskine. New York: Dodd Mead, 1929, II, 118–38.

Re-creation of a lecture given at Tokyo University sometime between 1896 and 1902. A close analysis of Herrick's style and philosophy; argues a similarity with Japanese verse.

Henley, William E. "Herrick: His Muse, His Moral, His Piety." *Views and Reviews.* London: David Nutt, 1890, pp. 112–15.

Appreciative remarks on the clarity of vision, the detailed description, and the emphasis on transiency in *Hesperides;* the sincerity, grace, and Spanish quality of *Noble Numbers.*

I., W. F. Query regarding Herrick. *Gentleman's Magazine,* 66 (1796), 384–85. Answered by "Eugenio," ibid., pp. 461–62; "Leviter Eruditus," ibid., pp. 545–46; and O. D., ibid., p. 736.

An exchange important to the nineteenth-century revival of interest in Herrick.

Macdonald, George. *England's Antiphon.* London: Macmillan, 1868, pp. 163–71.

Noble Numbers placed in the context of the history of English religious poetry. Stresses the uneven quality of Herrick's verse, but concentrates on the humor, tenderness, and homely detail.

Morton, Edward Payson. "Robert Herrick." *MLN,* 21 (1906), 96.

Calls attention to a Herrick reference in *Naps upon Parnassus* (1658).

N[ichols], J. "Letters of Robert Herrick the Poet." *Gentleman's Magazine,* 67 (1797), 102–03.

Records a note of debt and the text of two letters from the poet to his uncle, Sir William Hearick [*sic*].

Palgrave, F. T. "Robert Herrick." *Macmillan's Magazine,* 35 (1877), 475–81.

Rpt. in *Living Age,* 133 (1877), 349–54, and in Palgrave, ed. *Chrysomela.* London: Macmillan, 1877.

A general essay placing Herrick among his predecessors and contemporaries, but noting his uniqueness. Argues that his classicism derives from his simplicity, sanity, insight, sincerity, and grace.

Phillips, Edward. *Theatrum Poetarum.* London: for Charles Smith, 1675, Pt. II, p. 162.

Notes Herrick as a poet of about the same fame as Robert Heath; finds the pastoral qualities in his poems to be their most pleasing feature.

Pollard, Alfred W. "Herrick and His Friends." *Macmillan's Magazine,* 67 (1892), 142–48.

Rpt. in *Living Age,* 196 (1893), 220–26, and in Pollard's *Old Picture Books.* London: Methuen, 1902, pp. 200–15.

A survey of Herrick's life and a discussion of his patrons and the people mentioned in his poems.

————. "Herrick Sources and Illustrations." *The Modern Quarterly of Language and Literature,* 1 (1898), 175–84.

Detailed notes on 112 Herrick sources, not all of which have made their way into modern editions.

————. "A Poet's Studies." *Old Picture Books.* London: Methuen, 1902, pp. 216–26.

A survey of Herrick's indebtedness to classical and contemporary writers as evidence of his conscious artistry.

Reed, Edward B. "Herrick's Indebtedness to Ben Jonson." *MLN,* 17 (1902), 478–83.

Concentrates on Herrick's formal imitations of Jonson.

Robertson, J. M. "Herrick." *Criticisms.* London: A. and H. Bradlaugh Bonner, 1902, pp. 1–13.

A judicious answer to Swinburne's introductory essay in the Pollard edition of Herrick (Section I).

Saintsbury, George. *A History of Elizabethan Literature.* London: Macmillan, 1891.

Expresses the usual Victorian distaste for Herrick's epigrams; but praises *Hesperides,* which he does not find pagan, and *Noble Numbers,* which he does not find insincere.

————. *A History of English Prosody.* London: Macmillan, 1908. 2nd ed., 1923.

Rpt. New York: Russell and Russell, 1961.

A brief discussion of the characteristics of Herrick's prosody.

Southey, Robert. *Southey's Common-Place Book.* 4th Ser. Ed. John Wood Warter. London: Longman, 1850, pp. 303–05.

A severe attack on Herrick as a coarse-minded writer of trash whose emblem should be "a stinking cabbage-leaf" and who is wholly undeserving of the reputation he has attained.

Swinburne, A. C. See Pollard's edition of Herrick, Section I.

Warre, C. F. See Anon., *Edinburgh Review*.

Weatherly, Cecil. "Robert Herrick." *The Spirit Lamp*, 10 March 1893, pp. 67–71.

> Largely an appreciative essay, but with useful reminders of Herrick's wide range and rhythmic variety.

Winstanley, William. "Robert Herric [*sic*]." *The Lives of the Most Famous English Poets*. London: for Samuel Manship, 1687.

> Rpt. in facsimile, with an introduction by William Riley Parker, Gainesville, Florida: Scholar's Facsimiles and Reprints, 1963, pp. 166–67.

> Not a life, but rather a brief assessment of the poems; Herrick called "one of the Scholars of the middle Form."

Wood, Anthony à. "Robert Heyrick [*sic*]." *Athenae Oxonienses*. London: for Thomas Bennet, 1691. Ed. Philip Bliss. London: for F. C. and J. Rivington et al., 1813, III, cols. 250–52.

> Mistakenly discusses Herrick as an Oxford alumnus; notes that *Hesperides* and *Noble Numbers* made Herrick "much admired in the time when they were published," especially among Royalists. Wood's account corrected by Bliss, who praises *Hesperides* and applauds its revival.

B. SINCE 1910

Aiken, Pauline. "The Influence of the Latin Elegists on English Lyric Poetry, 1600–1650." *University of Maine Studies*, 2nd Ser. No. 22. Orono: University of Maine, 1932.

> One of the two fullest studies of Herrick's indebtedness to the Latin elegiac traditions (see McEuen); marred by not always recognizing Herrick's innovations.

> Review: Henry W. Prescott, *MP*, 30 (1932), 109–10.

Allen, Don Cameron. "Herrick's 'Rex Tragicus.' " *Studies in Honor of DeWitt T. Starnes*. Ed. Thomas P. Harrison et al. Austin: University of Texas Press, 1967, pp. 215–25.

Rpt. in Allen's *Image and Meaning: Metaphoric Traditions in Renaissance Poetry*. Enlarged ed. Baltimore: Johns Hopkins University Press, 1968, pp. 138–51.

Sees Herrick's poem as contemplating the Passion as spectacle and theatre; notes that the surprising comparison of Christ with Roscius, the great Roman comedian, may draw upon a rich tradition which transformed tragedy into comedy and saw Christ as the first of the "fools in Christ."

Asals, Heather. "King Solomon in the Land of *Hesperides*." *TSLL*, 18 (1976), 362–80.

Finds that biblical proverb, common proverb, and classical epigram figure in individual poems and in the total conception of *Hesperides*. Argues that Herrick borrows and transforms materials from the Solomonic books: Proverbs, Ecclesiastes, and the Canticles.

Ault, Norman. See Edward N. Hooker.

Bateson, F. W. *English Poetry and the English Language*. Oxford: Clarendon Press, 1934.

2nd ed. New York: Russell and Russell, 1961.

Brief discussion of *"Delight in Disorder,"* concluding that the poem is "essentially a plea for paganism."

Beer, David F. " 'The Countries Sweet Simplicity': Devonshire Life in the Poetry of Robert Herrick." Diss. New Mexico, 1972. *DAI*, 33 (1972), 2884A.

Relates Herrick's poems to the people, practices, and situations of Dean Prior and its surroundings. Stresses the realistic homeliness of those poems which deal with country life, a style allegedly reflecting the poet's real experiences in Devon.

Belgion, Montgomery. See C. S. Lewis.

Berman, Ronald. "Herrick's Secular Poetry." *ES*, 52 (1971), 20–30.

Rpt. in *Ben Jonson and the Cavalier Poets*. Ed. Hugh Maclean. New York: Norton, 1974, pp. 529–40.

Sees Herrick as having a "hieroglyphick" method, recognizing that all things are related and exist in correspondence to each other. Finds that in *Hesperides* the transitoriness of human beauty contrasts with the perfected beauty of the divine, making the concern with nature and mutability not pagan, but orthodox in reaching the reality beyond appearances. Important.

Boss, Judith E. "Robert Herrick's Epigrams and *Noble Numbers*." Diss. Texas Christian, 1971. *DAI*, 32 (1972), 4553A.

Emphasizes the Christian tenor of Herrick's work, seeing it as more Anglican than pagan in its eclecticism. Argues that Herrick's poetry gains depth through its use of allegorical and microcosmic correspondences.

Briggs, K. M. *The Anatomy of Puck*. London: Routledge and Kegan Paul, 1959.

Brief discussion of Herrick's fairy poems.

Broadbent, J. B. *Poetic Love*. London: Chatto and Windus, 1964.

Rpt. New York: Barnes and Noble, 1965.

Herrick categorized as a decadent Spenserian whose love poems lack sexuality; finds their "pretty lewdness" boring.

Bronson, Bertrand. "Literature and Music." *Relations of Literary Study*. Ed. James Thorp. New York: Modern Language Association, 1967, pp. 127–50.

Points out Herrick's experimentations with the ballad form in his skillful use of hold and pause and in his introduction of additional rhymes and extra feet. Concludes that "Herrick, for all his fastidious classicism, was in familiar touch with the popular singing tradition."

Brooks, Cleanth. *Modern Poetry and the Tradition*. Chapel Hill: University of North Carolina Press, 1939.

A note on Herrick's use of sheer verbal wit in two poems, illustrating the convergence of the two so-called "schools" of Donne and Jonson.

———. "What Does Poetry Communicate?" *The Well Wrought Urn*. New York: Harcourt, 1947, pp. 62–69.

A seminal essay on "Corinna's *going a Maying*" as a complex May-Day rite. Still the best study of this major poem. (See Roy Harvey Pearce.)

Bush, Douglas. *English Literature in the Earlier Seventeenth Century, 1600–1660.* Oxford: Clarendon Press, 1945.

2nd ed., rev., 1962.

A valuable general summary of Herrick's characteristics, emphasizing the seriousness of his poetry, its tensions, and its instinctive ceremonialism. Some significant reappraisals in the second edition.

———. *Mythology and the Renaissance Tradition in English Poetry.* Minneapolis: University of Minnesota Press, 1932.

Rev. ed., New York: Norton, 1963.

Argues that Herrick domesticates mythology with an abundance of realism, but finds his mythological figures less alive and more literary than Drayton's.

Cain, T. G. S. "The Bell/White MS: Some Unpublished Poems." *ELR,* 2 (1972), 260–70.

Discussion of a miscellany of seventeenth-century poetry in which Herrick is represented by some works which may be imitations and by a previously unattributed poem entitled "Herrack [*sic*] on a Kisse to his M^{rs}."

———. "Herrick." *EIC,* 26 (1976), 156–68.

Review article on the books by Scott, Deming, and DeNeef. Contains some important correctives.

———. "The Poetry of Robert Herrick." Diss. Cambridge, 1972.

Finds beneath the grace of *Hesperides* a persistent concern with human transience which the book as a whole is designed to counter through the exploitation of such strategies as the enduring nature of poetry, the stasis of ceremony, the continuity of pagan and Christian religious experience, and the regeneration of mankind through marriage.

Candelaria, Frederick H. "The *Carpe Diem* Motif in Early Seventeenth-Century Lyric Poetry with Particular Reference to Robert Herrick." Diss. Missouri, 1959. *DA,* 20 (1960), 2796–97.

Traces the motif from classical literature through medieval works to its important resurgence in the Renaissance. Discusses Herrick's use of the theme in both secular and religious poems. Comments on the use of the motif by Herrick's contemporaries, both major and minor poets.

————. "Ovid and the Indifferent Lovers." *RN*, 13 (1960), 294–97.

Sees the fourth elegy of the second book of *Amores* as the model for the pose of the indifferent lover in poems by Marlowe, Donne, Suckling, and Herrick.

Capwell, Richard L. "Herrick and the Aesthetic Principle of Variety and Contrast." *SAQ*, 71 (1972), 488–95.

Argues that *Hesperides* is deliberately arranged according to the established artistic principles of variety and contrast.

Chambers, A. B. "Herrick and the Trans-shifting of Time." *SP*, 72 (1975), 85–114.

Argues that Herrick, simultaneously a classical poet and a Christian priest, both views the imperfections of time and contemplates the perfection of eternity, thus achieving an ambivalent complexity. Important.

Chemin, Camille. "Robert Herrick (1591–1674)." *Revue Pédagogique*, 63 (1913), 54–72.

A discussion of Herrick's life and the themes of his poetry; nothing particularly original. Occasioned by Delattre's 1911 study.

Chute, Marchette. *Two Gentle Men: The Lives of George Herbert and Robert Herrick.* New York: Dutton, 1959; London: Secker and Warburg, 1960.

A sound and readable biography. See also "How a Book Grows," *LJ*, 84 (1959), 2431–32; and "A Biographer and Two Dear Friends She Never Met," *NYHTBR*, 27 December 1959, p. 1.

Reviews: Mark Van Doren, *NYHTBR*, 13 September 1959, p. 3; Samuel F. Morse, *NYTBR*, 13 September 1959, p. 6; *TLS*, 4 March 1960, p. 146; *SCN*, 17 (1959), 28–29; Charles Rollo, *Atlantic*, 204 (October 1959), 118–19.

Colie, Rosalie L. *The Resources of Kind: Genre-Theory in the Renaissance.*

Ed. Barbara K. Lewalski. Berkeley: University of California Press, 1973.

Illuminating and suggestive brief discussion of Herrick's reliance on and subversion of the expectations of genre, focusing on *"The Argument of his Book."*

[Croft, P. J.] "Robert Herrick's Commonplace Book (Lot 146)." *Bibliotheca Phillippica: Catalogue of the Celebrated Collection of Manuscripts Formed by Sir Thomas Phillipps, Bt. (1792–1872).* London: Sotheby, 28–29 June 1965, pp. 66, 123–35.

Detailed description of Phillipps MS.12341*, claiming without reservation that portions of the miscellany are in the hand of Robert Herrick and arguing the superiority of the manuscript's texts over other known texts of the poems it contains.

————. Untitled letter to the editor. *PBSA,* 66 (1972), 421–26.

Takes issue with Norman Farmer's reservations regarding the "Herrick Commonplace Book." (See Farmer's *PBSA* article.)

Crum, Margaret. "An Unpublished Fragment of Verse by Herrick." *RES,* 11 (1960), 186–89.

Points out unique contributions to the text of Herrick in the recently acquired Bodleian MS. Eng. Poet. c. 50.

Dearmer, Percy. *Songs of Praise Discussed.* London: Oxford University Press, 1933.

Brief notes on the musical adaptations of *"Mattens, or morning Prayer,"* *"The white Island,"* and *"Another Grace for a Child."*

Delattre, Floris. *English Fairy Poetry.* London: H. Froude, 1912.

Sees Herrick as culminating a tradition which includes Shakespeare, Jonson, and Drayton. Argues that most of the poems in *A Description of the King and Queene of Fayries* (1634) imitate Herrick's contribution to that volume, *"A Description of his Dyet."* Suggests that Herrick may have intended a fairy epic, since his fairy poems all fit together.

————. *Robert Herrick: Contribution à l'Etude de la Poésie Lyrique en Angleterre au Dix-septième Siècle.* Paris: F. Alcan, 1911.

An appreciative survey of Herrick's poetry, sensitive to its complexities and to the traditions upon which it is based, but overimpressionistic and inclined to overemphasize the autobiographical aspects of the poems. Superior to Moorman's comparable work, but dated.

Reviews: F. S. Boas, *MLR*, 9 (1914), 530–32; Bernard Fehr, *Beiblatt zur Anglia*, 26 (February 1915), 55–59.

Deming, Robert H. *Ceremony and Art: Robert Herrick's Poetry.* De Proprietatibus Litterarum, Series Practica, 64. The Hague and Paris: Mouton, 1974.

Attempts to place Herrick's poetry in its literary, historical, social, and artistic milieu. Emphasizes the ritualistic and ceremonial elements.

Reviews: Walter R. Davis, *SEL*, 15 (1975), 192–93; Robert Wilcher, *YES*, 6 (1976), 256–57; and the review articles by Cain and Claude J. Summers.

————. "The Classical Ceremonial in the Poetry of Robert Herrick." Diss. Wisconsin, 1965. *DA*, 26 (1966), 5430–31.

Argues that Herrick is "classical" not "pagan" in that he uses the ceremonies and rites of both the classical and the Christian worlds to affirm his devotion to an older and more stable order in the face of Puritan opposition, merging liturgical and sacramental ceremonial with their classical counterparts.

————. "Herrick's Funereal Poems." *SEL*, 9 (1969), 153–67.

Sees the part-classical, part-Christian death rites in Herrick's poems as ceremonies which give lasting significance to the deceased and link the mortal world of the poems to the immortal world of art.

————. "Robert Herrick's Classical Ceremony." *ELH*, 34 (1967), 327–48.

Argues that the Christian and the classical details in Herrick's ceremonial poems merge in an imaginative blend—compatible with Christianity—which evidences the poet's devotion to an older, more stable time.

————. "The Use of the Past: Herrick and Hawthorne." *JPC*, 2 (1968), 278–91.

Compares "Corinna's *going a Maying*" with "The May-Pole of Merry Mount" as responses to the conflict between Christianity and naturalism, noting that Herrick—unlike Hawthorne's Puritans—was able to accommodate the claims of paganism within his vision.

DeNeef, A. Leigh. "The Ceremonial Mode of Poetic Expression in Robert Herrick's *Hesperides*." Diss. Pennsylvania State, 1969. *DAI*, 30 (1970), 4981A–82A.

Asserts that the poetic ceremonial, which transforms human actions into rituals and enlists the reader's participation in them by getting him to affirm their value, is employed by Herrick to celebrate certain moments of human experience in the face of death and mutability. Concludes that the ultimate subject and concern of this mode of expression is poetry itself and its function within the framework of human experience.

———. "Herrick and the Ceremony of Death." *RenP*, 1970, pp. 29–39.

Sees Herrick creating a realm of stasis, immutable and transcendent, which renders death of more significance than simply an inevitable natural fact.

———. "Herrick's 'Corinna' and the Ceremonial Mode." *SAQ*, 70 (1971), 530–45.

Attributes the success of Herrick's poem to its ceremonial mode, which heightens and sanctifies, celebrates and demands celebration in return.

———. *"This Poetick Liturgie": Robert Herrick's Ceremonial Mode.* Durham, N. C.: Duke University Press, 1974.

Sees the artistic process throughout *Hesperides* as controlled by a conscious poetic ceremonial which isolates instants of human experience and transforms them into significant celebratory rituals in which both poet and reader participate. Important.

Reviews: Walter R. Davis, *SEL*, 15 (1975), 193–94; Robert B. Hinman, *SCN*, 33 (1975), 93–94; A. B. Chambers, *JEGP*, 75 (1976), 417–19; Paulina Palmer, *YES*, 6 (1976), 258–59; Claude J. Summers, *MP* (1978), in press; and the review articles by Cain and Claude J. Summers.

Ditsky, John M. "A Case of Insufficient Evidence: L. C. Martin's 'R.H.' Poems and Herrick." *BSUF*, 11 (1970), 54–59.

Argues that the seventeen poems ascribed to "R. H." in a seventeenth-century commonplace book, and thought by Martin to be Herrick's, ought to be removed from editions of Herrick. Concludes that by Martin's own criteria for internal evidence, "R. H." was hardly capable of creating the distinctive poetry which is Herrick's.

Easton, Emily. *Youth Immortal: A Life of Robert Herrick.* Boston and New York: Houghton Mifflin, 1934.

A romantic reconstruction of Herrick's life as suggested by the poetry. Interesting, but not scholarly or critical.

Reviews: Stark Young, *New Republic,* 79 (1934), 290–91; *Christian Science Monitor,* 15 August 1934, p. 10.

Eliot, T. S. "What Is Minor Poetry?" *SR*, 54 (1946), 1–18.

Rpt. in Eliot's *On Poetry and Poets.* London: Faber and Faber; New York: Farrar, Straus, 1957, pp. 34–51.

A seminal essay which touches Herrick only in passing, but which refocuses much of the controversy over Herrick's "major–minor" status. Argues implicitly that compared with Herbert and Campion, Herrick falls somewhere in the middle, with Herbert the most "major."

Evans, Willa M. *Henry Lawes.* New York: Modern Language Association, 1941.

Rpt. Milwood, N. Y.: Kraus Reprint Corp., 1966.

Argues that Lawes's "No Constancy in Man" perfectly matches Herrick's *"The Curse. A Song"* in meaning and delicacy; suggests that Lawes's "My Mistris blushed" belongs to the Herrick canon.

Farmer, Norman K., Jr., ed. *Poems from a Seventeenth-Century Manuscript with the Hand of Robert Herrick.* Monograph bound into *TQ,* 16, no. 4 (Winter 1973), paged separately.

Photographic reproductions of the portions of Phillipps MS. 12341* which contain poetry, with facing printed transcripts (a few of which are faulty). An introduction which accepts one of the hands in the MS as Herrick's (cf. Farmer's *PBSA* article) and surveys the contents of the collection, providing the historical contexts of the topical poetry. Important.

―――. "Robert Herrick and 'King Oberon's Clothing': New Evidence for Attribution." *YES*, 1 (1971), 68–77.

Argues that "King Oberon's Clothing," usually attributed to Sir Simeon Steward, is probably by Herrick.

―――. "Robert Herrick's Commonplace Book? Some Observations and Questions." *PBSA*, 66 (1972), 21–34.

A thoughtful study of Phillipps MS. 12341* urging caution in identifying one of its hands as Herrick's and in attributing some of the anonymous poems in it to Herrick (see Croft's letter in response and Farmer's monograph). Important for its general remarks on seventeenth-century MS miscellanies, as well as for Herrick studies in particular.

Fletcher, G. B. A. "Herrick and Latin Authors." *N&Q*, NS 6 (1959), 231–32.

Adds a few Latin sources to Martin's list.

Forsythe, R. S. " 'The Passionate Shepherd' and English Poetry." *PMLA*, 40 (1925), 692–742.

Primarily a study of the sources of and influences on Marlowe's poem, but discusses Herrick's use of the pastoral invitation to love and cites three poems as illustration.

Friederich, Werner P. *Spiritualismus und Sensualismus in der Englischen Barocklyrik*. Wein und Leipzig: W. Braumüller, 1932.

Extensive references to Herrick throughout a discussion of the conflict between spiritual and worldly values and attitudes, an opposition which Friederich finds characteristic of the baroque. Argues a new, concrete anti-Petrarchan attitude toward love in the Cavaliers and discusses the themes of transience, *carpe diem*, sin, and damnation.

Review: H. Glunz, *Beiblatt zur Anglia*, 48 (June 1937), 176–83.

Gaertner, Adelheid. *Die englische Epithalamienliteratur im siebzehnten Jahrhundert und ihre Vorbilder*. Coburg: A. Druck, 1936.

Discusses the influence of Catullus and Jonson on Herrick's epithalamia.

Gertzman, Jay A. "Robert Herrick's *Hesperides:* A Study of the Materials and Intentions of a Seventeenth-Century Lyric Poet." Diss. Pennsylvania, 1972. *DAI,* 33 (1972), 1682A.

Emphasizes the recreative, playful qualities of Herrick's poetry, as exemplified in the pervasive concept of "cleanly-wantonnesse," in the delineation of the ideal of *otium* and the primitivism of the Golden Age as they exist in the *locus amoenus* of *Hesperides,* and in the *beatus ille* verses which set in perspective the cleanly-wanton emotional ambience of *Hesperides.*

————. "Robert Herrick's Recreative Pastoral." *Genre,* 7 (1974), 183–95.

Argues that in *Hesperides* "we find a very definite pastoral sensibility, but one in which mood predominates over didactic intent, and in which Christian ceremonies are used to suggest the goodness of sensual pleasure."

————. See Roger B. Rollin, *N&Q.*

Gilbert, Alan H. "Robert Herrick on Death." *MLQ,* 5 (1944), 61–68.

Stresses the preoccupation with mortality in Herrick, counteracting the tendency to see him exclusively as a "faery poet"; emphasizes the doom of judgment day as a recurrent theme in *Hesperides.*

Glaser, Joseph A. "Recent Herrick Criticism: Sighting in on One of the Most Elusive of Poets." *CLAJ,* 20 (1976), 292–302.

Review article which concludes that much learning and sensitivity mark recent Herrick criticism, but an altogether successful reading of his work has yet to be published.

Godshalk, William L. "Art and Nature: Herrick and History." *EIC,* 17 (1967), 121–24.

A reply to Ross, *EIC.* Argues that in his view of a synthetic harmony of art and nature, Herrick is a traditionalist rather than an innovator, seeing a close relationship between the two, but not setting up art as a norm and nature as a corruption.

Haight, Elizabeth Hazelton. "Robert Herrick: The English Horace." *Classical Weekly*, 4 (8 April 1911), 178–81; (22 April 1911), 186–89.

While not denying the influence of Virgil, Anacreon, Catullus, and Martial, argues that Herrick's greatest debt is owed to Horace.

Halli, Robert W., Jr. "A Study of Herrick's *Hesperides*." Diss. Virginia, 1972. *DAI*, 33 (1972), 3584A–85A.

Emphasizes four principles: active reader response, which provides organic unity to *Hesperides* and to individual poems; variety, which suggests *Hesperides* as an *imitatio dei*; contrast; and context or resonance. Devotes attention to the contrast of beauty and ugliness and to the tension between life and death in Herrick's work.

Hallström, Per. *Konst och Liv: Litterära och Politiska Essayer*. Stockholm: Albert Bonniers Förlag, 1919, pp. 65–97.

Brief biography and appreciative critical comments stressing Herrick's lighthearted love of nature and the musicality, freshness, and warmth of his verse.

Hamer, Enid. *The Metres of English Poetry*. New York: Macmillan, 1930.

Discusses Herrick's use of ballad stanza, enjambement, variations in iambic stanza form, trisyllabic meters, and the ode.

Hamilton, George Rostrevor. *English Verse Epigram*. Writers and Their Work, No. 188. London: Longmans, 1965.

Argues that despite an unevenness, Herrick is one of the finest English epigrammatists, showing in his best epigrams an exquisite delicacy and a rare sensitivity to the shape and sound of words.

Heath-Stubbs, John. *The Ode*. London: Oxford University Press, 1969.

Credits Herrick with developing the ode in an interesting way by making of it a "miniature in which the necessary genuflexion to the Horatian altar does not destroy the lightness of tone."

Heinemann, Alison K. T. "The Style of Robert Herrick's Lyrics." Diss. Delaware, 1971. *DAI*, 32 (1972), 6377A.

Analyzes the tone, structure, poetic language, and versification of the lyric poetry. Emphasizes Herrick's balanced view, sense of formal design, ironic wit, and technical perfection.

Hess, M. Whitcomb. "Nature and Spirit in Herrick's Poetry." *The Personalist*, 27 (1946), 299–305.

Supports Gosse's contention that Herrick was the first English pastoral poet and insists that he was one for whom nature was always the book of God's creation. (See Gosse, Section IIIA.)

Hibbard, G. R. "The Country House Poem of the Seventeenth Century." *JWCI*, 19 (1956), 159–74.

Discusses *"A Country life"* and *"A Panegerick to Sir* Lewis Pemberton" as part of a tradition established by Jonson's "To Penshurst." Argues that *"A Panegerick"* embodies an understanding of the social, moral, and religious sanctions on which its view of country life rests. Amplified by Charles Molesworth, "Property and Virtue: The Genre of the Country-House Poem in the Seventeenth Century," *Genre*, 1 (1968), 141–57.

Hinman, Robert B. "The Apotheosis of Faust: Poetry and New Philosophy in the Seventeenth Century." *Metaphysical Poetry*. Ed. Malcolm Bradbury and David Palmer. Stratford-upon-Avon Studies 11. London: Edward Arnold, 1970; Bloomington: Indiana University Press, 1971, pp. 149–80.

Sees Herrick, like the new philosophers, reaching out from commonplace phenomena toward ultimate significance, fusing sacramentalism and empiricism in imaginative creation. Important.

Hollander, John. *The Untuning of the Sky: Ideas of Music in English Poetry, 1500–1700*. Princeton: Princeton University Press, 1961.

Rpt. New York: Norton, 1970.

Sees Herrick's use of musical paraphernalia in his poems as directed toward augmenting the repertory of objects and events listed in *"The Argument of his Book."*

Höltgen, Karl Josef. "Herrick and Mrs. Wheeler." *TLS*, 17 March 1966, p. 228.

Identifies the subject of *"To his Kinswoman, Mistresse* Penelope Wheeler" and *"Another upon her."*

———. "Herrick, the Wheeler Family, and Quarles." *RES*, 16 (1965), 399–405.

Presents information on Herrick's "Amarillis," Elizabeth Wheeler, whose brother John was mourned in an elegy by Francis Quarles.

Hooker, Edward N. "Herrick and Song-Books." *TLS*, 2 March 1933, p. 147.

Argues that Herrick's poems were not totally inaccessible or neglected in the eighteenth century, pointing out their inclusion in song books, miscellanies, and periodicals. Answered by Norman Ault (20 April, p. 276), who takes issue with Hooker's conclusions. A response by Hooker (1 June, p. 380) answered by Ault (22 June, p. 428).

Howarth, R. G. "Attributions to Herrick." *N&Q*, NS 5 (1958), 249.

Disputes Herrick's authorship of several poems attributed to him in MSS.

———. "An Early Elevation of Herrick." *N&Q*, NS 2 (1955), 341.

Calls attention to Richard James' *The Muses Dirge . . .* (1625), which links Herrick with Jonson and Drayton.

———. "Notes on Skelton." *N&Q*, 193 (1948), 186.

Takes issue with Dyce's observation that Herrick occasionally employs "Skelton's favorite metre." (See Alexander Dyce, ed. *The Poetical Works of J. Skelton.* London: T. Rodd, 1843, I, cxxix.)

———. "Two Poems by Herrick?" *N&Q*, NS 2 (1955), 380–81.

Suggests that two poems extracted in Joshua Poole's compilation, *The English Parnassus . . .* (1657), may be Herrick fragments. Answered by J. C. Maxwell (ibid., p. 500), who points out that one of the alleged Herrick fragments is from Jonson's *Sejanus*.

Hughes, Richard E. "Herrick's 'Hock Cart': Companion Piece to 'Corinna's Going A-Maying.' " *CE*, 27 (1966), 420–22.

Sees *"The Hock-cart"* as completing the Eleusinian ritual celebration begun by "Corinna," the spring poem celebrating fertility and the autumn poem celebrating the bounty of Dionysus. (See Rollin, *CEA Critic.*)

Huson, Dorothy M. "Robert Herrick's *Hesperides* Considered as an Organized Work." Diss. Michigan State, 1972. *DAI*, 33 (1973), 275A–76A.

Sees *Hesperides,* including *Noble Numbers,* as a seven-part *confessio* detailing Herrick's progress toward truth and religious faith.

Ishii, Shonosuke. *Essays on Robert Herrick with a Selection from His Hesperides Done into Japanese.* Tokyo: Kenkyusha, 1968.

Eleven essays and ten notes, in Japanese, with English synopses. Emphasizes Herrick's delicacy, polish, simplicity, and sweetness.

Review: *SCN*, 26 (1968), 76.

———. *The Poetry of Robert Herrick.* Renaissance Monographs 1. Tokyo: The Renaissance Institute, 1974.

Substantially the preceding study revised and translated into English.

Reviews: Walter R. Davis, *SEL*, 15 (1975), 192; Helen Marlborough, *SCN*, 33 (1975), 94–95.

Jenkins, Paul R. "Rethinking What Moderation Means to Robert Herrick." *ELH*, 39 (1972), 49–65.

Sees Herrick's avoidance of extremes as a method of enhancing appetite, rather than as an expression of the old humanist impulse toward the mean.

———. "Robert Herrick's Poems." Diss. University of Washington, 1970. *DAI*, 31 (1971), 3505A.

Investigates Herrick's achievement through questions about his range of response, vocabulary and style, poetic forms, literary ancestry, etc. Concludes that in Herrick's poems, unlike in Donne's, meaning is a matter of syntax.

Jonas, Leah. *The Divine Science.* New York: Columbia University Press, 1940.

Argues a shift in emphasis from subject to style in Herrick, a transition representative of later seventeenth-century poetry; stresses Herrick's concern with perfect form within a limited field, his musicality and delicate sensitivity, and the strong satiric strain in the epigrams.

Judson, A. C. "Robert Herrick's Grave." *N&Q*, 142 (1922), 426–27, 487.

Conjectures that one of the stone coffins known to exist beneath a new flooring (1917) at Dean Prior may be Herrick's; gives information on the burial of incumbents inside their churches *ca.* 1674.

―――. "Robert Herrick's Pillar of Fame." *Texas Review,* 5 (1920), 262–74.

Reviews Herrick scholarship, commenting in detail on the Moorman and Delattre studies; argues that Herrick's fame is justifiably based on the personal note in his poetry, its variety, simplicity, and melody.

Kimbrough, Joe Arthur. "A Critical Study of Robert Herrick." Diss. Illinois, 1965. *DA,* 26 (1965), 1023–24.

Sees Herrick as the most Elizabethan of the Caroline poets, attracted to ritual and ceremonial; argues that his greatest strength is in the felicitous expression of the tangible and that his inability to deal with abstractions causes him to be unsuccessful as a devotional poet.

Kimmey, John L. "Order and Form in Herrick's *Hesperides.*" *JEGP,* 70 (1971), 255–68.

Argues that *Hesperides* is a consciously designed whole, its unity achieved through the persona, subject matter, and poetic forms; sees the book as Herrick's attempt to represent completely and coherently the secular and religious world of his experience.

―――. "Robert Herrick's Persona." *SP,* 67 (1970), 221–36.

Finds Herrick's persona in *Hesperides* a fictive character who unifies the disparate poems by playing three roles: the poet, the aging lover, and the exiled Londoner; the persona in *Noble Numbers* seen to be that of a suffering devotee.

―――. "Robert Herrick's Satirical Epigrams." *ES,* 51 (1970), 312–23.

Argues that the epigrams, carefully developed and seriously satirical, concentrate on three weaknesses of man: physical imperfections, social and professional foibles, and gross sins; finds the epigrams presenting the reverse side of the good and happy life, thus expanding the world of *Hesperides.*

Leavis, F. R. "English Poetry in the 17th Century." *Scrutiny,* 4 (1935), 236–56.

Rpt. in *Revaluation*. London: Chatto and Windus, 1936; rpt. New York: Norton, 1963, pp. 10–36.

Finds Herrick "trivially charming"; a further discussion in *Revaluation* (pp. 39–41) contrasting Herrick's *"The Funerall Rites of the Rose"* with Marvell's "See how the flowers, as at parade" and arguing that Herrick's poem lacks the strength and the urbane wit of Marvell's.

Lefkowitz, Murray. *William Lawes*. London: Routledge and Kegan Paul, 1960.

Brief discussions of Lawes's settings of *"To the Virgins"* and "Charon *and* Phylomel, *a Dialogue sung,"* the latter especially interesting for its dramatic recitative. Lists MS and early printed copies of Lawes' compositions, including settings of seven Herrick poems.

Legouis, Émile. "Robert Herrick." *Revue des Cours et Conférences, Vingtième Année, Première Série* (1912), 361–67, 490–501.

A detailed biographical sketch and an appreciative discussion of the style, content, and organization of *Hesperides*, stressing Herrick's taste for disorder; emphasizes the diversity of subject matter and form.

Lewis, B. Roland. *Creative Poetry*. Stanford: Stanford University Press, 1931.

A discussion of the organic principles of creative English poetry; uses four Herrick selections with critical remarks to illustrate arguments on theme, organic rhythm, and organic pattern.

Lewis, C. S., and E. M. W. Tillyard. *The Personal Heresy: A Controversy*. London: Oxford University Press, 1939.

Rpt. 1965.

The first three essays rpt. from *E&S*, 19 (1934), 20 (1935), and 21 (1936). Uses *"Upon* Julia's *Clothes"* in four essays debating whether poetry should be treated as the expression of the poet's personality or as a presentation of "things." Challenged by Montgomery Belgion, "The Poet's Name," *SR*, 54 (1946), 635–49.

Loane, G. G. "Herrick's Sources." *N&Q*, 177 (1940), 224–25.

Sources and analogues for some fifteen lines from *Hesperides* and *Noble Numbers*.

Lossing, M. L. S. "Herrick: His Epigrams and Lyrics." *UTQ*, 2 (1933), 239–54.

Concludes that the coarse epigrams and the simple poems of *Noble Numbers* have in common with the delicate lyrics of *Hesperides* an immediate presentation of sensation.

Macaulay, Rose. *Some Religious Elements in English Literature*. London: Hogarth Press, 1931.

Stresses the dualistic conflict between Herrick's religious and his profane verse.

————. *They Were Defeated* [American title, *The Shadow Flies*]. London and New York: Harper, 1932.

A novel in which Herrick is a major character; rich in its pictures of Devonshire customs and the Cambridge University environment, of religious and political issues, and of the literary figures who were Herrick's contemporaries.

Maddison, Carol. *Apollo and the Nine: A History of the Ode*. London: Routledge and Kegan Paul, 1960.

Sees Herrick as unique in English literature, being a consummate classicist, a perfect artist, and a lover of the physical; argues that he is fundamentally Anacreontic; uses "Corinna's *going a Maying*" to illustrate Herrick's ability to adapt rather than simply to imitate the ancients.

Mandel, Leon. *Robert Herrick: The Last Elizabethan*. Chicago: Argus Press, 1927.

A biographical and critical study; marred by errors of fact and an inconsistent critical perspective. Of slight value.

Marcus, Leah Sinanoglou. "Herrick's *Noble Numbers* and the Politics of Playfulness." *ELR*, 7 (1977), 109–26.

Argues that *Noble Numbers*, reacting against Puritanism and emphasizing age-old customs, affirms Herrick's commitment to a Laudian Anglican vision. Relates the poems to the *Book of Sports* controversy and concludes that Herrick's consciousness of the frailty of the Merry England ideal adds depth and urgency to his argument.

Mattson, Barbara D. "A Study of Robert Herrick's *Hesperides.*" Diss. Minnesota, 1972. *DAI*, 33 (1973), 6319A.

Finds *Hesperides* complex, learned, and unified. Discusses Herrick's "art," variety of subject matter, "masculine sensibility," and controversial epigrams.

Maxwell, J. C. See Howarth, "Two Poems by Herrick?"

Maxwell, Sue. "Robert Herrick: The Metrician." *Poet Lore*, 52 (1946), 353–59.

A discussion of Herrick's metrical versatility.

McCall, Joseph Darryl, Jr. "Factors Affecting the Literary Canon." Diss. Florida, 1958. *DA*, 19 (1959), 1744.

Uses *Hesperides* in a description of the process through which a book may go between its publication and its recognition as a "classic."

McEuen, Kathryn A. *Classical Influence upon the Tribe of Ben.* Cedar Rapids: Torch Press, 1939.

Rpt. New York: Octagon, 1968.

A study of the classical elements in the nondramatic poetry of Jonson and his circle. Contains a detailed analysis of Herrick's indebtedness to eleven classical writers. (Cf. Aiken.)

McGovern, Robert J. "A Trust to Good Verses: Robert Herrick's Poetics of Self." Diss. Case Western Reserve, 1968. *DAI*, 30 (1970), 3911A.

Places Herrick at the beginning of a line of poets such as Wordsworth, Whitman, and Cummings, who saw poetry as an epiphany of the poet.

McPeek, James A. S. *Catullus in Strange and Distant Britain.* Cambridge: Harvard University Press, 1939.

Sees a resemblance between Catullus and Herrick in specific motifs, poems, and diction, but denies any specific influence.

Mellers, Wilfrid. *Harmonious Meeting: A Study of the Relationship Between English Music, Poetry, and Theatre, c. 1600–1900.* London: Dennis Dobson, 1965.

Brief discussion of Henry Lawes's setting of "*The Primrose*," emphasizing the "conscious artifice" in feeling and in technique.

Miner, Earl. *The Cavalier Mode from Jonson to Cotton*. Princeton: Princeton University Press, 1971.

Brief, appreciative, often perceptive discussions of such issues in Herrick's poetry as politics, time, ceremony, and friendship. Important.

Minich, Paul A. "An Analysis of a Perfect Poetic Kingdom: Robert Herrick's *Hesperides*." Diss. SUNY–Buffalo, 1972. *DAI*, 33 (1973), 5133A.

Argues that *Hesperides* both expresses and embodies Herrick's grasp of himself as a creator psychically inhabiting an imaginative linguistic creation.

Molesworth, Charles. See G. R. Hibbard.

Moorman, Frederick W. *Robert Herrick. A Biographical and Critical Study*. London and New York: John Lane, 1910.

Rpt. New York: Russell and Russell, 1962.

The first full-scale study of Herrick's life and work; now outdated and showing very much the impress of its age, but not without substance.

Reviews: *Nation*, 91 (1910), 317–18; *Saturday Review*, 109 (1910), 498–99; *Spectator*, 104 (1910), 770; John Lane, *Athenaeum*, 14 May 1910, p. 576; [Arthur Clutton-Brock], *TLS*, 25 August 1910, pp. 297–98, expanded in *More Essays on Religion*. London: Methuen, 1927, pp. 24–34; Bernard Fehr, *Beiblatt zur Anglia*, 22 (August 1911), 225–28.

Moranville, Sharelle. "The Self and Soul in Robert Herrick's Poetry." Diss. Kent State, 1971. *DAI*, 32 (1972), 5192A.

Finds that while Herrick's best poetry emphasizes the temporal world, it does so within a Christian context. Stresses Herrick's concern with the special obligations of the poet, whose gift can gain him a "limited immortality" of the self, a goal always balanced against the true immortality of the soul.

M[ore], P[aul] E[lmore]. "Herrick." *Nation*, 95 (1912), 378–81.

Brief but judicious essay on Herrick's life and, in particular, the classical resonances of his work. Nominally in response to the critical studies by Delattre and Moorman.

Musgrove, Sydney. *The Universe of Robert Herrick.* Auckland University College Bulletin No. 38, English Series No. 4. Auckland: Pelorus Press, 1950.

Rpt. Folcroft, Pa.: Folcroft Library Editions, 1971.

Sees Herrick as neither trivial nor pagan; argues that he is a poet of only slightly less stature than the greatest; concludes that Herrick is a seventeenth-century Christian who constantly evokes the physical world and simultaneously transcends it. Important.

Review: *TLS*, 10 August 1951, p. 501.

Naylor, E. W. "Three Seventeenth Century Poet-Parsons and Music." *Proceedings of the Musical Association*, Fifty-Fourth Session (1927–28), pp. 93–113.

Discusses Herrick's familiarity with the music and musicians of his age and notes the many references to music in his lyrics.

Newton, Edward. "In Dimpled Devonshire." *YR*, NS 19 (1930), 762–72.

Describes a visit to Exeter and Dean Prior; surveys the Herrick bibliography. Inconsequential, but a charming example of its kind.

Nixon, Paul. "Herrick and Martial." *Classical Philology*, 5 (1910), 189–202.

Notes a considerable debt to Martial in Herrick's choice of *topoi* and in the imitation of particular lines, but concludes that the points of similarity, although numerous, are "relatively unimportant"; extensive citing of parallels.

Oram, William A. "The Disappearance of Pan: Some Uses of Myth in Three Seventeenth-Century Poets." Diss. Yale, 1973. *DAI*, 34 (1973), 3423A.

Argues that Herrick, more than either Drayton or Milton, secularizes myth, treating poetry and mythmaking as a kind of play and ignoring the traditional demand that myth be "true" to the higher realities of the spirit.

Ozark, Joan M. "Faery Court Poetry of the Early Seventeenth Century." Diss. Princeton, 1973. *DAI*, 34 (1974), 5115A–16A.

Argues that the fairy poems of William Browne, Herrick, Simeon Steward, and Drayton "are peculiarly devoid of folklore and distinctively emphasize literary traditions." Contains extensive analyses of *"The Fairie Temple:* or, Oberons *Chappell,"* "Oberons *Feast,"* and "Oberons *Palace."*

Pace, George B. "The Two Domains: Meter and Rhythm." *PMLA*, 76 (1961), 413–19.

Uses *"Upon* Julia's *Clothes"* to illustrate how linguistic metrics aid interpretation; subjects *"The Amber Bead"* to rhythm analysis.

Pearce, Roy Harvey. " 'Pure' Criticism and the History of Ideas." *JAAC*, 7 (1948), 122–32.

Sees Brooks's explication of "Corinna's *going a Maying"* as incomplete, failing as it does to recognize the problem of the naturalistic onslaught on religious faith in the earlier seventeenth century and thus neglecting the poem's normative ideological structure. (See Brooks, *The Well Wrought Urn.*)

Piepho, Edward Lee. " 'Faire, and Unfamiliar Excellence': The Art of Herrick's Secular Poetry." Diss. Virginia, 1972. *DAI*, 33 (1972), 3664A–65A.

Stresses the importance of art and play in creating fabulous worlds and rendering wondrous the everyday world in *Hesperides*, realms which are experienced through art. Surveys Herrick's artistry in developing stock themes, situations, and conceits.

Press, John. *Robert Herrick*. Writers and Their Work, No. 132. London and New York: Longmans, 1961.

Somewhat condescending monograph which emphasizes Herrick's lyrical gift and minimizes the depth of his vision.

Rau, Fritz. "Kleine Beiträge: Robert Herrick." *NS*, 4 (1955), 357–63.

Impressionistic, often inaccurate account of Herrick's poetry and reputation.

Reed, Mark L. "Herrick Among the Maypoles: Dean Prior and the *Hesperides*." *SEL*, 5 (1965), 133–50.

Charges that the influence of Dean Prior on Herrick's verse has been overestimated; concludes that Herrick's poems grow from and sing of England in general.

Regenos, Graydon W. "The Influence of Horace on Robert Herrick." *PQ*, 26 (1947), 268–84.

Argues an extensive influence of Horace in form, subject matter, and feeling. Extensive citation of parallel passages.

Richmond, Hugh M. *The School of Love: The Evolution of the Stuart Love Lyric*. Princeton: Princeton University Press, 1964.

Occasionally uses Herrick's poems as examples; good analysis of *"To the Virgins."*

Roeckerath, Netty. *Der Nachruhm Herricks und Wallers*. Kölner Anglistische Arbeiten, 13. Band. Leipzig: Bernhard Tauchnitz, 1931.

Traces the reputations of the two poets as a study in the history of literary taste.

Reviews: *TLS*, 30 April 1931, p. 347; Frederick T. Wood, *ES*, 15 (1933), 197–98.

Rollin, Roger B. "The Decorum of Criticism and Two Poems by Herrick." *CEA Critic*, 31 (1969), 4–7.

Accuses Lougy, Clark, Rea, and Hughes of violating various principles of critical decorum in their interpretations of *"The Hock-cart"* and "Corinna's *going a Maying*." (See Hughes, above; Lougy, Clark, and Rea, Section IV.)

———. *Robert Herrick*. TEAS, 34. New York: Twayne; London: Bailey Bros., 1966.

Argues that Herrick's pastoral vision provides intellectual unity to *Hesperides* and that his comprehensive aesthetic, including both serious and light elements, gives focus, order, and originality to his world view. Important.

Reviews: Brian Short, *SCN*, 25 (1967), 12–13; H. L. Richmond, *CL*, 22 (1970), 81–85.

————. "Robert Herrick and the Pastoral Tradition." Diss. Yale, 1960.

Confronts the critical controversy over Herrick's achievement by analyzing representative poems and considering the unity and variety of *Hesperides*. Concludes that, by T. S. Eliot's standards, Herrick is a "major" poet whose work embodies a "unity of underlying pattern" through its unique synthesis of the pastoral tradition.

————. "A Thief in Herrick's *Hesperides*." *N&Q*, NS 14 (1967), 343–45.

Notes that Robert Chamberlain, a poet of comparable temperament but none of the genius of Herrick, plagiarized several of Herrick's verses, especially from *"A Country life."* Amplified by Jay A. Gertzman, *N&Q*, NS 20 (1973), 182–84.

Ross, Richard J. "Herrick's Julia in Silks." *EIC*, 15 (1965), 171–80.

Concentrates on the one poem, but shows that the effect of many poems by Herrick is the vibrant culmination of the natural and the artful brought into a complete harmony. Answered by Godshalk.

————. " 'A Wild Civility': Robert Herrick's Poetic Solution of the Paradox of Art and Nature." Diss. Michigan, 1958. *DA*, 19 (1958), 1390–91.

Sees the alternating realism and idyllicism of the earlier lyrics as culminating in the balanced serenity of the latter part of *Hesperides*; argues that Herrick's prime achievement is a realistic idealism achieved through artful naturalness.

Røstvig, Maren-Sofie. *The Happy Man: Studies in the Metamorphoses of a Classical Ideal, 1600–1700*. Oslo: Akademisk Forlag; Oxford: Basil Blackwell, 1954.

Brief discussion of Herrick's poems on country life.

Roth, Frederic H., Jr. " 'Heaven's Center, Nature's Lap': A Study of the English Country-Estate Poem of the Seventeenth Century." Diss. Virginia, 1973. *DAI*, 34 (1974), 5120A–21A.

Discusses Herrick's country-estate poems as imitations of Jonson's. Sees the whole genre as reflecting "a philosophic consciousness, moralizing impulse, and acute awareness of shifting social patterns in a rapidly changing England."

Rowley, Victor Curtis, Jr. "Artifact, Author, and Audience in Robert Herrick's *Hesperides*." Diss. Ohio State, 1973. *DAI*, 34 (1974), 5121A–22A.

Studies the rhetorical components of *Hesperides*, "the *I*, the *it*, and the *you*," which make the book a vehicle of communication.

Ruggles, Melville J. "Horace and Herrick." *CJ*, 31 (1936), 223–34.

Rejects Catullus in favor of Horace as the Roman poet most like Herrick; cites parallel passages and identifies parallel themes and attitudes.

Salomon, Louis B. *The Devil Take Her: A Study of the Rebellious Lovers in English Poetry*. Philadelphia: University of Pennsylvania Press, 1931.

A largely descriptive account of the tradition, with considerable attention throughout to Herrick's place within it.

Schleiner, Louise. "Herrick's Songs and the Character of *Hesperides*." *ELR*, 6 (1976), 77–91.

Discusses the popularity of Herrick as a writer of song texts and explores his methods of turning song texts into lyrics to be read. Concludes that much of "the effect of lightness" in *Hesperides* is caused by an "expressive bareness or suggestiveness" appropriate to song texts rather than to printed poems. Appends a useful list of seventeenth-century musical settings of Herrick's poems.

Scott, George Walton. *Robert Herrick*. London: Sidgwick and Jackson, 1974.

A much padded biography, heavily dependent on Moorman and Chute, augmented with amateurish explications of several poems.

Reviews: Ted-Larry Pebworth, *SCN*, 33 (1975), 95; and the review article by Cain.

Shafer, Robert. *The English Ode to 1660*. Princeton: Princeton University Press, 1918.

Brief attention given to five poems which Herrick entitled odes, noting their formal relationship to his other poems. Limited, but useful.

Smith, G. C. Moore. "Herrick's 'Hesperides.' " *MLR*, 9 (1914), 373–74.

Speculation over the various possible meanings of "Hesperides."

———. "Some Notes on Herrick." *N&Q*, 12th Ser. 1 (1916), 205.

Twelve suggested emendations, analogues, sources, and explications.

Starkman, Miriam K. "*Noble Numbers* and the Poetry of Devotion." *Reason and the Imagination: Studies in the History of Ideas, 1600–1800*. Ed. J. A. Mazzeo. New York: Columbia University Press; London: Routledge and Kegan Paul, 1962, pp. 1–27.

Argues that *Noble Numbers* is a large metrical prayerbook which domesticates worship and reenacts it in personal and humanistic terms. Important.

Stauffer, Donald A. *The Nature of Poetry*. New York: Norton, 1946.

Brief discussion of the complexity of *"Upon* Julia's *Clothes."*

Summers, Claude J. "Herrick's Ceremonialism." *SCN*, 34 (1976), 87–88.

Review article concentrating on the books by Deming and DeNeef and placing the issue of ceremonialism within the larger context of recent Herrick criticism.

Summers, Joseph H. "Gentlemen of the Court and of Art." *The Heirs of Donne and Jonson*. New York: Oxford University Press, 1970, pp. 41–75.

Argues that Herrick is more than an imitator of Jonson and concludes that while many of Herrick's poems are facile, silly, arch, grotesque, and unconvincing, others exhibit a unique polish and perfection.

Swardson, Harold Roland, Jr. "Herrick and the Ceremony of Mirth." *Poetry and the Fountain of Light: Observations on the Conflict Between Christian and Classical Traditions in Seventeenth-Century Poetry*. Columbia: University of Missouri Press; London: Allen and Unwin, 1962, pp. 40–63.

Views the religious terms in Herrick's secular poetry as working to heighten and ritualize worldly experience. Finds that Herrick also involves Christian elements in the atmosphere of his mirthful natural world.

Review: *TLS*, 2 November 1962, p. 842.

———. "A Study of the Tension Between Christian and Classical Traditions in Seventeenth-Century Poetry." Diss. Minnesota, 1956. *DA*, 17 (1956), 1559.

An earlier version of the preceding entry.

Tanner, James T. F. "Robert Herrick's Flower Poems." *Dickinson Review*, 2 (1970), 25–34.

Impressionistic discussion of the flower poems, emphasizing "those aspects of Herrick's poetry which appeal to young people; subjects such as falling in love, enjoying life while it lasts; the bloom of youth which quickly fades."

Thompson, Elbert N. S. "The Octosyllabic Couplet." *PQ*, 18 (1939), 257–68.

Discusses the seventeenth-century modification of the couplet in accordance with musical principles in order to create subtle and pleasing rhythms; notices Herrick's accomplishments in this area.

Thompson, W. Meredith. *Der Tod in der englischen Lyrik des siebzehnten Jahrhunderts.* Sprache und Kultur der Germanischen und Romanischen Völker. Anglistische Reihe. Band 20. Breslau: Verlag Priebatsch's Buchhandlung, 1935.

Sees Herrick as an epicurean in his attitude toward death, standing between the Cavalier and Anglican poets; concludes that his brooding over death is not so much fear as it is Christian acceptance.

Tillyard, E. M. W. See C. S. Lewis.

Trogdon, William L. "Classical Mythology in the Poetry of Robert Herrick." Diss. Missouri–Columbia, 1973. *DAI*, 35 (1974), 1065A–66A.

Examines the contribution of mythology to the art of individual poems and to the Hesperidean vision, a vision which attempts to make sense of mutability. Includes as appendices a list of poems containing myth, an index of myth allusions, a chronology of the mythological poems, and a frequency chart of myth references.

Tufte, Virginia. *The Poetry of Marriage: The Epithalamium in Europe and Its Development in England.* University of Southern California Studies in Comparative Literature, II. Los Angeles: Tinnon-Brown, 1970.

Brief discussion of Herrick's epithalamia, which "demonstrate that an inventive poet may still give new life to old motifs."

Turman, Margaritha. *Die Farbenbezeichnungen in der Dichtung der englischen Renaissance.* Reval: Estländische Druckerei Akt.-Ges, 1934.

Sees Herrick both as a typical Cavalier in his use of vivid colors for effects of hyperbole and preciosity and as a representative of the movement toward more naturalistic uses of color.

Tuve, Rosemond. *Elizabethan and Metaphysical Imagery.* Chicago and London: The University of Chicago Press, 1947.

Includes many examples from Herrick in her illustrations and analyses of seventeenth-century poetics.

Van Doren, Mark. "A Visit to the Home of Robert Herrick." *Reporter,* 22 March 1956, pp. 47–49.

Impressionistic but appreciative account of Herrick and of Dean Prior.

Waddy, Reginald. "Elizabethan Lyrics and Love-Songs." *Proceedings of the Musical Association,* Thirty-eighth Session (1911–12), pp. 21–39.

Includes a brief discussion of musical settings of Herrick's lyrics and a list of poems which could profitably be set to music.

Walton, Geoffrey. "The Cavalier Poets." *From Donne to Marvell.* The Pelican Guide to English Literature, III. Ed. Boris Ford. Harmondsworth and Baltimore: Penguin, 1956, pp. 160–72.

Finds Herrick possessed of a charmingly fanciful but simple sensibility, his poems lacking complexity, polished technique, and emotional discipline.

Ward, Joseph Heald. "Herrick's Debt to Andrew Willet." *N&Q,* 12th Ser. 5 (1919), 37.

Asserts Herrick's familiarity with Willet's *Synopsis Papismi* (1592; expanded 1594, 1600, 1613), but does not identify the edition which Herrick might have seen.

Warren, Austin. "Herrick Revisited." *MQR,* 15 (1976), 245–67.

A charmingly written essay which is the culmination of sixty years' acquaintance with Herrick. Concerns his "unifying personality," the nature of his religion, and his rank as a poet.

Wasserman, Earl R. *Elizabethan Poetry in the Eighteenth Century*. Illinois Studies in Language and Literature, XXXII, Nos. 2–3. Urbana: University of Illinois Press, 1947.

Traces the popularity of Herrick's lyrics from 1650 to 1800.

Wells, Henry W. *New Poets from Old. A Study in Literary Genetics*. New York: Columbia University Press, 1940.

Traces the influence of earlier poetry on early twentieth-century poets; has references to Herrick throughout and discusses in detail his influence on W. H. Davies.

Wentersdorf, Karl P. "Herrick's Floral Imagery." *SN*, 36 (1964), 69–81.

Finds Herrick's floral imagery to be Dionysian, symbolizing sensuality, transience, and the annual renewal of nature; concludes that Herrick's outlook was more pagan than Christian.

Whitaker, Thomas R. "Herrick and the Fruits of the Garden." *ELH*, 22 (1955), 16–33.

Sees Herrick's verse as moving in two imperfectly coordinated worlds, the Christian and the qualified Dionysian; finds his symbolism crystallizing in art the situation of man: immersed in natural flux, yet realizing and thereby transcending that immersion, demanding an escape into the ideal realm of art. Important.

Whitehead, J. G. O. "The Tudor Rose." *The Coat of Arms* (London), 10 (1968), 110–15.

Argues that Herrick's description of Julia's "Strawberry and Creame" breasts (H-440) alludes to the Tudor rose and its ideals of wisdom, justice, and the common weal. Unconvincing.

Wilkinson, L. P. *Horace and His Lyric Poetry*. Cambridge: Cambridge University Press, 1945.

Takes notice, in passing, of Horatian details and tonal qualities in Herrick's verse.

Willey, Basil. "Robert Herrick: 1591–1674." *Church Quarterly Review*, 156 (1955), 248–55.

Condescending but appreciative tribute occasioned by the restoration of Herrick's epitaph for his niece Elizabeth in St. Margaret's, Westminster (see Howarth and Smyth, *"Upon his kinswoman Mistris Elizabeth Herrick,"* Section IV).

Williams, Raymond. *The Country and the City*. New York: Oxford University Press, 1973.

Superficial discussions of *"The Hock-cart"* and *"A Thanksgiving to God, for his House."*

Witt, Robert W. "Building a Pillar of Fame." *UMSE*, 13 (1972), 65–83.

A survey of the folklore elements in Herrick's poetry, concluding that through use of them the poet builds an earthly immortality. Slight.

Woodward, Daniel H. "Herrick's Oberon Poems." *JEGP*, 64 (1965), 270–84.

Sees the three Oberon poems as forming a fairy epithalamion which contributes substantially to *Hesperides* by providing a miniature mythology within the larger mythology of the garden; finds several of the central themes of *Hesperides* in them and calls attention to the comic skill with which they were written.

IV. Separately Published Notes on Individual Poems

"A Meditation for his Mistresse" (H-216)
Heinemann, Alison. *"Balme* in Herrick's 'A Meditation for His Mistresse.' "* ELN*, 8 (1971), 176–80.

"An Ode for him" [i.e., Ben Jonson] (H-911)
Kirby, Thomas A. "The Triple Tun." *MLN*, 62 (1947), 191–92.

"Another Grace for a Child" (N-95)
C., T. S. *Expl*, 3 (1945), query 17.
Mill, Anna Jean. *Expl*, 3 (1945), item 61.

"The Argument of his Book" (H-1)
DeNeef, A. Leigh. "Herrick's 'Argument' and Thomas Bastard." *SCN*, 29 (1971), 9–10.
Hirsch, Edward L. *Expl*, 2 (1943), item 11.

"The Carkanet" (H-34)
Huttar, Charles A. *Expl,* 24 (1965), item 35.
Sanders, Charles. *Expl,* 23 (1964), item 24.

"Ceremonies for Candlemasse Eve" (H-892)
Jones, Tom. "Herrick on the Yew." *N&Q,* NS 12 (1909), 78.
Tyner, Raymond. "Herrick's 'Crisped Yew.' " *N&Q,* NS 12 (1965), 380–81.

"Cherry-pit" (H-49)
Miller, Frances Schouler. *TLS,* 27 December 1934, p. 921.
  Notices an eighteenth-century plagiarism of the poem.

"Corinna's going a Maying" (H-178)
Candelaria, Frederick H. "Ronsard and Herrick." *N&Q,* NS 5 (1958), 286–87.
Rea, J. "Persephone in 'Corinna's Going A-Maying.' " *CE,* 26 (1965), 544–46. (See Rollin, *CEA Critic,* Section IIIB.)
Toback, Phyllis Brooks. "Herrick's 'Corinna's Going A-Maying' and the Epithalamic Tradition." *SCN,* 24 (1966), 13.

"Delight in Disorder" (H-83)
Shadoian, Jack. *Studies in the Humanities,* 2 (1971), 23–25.
Spitzer, Leo. *MLN,* 76 (1961), 209–14; rpt. in *Essays on English and American Literature.* Ed. Anna Hatcher. Princeton: Princeton University Press, 1962, pp. 132–38.

"The Hag" (H-643)
Cronin, James E. " 'The Hag' in 'The Cloud.' " *N&Q,* 195 (1950), 341–42.
Richards, Irving T. "A Note on Source Influences in Shelley's *Cloud* and *Skylark." PMLA,* 50 (1935), 562–67.

"His wish" (H-938)
Cobb, W. F. "Herrick and Martial." *The Academy,* 52 (1897), 138.
Jerram, C. S. "Herrick and Martial." *The Academy,* 52 (1897), 155.

"The Hock-cart, or *Harvest home"* (H-250)
Clark, Paul O. *Expl,* 24 (1966), item 70. (See Rollin, *CEA Critic,* Section IIIB; and Lougy, below.)
Cowan, S. A. *SCN,* 25 (1967), 68–70.
Lougy, Robert. *Expl,* 23 (1964), item 13. (See Rollin, below; Clark, above; and Rollin, *CEA Critic,* Section IIIB.)
Rollin, Roger B. "Missing 'The Hock Cart': An Explication Re-explicated." *SCN,* 24 (1966), 39–40. (See Lougy, above.)

"Julia's *Petticoat*" (H-175)

Low, Anthony, "The Gold in 'Julia's Petticoat': Herrick and Donne." *SCN*, 34 (1976), 88–89. (Answered by Patrick, below.)

Patrick, J. Max. "The Golden Leaves and Stars in 'Julia's Petticoat': A Reply to Anthony Low." *SCN*, 34 (1976), 89–91. (See Low, above.)

"*The mad Maids song*" (H-412)

D'Avanzo, Mario L. *AN&Q*, 4 (1965), 55.

"*The Primrose*" (H-580)

Howarth, R. G. "A Song of Herrick's Altered by Burns." *N&Q*, 175 (1938), 153.

"*To Dean-bourn*" (H-86)

Boas, F. S. "A Herrick Reading." *MLR*, 8 (1913), 92–93.

Moorman, Frederick W. "A Herrick Reading." *MLR*, 7 (1912), 519.

"*To* Electra" (H-663)

Cohen, Hennig. *Expl*, 17 (1959), item 44.

"*To* Master Denham, *on his Prospective Poem*" (H-673)

Tyner, Raymond. *Expl*, 23 (1965), item 72.

"*To the Virgins, to make much of Time*" (H-208)

Bache, William B. "Experiment with a Poem." *CollL*, 1 (1974), 64–66. Pedagogical use of the poem.

[Editors.] *Expl*, 1 (1942), item 2.

Halli, Robert W., Jr. "Affective Stylistics and Gathering Rosebuds." *Notes on Teaching English*, 1, no. 2 (1974), 1–2.

Leeper, Alexander. *N&Q*, 8th Ser. 8 (1895), 374. Identifies a source in Philostratus.

Mollenkott, Virginia R. " 'Gather Ye Rosebuds': An Expanded Interpretation." *C&L*, 23, no. 3 (1974), 47–48.

Simmons, J. L. "Marvell's 'The Picture of Little T. C. in a Prospect of Flowers.' " *Expl*, 22 (1964), item 62. An allusion to Herrick's poem in Marvell's.

Staudt, Victor P. "Horace and Herrick on Carpe Diem." *Classical Bulletin*, 33 (1957), 55–56.

"*To Violets*" (H-205)

Lyde, L. W. Letter to the Editor. *The Observer* (London), 22 March 1936, p. 13.

"The Tythe. To the Bride" (H-581)

DeNeef, A. Leigh. "Herrick and John Heywood." *N&Q*, NS 17 (1970), 408.

"Upon his kinswoman Mistris Elizabeth Herrick" (H-376)

Howarth, R. G. "Herrick's Epitaph on his Niece Elizabeth." *N&Q*, NS 2 (1955), 341–42.

Smyth, Charles. "A Herrick Epitaph." *TLS*, 13 May 1955, p. 253.

"Upon Julia's Clothes" (H-779)

Coffin, Lawrence. *CP*, 6, no. 2 (1973), 56–59.
    A discussion of "liquefaction."

Daniels, Earl. *Expl*, 1 (1943), item 35. (Answered by Henry.)

Harris, William O. *Expl*, 21 (1962), item 29.

Henry, Nat. *Expl*, 5 (1947), item 46. (Challenges Daniels.)

———. *Expl*, 14 (1955), item 15. (Challenges Schneider.)

Leiter, Louis H. *MLN*, 73 (1958), 331.

———. *Expl*, 25 (1967), item 41.

Merchant, Paul. "A Jonson Source for Herrick's 'Upon Julia's Clothes.' " *N&Q*, NS 21 (1974), 93.
    A song in *Epicoene* (1.1.97–102).

Preston, Michael. *Expl*, 30 (1972), item 82.
    A source in Ovid's *Amores*.

Schneider, Elisabeth. *Expl*, 13 (1955), item 30. (See Henry.)

Schuchter, J. D. *Expl*, 25 (1966), item 27.

Weeks, Lewis E., Jr. *CEA Critic*, 25 (1963), 8.

Weinberg, Gail S. *Expl*, 27 (1968), item 12.

"Upon Julia's Voice" (H-67)

Dormer, J., F. G. Stephens, and Alexander Leeper. "Herrick's *Hesperides*: 'Lutes of Amber.' " *N&Q*, 105 (1902), 408–09, 471; 106 (1903), 17, 95, 336, 511.

"Upon Spur" (H-1099)

Botting, Roland B. *MLN*, 44 (1929), 106–07.
    A source study.

Notes on the Contributors

GORDON BRADEN, Assistant Professor of English at the University of Virginia, is a specialist in classical and Renaissance literature. He is the author of *The Classics and English Renaissance Poetry: Three Case Studies* and of articles on Seneca and Spenser.

T. G. S. CAIN has been Lecturer in English Literature at the University of Newcastle upon Tyne since 1970. He read English at Gonville and Caius College, Cambridge, and earned his Ph.D. there with a dissertation on Herrick. He has published articles on sixteenth- and seventeenth-century poetry and a recent book on the fiction of Tolstoy.

A. LEIGH DENEEF, Associate Professor of English, Duke University, is the author of *'This Poetick Liturgy': Robert Herrick's Ceremonial Mode* and *The Poetics of Orpheus: An Edition and Study of 'Orpheus His Journey to Hell,' 1595*. His special interests are sixteenth- and seventeenth-century lyric poetry and literary theory.

A. E. ELMORE read the paper selected to celebrate the Herrick tercentenary at the 1974 meeting of the Modern Language Association, "Herrick and the Poetry of Allusion." He has published essays in the *Fitzgerald/Hemingway Annual* and in *The Sewanee Review* and has a book on *The Great Gatsby* forthcoming. He was Associate Professor of English at Hampden-Sydney College but is now studying law.

NORMAN K. FARMER, JR., has published several articles on Herrick and an edition of the Commonplace Book believed by some to have belonged to the poet. His other writings deal with genre-theory of seventeenth-century poetry, the work of Fulke Greville, and the relationship between art and literature. Associate Professor of English at the University of Texas at Austin, he specializes in the poetry and drama of the sixteenth and seventeenth centuries and interdisciplinary studies.

ACHSAH GUIBBORY is Associate Professor of English at the University of Illinois at Urbana-Champaign. She is on the editorial board of the *Journal of English and Germanic Philology* and has published articles and notes on Jonson, Bacon, Browne, Milton, and Dryden. She is currently at work on a longer study of the views of history and time in seventeenth-century English literature.

SHONOSUKE ISHII helped to found both The Society of Seventeenth-Century Studies and The Renaissance Institute in Japan and is co-editor of the latter's publications. Currently Professor of English at Soka University, Tokyo, he previously taught at Tokyo Gakugei University and Shirayri Women's College. He has published, chiefly on English poets and poetry, in both the Japanese and English languages and is the author of *The Poetry of Robert Herrick*.

DOROTHY LEE, Associate Professor of Comparative Literature at the University of Michigan–Dearborn, formerly taught at Wayne State University and Henry Ford Community College. Her essay on Afro-American drama was published in *Modern Drama*.

HELEN MARLBOROUGH is Assistant Professor of English at DePaul University where she teaches Renaissance literature and administers the writing program. From 1970 to 1976 she taught at Franklin and Marshall College. She earned her Ph.D. at Brown University with a dissertation on Ben Jonson.

VIRGINIA RAMEY MOLLENKOTT, Professor of English at William Paterson College of New Jersey, edits a quarterly bibliography for *Christianity and Literature* and serves on the executive committee of both the Modern Language Association Division on Religion and Literature and the Milton Society. She has published articles on Milton and Herbert, reviews in *Seventeenth-Century News,* and various essays for journals of education and religion. Her most recent book is *Women, Men, and the Bible.*

AVON JACK MURPHY is currently writing a book on John Dennis and has published an article on seventeenth-century critical verse and reviews of both modern fiction and literary criticism. He is Associate Professor of Language and Literature at Ferris State College.

WILLIAM ORAM is Assistant Professor of English at Smith College. He has written articles on Milton and Drayton and at present is at work on a book about the treatment of the royal court in Spenser and other English Renaissance poets.

J. MAX PATRICK is Professor of English at the University of Wisconsin–Milwaukee. He has taught at the universities of Manitoba, Buffalo, Emory, and Florida, and at Queens College (CUNY) and the New York University Graduate School. He was a visiting professor at the Centre d'Etudes Supérieures de la Renaissance (Tours) and at the Claremont Graduate School. He held Massey, Fulbright, Ford, and Newberry Library fellowships. Co-editor of *Seventeenth-Century News* and general editor of the Anchor and the Norton Seventeenth-Century Series, he has published editions of Milton, Herrick, Mallock, and Croll, and numerous articles.

TED-LARRY PEBWORTH is the principal organizer of the University of Michigan–Dearborn Biennial Renaissance Conferences and assistant editor of *Seventeenth-Century News*. Author of *Owen Felltham* and co-editor of *The Poems of Owen Felltham, 1604?–1668*, he has taught at Louisiana State University and the University of Illinois at Chicago Circle. Currently he is Professor of English Literature at the University of Michigan–Dearborn.

ROGER B. ROLLIN is the author of *Robert Herrick* and editor of a literature anthology, *Hero/Anti-Hero*. He has published articles on Herrick, Milton, critical theory, and American popular culture. From 1959 to 1975 he taught at Franklin and Marshall College and at present is William James Lemon Professor of Literature, Clemson University.

JOHN T. SHAWCROSS, Distinguished Professor of Literature, CUNY and the College of Staten Island, has published widely on seventeenth- and twentieth-century literature. He is the editor of *The Complete Poetry of John Milton* and *The Complete Poetry of John Donne*. His other onomastic studies deal with *Paradise Regained*, Andrew Marvell's poetry, and Hart Crane's *White Buildings*.

JAMES E. SIEMON has published articles on English Renaissance literature and has taught at the University of Washington and the University of Wisconsin–Madison. He is currently associated with the University of California at Los Angeles.

CLAUDE J. SUMMERS, Professor of English at the University of Michigan–Dearborn, is the author of *Christopher Marlowe and the Politics of Power*, co-editor of *The Poems of Owen Felltham, 1604?–1668*, and associate editor of *Seventeenth-Century News*. He has published articles on Marlowe, Jonson, Herrick, Vaughan, Marvell, and Christopher Isherwood, and serves on the executive committee of the Milton Society and on the MLA Delegate Assembly.

JAMES S. TILLMAN is the author of articles on Bacon, Burton, and Thoreau and is co-editor of an issue of *Studies in the Literary Imagination* devoted to seventeenth-century prose. He is Assistant Professor of English at Georgia State University.

Index to Herrick's Poems

This index is arranged to accord with that of *The Complete Poetry of Robert Herrick*, ed. J. Max Patrick (Garden City, N.Y.: Doubleday, 1963). The poem number assigned in Patrick's edition is supplied in parentheses when the entry refers to one of two or more poems with identical titles. Poem titles appear in small capitals; first lines in italics. Not listed are poems cited in the notes.